COLLEGE

NICKNAMES

AND OTHER INTERESTING SPORTS TRADITIONS

ON THE COVER:

Early collegiate football games were so rough that this satirical cartoon was captioned "Cheerful sport between the aesthetic young gentlemen of Princeton and Yale." Although the game had not been as violent as the cartoon suggested, in 1889 the captains of five Ivy League teams agreed to limit swearing and punching.

COLLEGE
NICKNAMES

AND OTHER INTERESTING SPORTS TRADITIONS

By Joanne Sloan and Cheryl Watts

VISION PRESS

P.O. Box 1106   3230 Mystic Lake Way   Northport, AL 35476

Vision Press
P.O. Box 1106
3230 Mystic Lake Way
Northport, Alabama 35476

Library of Congress Cataloguing-in-Publication Data

Sloan, C. Joanne, (Cheryl Joanne), 1947-
  College Nicknames / by C. Joanne Sloan and Cheryl S. Watts
      p. cm.
    ISBN 0-9630700-3-7 :
    1. College sports--United States--History. 2. Athletic
clubs--United States--Names--History. 3. Sports team
mascots--United States--History. I. Watts, Cheryl Sloan,
1968- . II. Title. III. Title: College nicknames.
GV351.S57 1992
796'.071'173--dc20   92-23714
                                                          CIP

Printed in the United States of America

To David, Tracy, Christopher, and McKenna

Acknowledgments

A number of people helped us in the preparation of this book. We first would like to thank the sports information directors at the schools included in *College Nicknames*. We relied on them for most of the material in the book. If not for their assistance, *College Nicknames* could not have been done.

For assistance with design, graphics, and other work involved in the book's production, we especially appreciate the contributions of Christopher Sloan, Wendel Sloan, Jim Stovall, Alan Dennis, Marian Huttenstine, and David Sloan.

Use of logos

Many universities have logos that are registered trademarks or are copyrighted and that may not be used without permission. We appreciate the assistance of the various sports information directors and other school officials who gave their consent to our use of the logos.

CONTENTS

From Anteaters and Antelopes to Zias and Zips ◆ 1

• Duke • Duquesne

E ◆ 83

East Carolina • East Stroudsburg • East Tennessee State • East Texas State • Eastern Illinois • Eastern Kentucky • Eastern New Mexico • Eastern Washington • Edinboro • Elon • Evansville

F ◆ 93

Fairfield • Fairleigh Dickinson • Ferris State • Florida • Florida A&M • Florida Atlantic • Florida Southern • Florida State • Fordham • Fort Hays State • Francis Marion • Fresno State

G ◆ 103

Gardner-Webb • George Mason • George Washington • Georgetown • Georgia • Georgia Southern • Georgia State • Georgia Tech • Gonzaga • Grambling • Grand Canyon • Grand Valley State • Guilford

H ◆ 115

Hampden-Sydney • Hampton • Harvard • Hawaii • Henderson State • Hillsdale • Hofstra • Holy Cross • Houston • Howard Payne

I ◆ 125

Idaho • Idaho State • Illinois • Illinois-Chicago • Illinois State • Indiana • Indiana State • Iona • Iowa • Iowa State • Ithaca

J ◆ 136

Jackson State • Jacksonville • Jacksonville State • James Madison • Johnson C. Smith

K ◆ 141

Kansas • Kansas State • Kent State • Kentucky • Kentucky Wesleyan

L ◆ 147

Lafayette • La Salle • Lehigh • Lenoir-Rhyne • Liberty • Linfield • Long Beach State • Long Island • Louisiana State • Louisiana Tech • Louisville • Loyola College • Loyola Marymount • Loyola University

M ◆ 159

Maine • Manhattan • Mankato • Mansfield • Marist • Mars Hill •

Marshall • Maryland • Maryland-Baltimore • Massachusetts •
McMurry • Memphis State • Mercer • Merrimack • Miami •
Michigan • Michigan State • Middle Tennessee • Millersville •
Minnesota • Mississippi • Mississippi College • Mississippi State
• Mississippi Valley State • Missouri • Missouri-Kansas City •
Monmouth • Montana • Moorhead • Mount Senario • Murray State

N ◆ 191

Navy • Nebraska • Nebraska-Omaha • Nevada-Las Vegas •
Nevada-Reno • New Hampshire • New Hampshire College •
New Mexico • New Mexico State • New Orleans • New York •
Newberry • Niagara • Nicholls State • North Alabama • North
Carolina • North Carolina-Charlotte • North Carolina-
Greensboro • North Carolina-Wilmington • North Carolina State
• North Dakota State • Northeast Louisiana • Northeastern •
Northeastern Illinois • Northern Arizona • Northern Colorado •
Northern Illinois • Northern Iowa • Northern Michigan •
Northwestern • Notre Dame

O ◆ 224

Ohio • Ohio State • Oklahoma • Oklahoma Baptist • Oklahoma
State • Old Dominion • Oregon • Oregon State • Otterbein

P ◆ 233

Pacific • Penn State • Pepperdine • Pittsburgh • Pittsburg State
• Portland State • Prairie View A&M • Presbyterian •
Princeton • Purdue

Q ◆ 244

Quincy

R ◆ 245

Radford • Randolph-Macon • Rice • Richmond • Rider • Robert
Morris • Rutgers

S ◆ 251

Saint Bonaventure • St. Cloud • Saint Francis • St. Joseph's • St.
Louis • Saint Mary's • St. Peter's • Sam Houston State • Samford
• San Diego State • San Francisco State • San Jose State • Seton
Hall • Shippensburg • Siena • Slippery Rock • South Alabama •
South Carolina • South Carolina State • South Dakota • South
Dakota State • South Florida • Southeast Missouri •

Southeastern Louisiana • Southern California • Southern Illinois • Southern Methodist • Southwest Missouri State• Southwest Texas State • Southwestern Louisiana • Stanford • Stephen F. Austin • Stetson • Sul Ross • Syracuse

T ◆ 282

Tarleton State • Temple • Tennessee • Tennessee-Martin • Tennessee Tech • Texas • Texas-Arlington • Texas-El Paso • Texas-Pan American • Texas-San Antonio • Texas A&I • Texas A&M • Texas Christian • Texas Lutheran • Texas Tech • Toledo • Towson State • Troy State • Tufts • Tulane • Tulsa

U ◆ 305

Utah

V ◆ 306

Valparaiso • Vanderbilt • Villanova • Virginia • Virginia Commonwealth • Virginia Military Institute • Virginia State • Virginia Tech • Virginia Union

W ◆ 315

Wabash • Wagner • Wake Forest • Washburn • Washington • Washington & Lee • Washington State • Wesleyan • West Chester • West Georgia • West Texas State • West Virginia • Western Carolina • Western Illinois • Western Kentucky • Western Michigan • Whittier • Wichita State • Widener • William & Mary • Williams • Wisconsin • Wisconsin-Green Bay • Wofford • Wyoming

X ◆ 340

Xavier

YZ ◆ 342

Youngstown State

Other Colleges and Nicknames ◆ 344

♦ ♦ ♦

From Anteaters and Antelopes to Zias and Zips

How many of the following questions about college nicknames and traditions can you answer?

1. Match the schools on the left with their nicknames on the right:

a. Amherst	a. Aggies
b. Eastern Kentucky	b. Badgers
c. Grambling	c. Colonels
d. Indiana State	d. Jayhawks
e. Kansas	e. Lord Jeffs
f. Mississippi	f. Rebels
g. North Carolina State	g. Sycamores
h. Portland State	h. Tigers
i. Texas A&M	i. Vikings
j. Wisconsin	j. Wolfpack

2. Name five schools that use the nickname "Tigers."

3. Name three schools that have at least two nicknames.

4. What college nickname was inspired by a 1940s Errol Flynn movie?

5. What university took its nickname from a ninth-century English king?

6. What school's mascot is based on a Walt Disney cartoon character?

7. What was the first college to play football in a foreign country?

8. Which two schools vie for the Little Brown Jug?

9. What university has won more national championships than any other school?

10. What college has appeared in more national football bowl games than any other school?

The answers to these questions, along with hundreds of other fascinating facts, are found in *College Nicknames*.

THE LEGACIES OF COLLEGE SPORTS

Many of our earliest memories come rushing back when we feel the cool breeze of an autumn football Saturday, hear the squeaking of tennis shoes on the parquet basketball floor, see the flurry of our school colors crash across the stadium in a "wave," find ourselves telling a joke about that school on the other side of the state, or smell the mingling aromas of hot dogs and popcorn. Such memories are relived every day, as generations pass the torch of school pride and the love of athletic competition to children and grandchildren, as with a sense of duty.

This legacy is often reflected in the fascinating stories that come from college campuses across the nation. The images of our alma maters and favorite teams—the nicknames, mascots, rivalries, legendary coaches, and other traditions—and the stories behind them become endearing to all who love college athletics. What true fan can't relate to the excitement of the coach of Wabash University at his team's performance, which led him to say "We're not very big, but we play like Little Giants" and thus be responsible for giving his school its nickname? What sports enthusiast doesn't find it interesting that Notre Dame's 1909 quarterback John Murphy's remark to his teammates—"What's the matter with you guys? You're all Irish and you're not fighting worth a lick" led to the school's nickname? What lover of tradition can't be moved by the story of Jackson State University's "Iron Thirteen," who, coached by their French teacher, went undefeated in football three years in the 1920s? What listener to sports tales can't be enthralled with the legendary story about Purdue in the late 1880s during football season enrolling eight boilermakers from the shops of the Monon Railroad?

In our immediate family, we have our own favorite stories and memories of college athletics. We are directly represented by the universities of Alabama, Texas, East Texas State, and Arkansas. Our extended family includes students, alumni, and faculty members of such varied schools as Georgia, Texas Tech, Missouri, Eastern New Mexico State, North Carolina State, Texas A&M, Louisiana Tech, and Northeast Louisiana.

For years, we have sat around dinner tables and in front of television sets, asking one another questions like: "Why is Kansas called the Jayhawks?" "Which is Auburn's real nickname—Tigers, War Eagles, or Plainsmen?" "What exactly does 'Boomer Sooner' mean?" and "Why do Iowa State's nickname and mascot have nothing in common?"

We've often wished there was a book that could answer such questions. When we decided that we should write that book, we wanted to answer those questions and provide the reader with some great stories at the same time. In that respect, the book wrote itself—many of the stories about nicknames, mascots, and other sports traditions that came pouring in from across the nation are fascinating!

WHERE NICKNAMES COME FROM

In researching *College Nicknames*, we discovered that the stories behind nicknames and mascots are both ordinary and outlandish. The most common athletic nicknames are Tigers, Bears, Bulldogs, Wildcats, Eagles, Cougars, Panthers, and Indians. Yet, there are such unique ones as Horned Frogs, Anteaters, Gauchos, Crimson Tide, Penguins, Javelinas, Catamounts, Purple Cows, Blue Hose, Camels, Kangaroos, Fighting Leathernecks, Violets, and Zips. At times, the nicknames and mascots are the same; at other times, they have little to do with one another.

One can't help but be intrigued by such nicknames, and the authors of this book have their own favorites. Perhaps you will be able to compose your own list of favorites after reading *College Nicknames*, but be forewarned that there are so many distinctive nicknames that you may have a difficult job doing that. We were tempted to try to list our 25 favorite, but decided the task was too great. We would have had to leave out too many wonderful ones.

As you can see from this partial list of nicknames and mascots, animals are a common source. There are schools, however, that are named for people (Colonials, John Harvard, Gaels), weather terms (Hurricanes, Rainbows), and even imaginary beings (Jayhawks, Griffins). Over the years, Indians and variations of the name (such as Savages, Warriors, Braves, and Chiefs) have been extremely popular with universities. As, however, the 1991 controversy over the nickname of the Atlanta Braves, the National League baseball team, showed, Indian monikers can create problems for the schools, when Native Americans often take offense at the wording. This controversy, though, is not new. Many colleges have dropped Indians and related nicknames for other monikers. The University of Massachusetts, for example, used to be called Redmen; now they are Minutemen. Nebraska-Omaha teams were once Indians, but are now Mavericks. Stanford likewise replaced its nickname of Indians with the Cardinal.

How did schools acquire their nicknames? The most common source was newspaper sports reporters. Editors and reporters for college and local newspapers have had a habit of giving a school a nickname in an article or column, and many times the school has followed suit and officially adopted the name. A close second in ways nicknames and mascots originate has been through student body contests. One documented instance shows that the nickname Sycamores (Indiana State) was entered into such a contest as a joke, only to be named the winner. Other frequent sources for nicknames include school yearbooks, committee and alumni recommendations, and excited statements by coaches.

Whether it has been a sophomore editor, a basketball coach, or a faculty committee that selected the nickname or mascot, the inspiration for that decision had to evolve. Although some choices may have been arbitrary (as, often with the popular choice of Tigers), most names originated from a logical source. The school, state, or region's history provided the inspiration for many monikers. Many a school's teams were once called Teachers, Professors, or Pedagogues because of its heritage as a teaching college. Other nicknames came from the history of their home state or region. This accounts for nicknames such as the Tennessee Volunteers and the Dayton Flyers. The geography of the area also provided inspiration for many schools, thus the Grand Canyon Antelopes and the Western Kentucky Hilltoppers.

Yet another source of inspiration is the athletic team's attitude or behavior. Just ask the Arkansas team which got its name after the coach referred to the team as "a wild band of razorbacks" or the North Carolina State team who received its nickname after a disgruntled fan complained to athletics officials that the school could never have a winning record as long as the players behaved—both on and off the field—like a wolfpack.

WHAT YOU'LL FIND IN THIS BOOK

The publication of this book coincides with exciting events happening in college sports across the nation. The 1990s ushered in centennial celebrations of athletic programs around the country; the 1890s saw football programs begin at Missouri (1890), Alabama (1892), Maine (1892), and Montana (1897), among others.

We hope that *College Nicknames* will introduce or reacquaint you with the stories behind college nicknames, mascots, colors, rivalries, historic games, trophies, bowl games, and the many other interesting sports traditions!

College Nicknames is not a definitive work, although it attempts to feature as many colleges as possible. The source for information, almost exclusively, was sports information directors or offices. All major NCAA schools were solicited for information, as well as other schools with strong sports traditions. Our intention was to present not only the athletic powerhouses—the Notre Dames, Florida States, USCs, Texases, Nebraskas, Oklahomas, Ohio States, Michigans, Alabamas, and the many others too numerous to name—but the lesser-known schools who still have interesting stories. Sometimes, in fact, small schools have the most intriguing nickname origins and traditions.

The body of this book includes stories about nicknames from 342 schools. For the truly avid fan, there is an appendix at the end that includes the nicknames of about 1,100 more.

The primary focus of *College Nicknames* is football, simply because it is the dominant sport at most colleges. Basketball, however, is featured at schools where it is the most popular sport. Other sports are spotlighted when the school has a particular tradition in that area. An attempt was made to list most of the national championships won by a school in all sports. Therefore, you will see mention of national championships in cross-country, tennis, rugby, volleyball—almost any sport you can think of.

While nicknames, in most cases, are the same for men's and women's teams, there are exceptions. We did not attempt to list all the alternate nicknames used by women's teams at universities. The fact that there is less information available about these nicknames was a factor in their exclusion.

The three categories in the book are Nicknames, Mascots, and Interesting Facts. We used the *nickname* designation to refer to the name the school's athletic teams go by. The *mascot* refers to the school's live or costumed representative at athletic events. The nickname and mascot are usually the same, although that is not always the case. When the mascot has a proper name, that is designated as well. *Interesting facts* refer to other stories regarding the school's sports programs. In this section you will find anecdotes and information about famous coaches and players, rivalries, trophies and other awards, legendary games, national championships, and other assorted details.

Adelphi

Nickname: Panthers
Mascot: Panther
Colors: Brown and Gold
Conference: New York Collegiate Athletic
Location: Garden City, N.Y.
Year founded: 1896

Nickname: Adelphi University's nickname dates back to 1946. That year, freshman Jim Young proposed both the name Panthers and the emblem. The athletic department accepted the name, and it was first used by the men's basketball team in a game against the Aggies of State University of New York Farmingdale Agricultural and Technical in January 1947.

Mascot: A student dressed in a black panther costume, complete with large eyes and teeth and long tail, entertains at athletic events.

Interesting Facts: In 1951, Adelphi head coach Al Davis introduced the four-man-line in football for the first time; Davis went on to lead the Super Bowl Champion Oakland Raiders.

Air Force

Nickname: Falcons
Mascot: Falcon
Colors: Blue and Silver
Conference:
Independent
Location: Colorado
Springs, Colo.
Year founded: 1954

Nickname: On September 25, 1955, the first class of cadets to enter the Air Force Academy, then in temporary quarters at Lowry Air Force Base in Denver, selected the falcon as the official nickname of the Cadet Wing. In making its choice, the class considered only nominees possessing characteristics which typified the combat role of the U.S. Air Force. The eagle, tiger, and falcon were among those considered. In the final vote, the falcon was selected over the tiger, and the eagle was passed over since it already was the national emblem. Some of the characteristics of the falcon which led to its selection were its speed, powerful and graceful flight, courage, keen eyesight, and noble carriage.

Mascot: When the cadets selected the falcon as the official mascot, they did not specify any particular species. As a result, any falcon can serve as the mascot. About 10 falcons are kept in the mews north of the cadet area. The majority are prairie falcons since they are native to Colorado.

The first mascot presented to the cadet wing was a peregrine falcon named Mach 1, given to the Academy on October 5, 1955. Although Mach 1 is still the official mascot name, each bird receives an individual name from the cadet falconers. Since July 1980, the official mascot has been Glacier, a white gyrfalcon.

Glacier was taken from a nest in the Seward Peninsula of Alaska by an Academy-sponsored search team.

Air Force also has a student mascot dressed in a blue and white falcon costume who performs at games.

Interesting Facts: Twelve cadet falconers, with four chosen from each freshman class at the end of the year to replace the seniors who will graduate, train and handle the falcons. Since 1965, flying demonstrations have been held at football and basketball games before thousands of spectators.

Akron

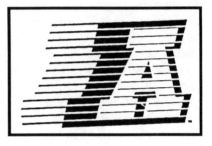

Nickname: Zips
Mascot: Zippy the Kangaroo
Colors: Blue and Gold
Conference: Independent
Location: Akron, Ohio
Year founded: 1870

Nickname: The University of Akron has one of the most unique nicknames in the nation. In 1925, when a campus contest was held to select a name, suggestions came from students, faculty, and alumni. On January 15, 1926, after a three-way vote—one by the student body, one by athletic lettermen, and one by local sports writers and faculty representatives—the winner was chosen. Freshman Margaret Hamlin's submission of Zippers won over Golden Blue Devils, Tip Toppers, Rubbernecks, Hillbillies, Kangaroos, and Cheveliers. Hamlin got her idea from a pair of rubber overshoes called Zippers, a brand name of The BF Goodrich Company. On September 13, 1950, athletic director Kenneth "Red" Cochrane announced that the nickname would be officially known as Zips. Two reasons have been offered for the name change: the shorter name was easier to use, and when zippers became a popular addition to men's trousers, there was an opportunity for puns.

Mascot: Because of a suggestion offered by Bob Savoy, student council member and All-American Zip diver, the Akron Student Council agreed on May 1, 1953, to declare the kangaroo the official mascot. Much resentment and apathy surfaced about the selection, which was chosen without a campuswide vote. The school newspaper, The *Buchtelite,* commented, "Granted, the kangaroo is unique, but then so is the hippopotamus, ostrich, and rhinoceros." Defenders of the kangaroo wrote back with "it is an animal that is fast, agile, and powerful with undying determination—all the necessary qualities of an athlete."

Since 1954, students have donned the Zippy kangaroo costume to perform at athletic events.

Interesting Facts: John Heisman, namesake for the Heisman Trophy annually awarded to the top collegiate football player in the country, was the first paid coach and athletic director at Buchtel College—the forerunner of The University of Akron. Under Heisman's coaching, the 1893 football team scored 276 points to establish an all-time Akron record that was not broken until 1969.

Since 1945, the Wagon Wheel Award has been given each year to the winner of the Akron-Kent State game. The Steel-Tire Trophy was initiated in 1976 to honor the winner of the Akron-Youngston State game.

Alabama

Nickname: Crimson Tide
Mascot: Big Al
Colors: Crimson and White
Conference: Southeastern
Location: Tuscaloosa
Year founded: 1831

Nickname: During the early 1900s, because of the football team's crimson jerseys, the

University of Alabama's defensive line was referred to as the Thin Red Line. In 1911, during a driving rainstorm when Alabama was playing Smith College, a sportswriter said the players looked like a swarming Crimson Tide. Alabama's school cheer, "Roll Tide Roll," comes from the nickname.

Mascot: Alabama's nickname and mascot are unrelated. The elephant mascot can be traced back to the 1926 Rose Bowl between Alabama and the University of Washington. The owner of a Birmingham trunk company gave each team member a large piece of luggage emblazoned with his company's symbol—a red elephant standing atop a suitcase. Reporters immediately noticed the suitcases and their symbol as the players disembarked from their train. Subsequently, in game stories, they began to compare the winning Tide team to a powerful herd of elephants.

In the 1960s, the first Big Al took part in games, although the mascot wasn't legitimized until 1979, when it was voted upon by students. Students try out each season to win the coveted Big Al title.

Fans and students have attempted to change the mascot to make it more compatible with the nickname. The mythological figure Trident was tried once, as was a simple wave; however, they never were popular.

Interesting Facts: Alabama has appeared in more national bowl games than any other college. Coach Wallace Wade led his teams to national football championships in 1925 and 1926. The University won national championships in 1961, 1964, 1965, 1973, 1978, and 1979, all under its legendary coach Paul "Bear" Bryant. Alabama ranks only behind Notre Dame and Oklahoma for most national championships (according to AP rankings). When Bryant retired after the 1982 season, he was the all-time leader in collegiate coaching victories with 323. Although his total has since been surpassed, Bryant still holds the record for the most victories among Division I-A coaches. The Paul Bryant Museum, which holds memorabilia from Bryant's 25 years at Alabama, is one of the state's main tourist attractions.

The Century of Champions celebration in 1992 honored the "Team of the Century," selected by Alabama football fans. First team honors went to Don Hutson (1932-34), Ozzie Newsome

(1974-77), John Hannah (1970-72), Vaughn Mancha (1944-47), Billy Neighbors (1959-61), Fred Sington (1928-30), Joe Namath (1962-64), Kenny Stabler (1965-67), Dwight Stephenson (1977-79), Bobby Marlow (1950-52), Johnny Musso (1969-71), Bobby Humphrey (1985-88), and Van Tiffin (1983-86).

The Alabama/Auburn "Iron Bowl" is one of the biggest rivalries in college football.

Cornelius Bennett won the Lombardi Award in 1986, and Derrick Thomas received the Butkus Award in 1988.

The women's gymnastics team won national titles in 1988 and 1991. The women's lacrosse team was national champion in 1988.

Alabama-Birmingham

Nickname: Blazers
Mascot: Beauregard T. Rooster
Colors: Green, Gold, and White
Conference: Great Midwest
Location: Birmingham
Year founded: 1969

Nickname: A poll of students and faculty selected Blazers as UAB's nickname during the planning for a varsity athletic program in 1977.

Mascot: Since the late 1970s, Beauregard T. Rooster has been the athletic mascot. A new mascot will be announced during the 1992-93 school year.

Interesting Facts: UAB joined the Great Midwest Conference, the newest NCAA Division I athletic conference, in 1990. The first season of play was the 1991-92 one.

The UAB athletic program, which began in 1977, has already experienced much success. The men's basketball program under

Coach Gene Bartow has never had a losing season and has participated in eight NCAA Tournament games and four NIT games. The Lady Blazers have won the Sun Belt and the Great Midwest Conferences. The baseball team, as well as the men's tennis team, won the 1991 Sun Belt championship.

Alaska-Anchorage

Nickname: Seawolves
Mascot: Seawolf
Colors: Green and Gold
Conference: Pacific West
Location: Anchorage
Year founded: 1977

Nickname: Originally nicknamed the Sourdoughs, UAA adopted Seawolves in 1977. Seawolves represent mystical sea creatures whose origin is associated with the Tlingit (pronounced Clink-it) Indians of Southeastern Alaska. The legend that exists about a seawolf is that anyone who sees one will experience good luck. What the seawolf looks like is left to one's imagination.

The Seawolf logo used today by UAA represents an adaptation of a traditional Alaskan totemic-like characterization of the mythical seawolf.

Mascot: A student costumed as the mythical seawolf serves as the school's mascot.

Interesting Facts: UAA played for the NCAA Division II men's basketball final in 1988 losing to Lowell (Mass.).

Alcorn State

Nickname: Braves
Mascot: Indian brave

Colors: Purple and Gold
Conference: Southwestern Athletic
Location: Lorman, Miss.
Year founded: 1871

Nickname: When Alcorn State University started competitive football in 1921, the area was inhabited by the Natchez Indians. The nickname, Braves, is in honor of the tribe.

Mascot: The school mascot is a student dressed in Indian garb who rides a horse.

Interesting Facts: Alcorn, the oldest land-grant college for blacks in the United States, first played football in 1922. In 1991 ASU played eleven football games on the road, more than any other team in the nation.

Alfred

Nickname: Saxons
Mascot: None
Colors: Purple and Gold
Conference: Empire Athletic Assoc.
Location: Alfred, N.Y.
Year founded: 1836

Nickname: Alfred University is named for King Alfred (849-899), Christian king of the West Saxons who ruled England from 871-899. Alfred was known not only for his successful victories over the Danes, but for his stimulation of learning among his war-ravaged people. Known as "The Education King," he took an active role in having Latin texts translated into Old English. He was probably responsible for the *Anglo-Saxon Chronicle*, the historical record which has proved so valuable to modern scholars.

The area around the school was settled by some of King Alfred's descendants. Because the land reminded them so much of their English homeland, they named it Alfred. Thus, the nickname honors the famous Saxon king.

Mascot: Although Alfred doesn't have a mascot, a Saxon is used for the athletic logo.

Allegheny

Nickname: Gators
Mascot: Gator
Colors: Blue and Gold
Conference: North Coast Athletic
Location: Meadville, Pa.
Year founded: 1815

Nickname: Until the 1920s, Allegheny College's athletic teams were called Hilltoppers, Methodists, and Blue and Gold. Then in April 1925, a group of Allegheny students published the first issue of a humor magazine which they named *Allegheny Alligator*. Choosing the name because of the alliteration, they wrote, "The name, Alligator, was selected not because the alligator is noted for its sense of humor, nor because the haunts of the above-mentioned critter are located in this vicinity, but purely and simple because of the 99.44 percent alliterative value of its orthography."

A column in the first issue of the magazine was called "Gator Gossip." In the fall of 1926, a new campus organization appeared called the Go-Get-Em Gator Club. At football games club members occupied a reserved section of the bleachers and acted as a nucleus for the cheering section. By the end of the decade, Allegheny's athletic teams were referred to as the Gators.

Mascot: A student dressed up in a gator costume entertains at athletic events.

Interesting Facts: The school won its first Division III national football championship in 1990 beating Lycoming, 21-14, in the Amos Alonzo Stagg Bowl in Bradenton, Florida.

The College won the 1983 national golf championship.

Allegheny President William H. Crawford addressed the formative meeting of the NCAA—the National Collegiate Athletic Association—on December 30, 1905. Crawford spoke about the ethical questions surrounding eligibility of players at this historic meeting.

Amherst

Nickname: Lord Jeffs
Mascot: None
Colors: Purple and White
Conference: Little Three
Location: Amherst, Mass.
Year founded: 1821

Nickname: J.S. Hamilton, Class of 1906, wrote the Amherst college song, "Lord Jeffery Amherst" that was traditionally sung after the football team scored; therefore, the school became known as the Lord Jeffs. The city of Amherst derived its name from Lord Jeffery Amherst, a general during the French and Indian War of 1756-63. When Amherst College was founded, the school simply assumed the name of the town.

During the 1991 Atlanta Braves/Tomahawk Chop debate, there was a brief movement at Amherst to have the nickname changed, but after alumni and students wrote letters to the student newspaper defending the name, nothing else was said.

Amherst athletic teams were once called Sabrinas as well as Lord Jeffs. The Sabrina was a campus statue that was routinely stolen. The nickname fell out of fashion in the 1960s and died completely when Amherst went coeducational in 1975.

Mascot: Amherst College has no official mascot, but one student traditionally dresses in 18th-century clothing and leads athletic spectators in various cheers.

Interesting Facts: Amherst College participated in the first intercollegiate baseball game, playing against Williams College in 1859. The school also has the distinction of having the oldest football program in the nation among small colleges.

Appalachian State

Nickname: Mountaineers
Mascot: Mountaineer
Colors: Black and Gold
Conference: Southern
Location: Boone, N.C.
Year founded: 1899

Nickname: Appalachian State University is located in the heart of the Blue Ridge Mountains; thus, the name Mountaineers was chosen.

Mascot: A costumed mountaineer, carrying a working long rifle, is a member of the school's cheerleading squad.

Interesting Facts: Since joining the Southern Conference, Mountaineer teams have won conference championships in football, men and women's basketball, baseball, volleyball, men and women's cross country, soccer, wrestling, men's and women's indoor and outdoor track, and men's and women's tennis.

Arizona

Nickname: Wildcats
Mascot: Wilbur T. Wildcat
Colors: Cardinal and Navy
Conference: Pacific 10

Location: Tucson
Year founded: 1885

Nickname: In 1914, Bill Henry, a student correspondent for the Los Angeles *Times* covering the Arizona-Occidental football game on the Occidental campus, penned the following about the losing team: "The Arizona men showed the fight of wildcats..." Back in Tucson, when the student body read the dispatch of the game, a resolution was immediately drawn up and passed that Arizona athletic teams would be called the Wildcats. Bill Henry, a senior at Occidental that year, became a renowned columnist for the L.A. *Times*, a war correspondent, and a news analyst for NBC. In 1964 he was honored as the "Father of the Arizona Wildcats" at the 50th Homecoming.

Mascot: The University of Arizona's first mascot in 1915 was Rufus von KleinSmid, a live bobcat named after the school's president. A gift of freshman Stanford Earl Brooks, Rufus was mascot only for a few months before it strangled itself on a chain that tethered the bobcat to a tree. The tradition of live cats continued until 1959 when Wilbur T. Wildcat, a costumed mascot, first appeared. Each year a student is chosen to wear the bobcat head at all the home football and basketball games. Because it was stolen at a basketball game in 1979 by a fraternity at the University of California at Berkeley, the bobcat head, valued at $500, remains in a secret spot between games. Now there are actually three heads that are used.

Interesting Facts: The University's most memorable athletic tradition is the slogan "Bear Down," given to the Wildcat teams by John "Button" Salmon, student body president and varsity athlete, shortly before he died in 1926 following an automobile accident. His last message to his teammates was "Tell them to bear down."

Established in 1979, the Big Game Trophy is the annual prize for the victor of the Arizona-Arizona State game. The Kit Carson Rifle is the trophy which is retained by the victor of the Arizona-New Mexico football rivalry. (A Springfield rifle, it is rumored to be that of the Indian leader Geronimo.)

Darryl Lewis won the Jim Thorpe Award as the top defensive back for Arizona in 1990.

Arizona won the Baseball College World Series in 1976, 1980, and 1986.

Arizona State

Nickname: Sun Devils
Mascot: Sun Devil
Colors: Maroon and Gold
Conference: Pacific 10
Location: Tempe
Year founded: 1885

Nickname: The Sun Devil is the third nickname in Arizona State University's history. When the second Tempe Normal football team opened play in 1889, the student body chose Owls for its moniker. Then when Tempe Normal became Arizona State Teachers College, the nickname was changed to Bulldogs.

The State Press, the student newspaper, ran frequent appeals during the fall of 1946 urging that the Bulldog be replaced by the Sun Devil. On November 8, 1946, the student body voted 819 to 196 to make the change.

Who first suggested the name? Some say it was civic leaders in Phoenix who banded together late in the summer of 1946 to build Arizona State sports programs; they took the name Sun Angels. The name Sun Devils was a natural complement. Others attribute it to Donn Kinzle, later athletic director, who was a Duke Blue Devil in his undergraduate days and liked the Devil symbol.

Mascot: In 1947 Sparky became the Sun Devil mascot. One story says that Phoenix attorney Walter E. Craig, who was then vice president of the Sun Angel Foundation, contacted former college classmate Bert Anthony, an illustrator who was working for Walt Disney, to create the character. Sparky was then reportedly sold to the university for $75 (for copyright purposes). In 1971, an ASU graduate designed a new Devil to replace Sparky, but his design was quickly turned down after it was described as a "nordic ogre."

Interesting Facts: Although Arizona State has not won a national football championship, it has experienced undefeated seasons. In 1970, the school had a 11-0 season and finished 8th in the AP standings; in 1975, it had a 12-0 year and finished 2nd in the nation.

The Sun Devil Stadium has been home to not only athletic events but also concerts and papal visits. A former landfill, the stadium will be the setting for Super Bowl XXVII in 1993.

ASU won the Baseball College World Series in 1965, 1967, 1969, 1977, and 1981.

ASU has a tradition of providing top quarterbacks to professional football. Two standouts have been Danny White of the Dallas Cowboys and Cleveland Brown's Mike Pagel.

Arkansas

Nickname: Razorbacks
Mascot: Big Red
Colors: Red and White
Conference: Southeastern
Location: Fayetteville
Year Founded: 1871

Nickname: When University of Arkansas students voted on school colors for its athletic teams in 1895, cardinal (a shade of deep red) garnered the most votes. The color gave the football team its first nickname; the team was called the Cardinals until the end of its unbeaten 1909 season. At a rally celebrating that winning season, head coach Hugo Bezdeck referred to his team as "a wild band of razorbacks." Sports reporters and fans began using the name, and it quickly became the official nickname.

Mascot: Arkansas is represented at games by a student dressed up in a razorback costume, as well as by a live mascot. The school didn't have a live mascot until the mid-1960s when fans donated a pig named Big Red. That pig and a second, Big Red II, were duroc hogs that died of heart attacks. In 1975, the Little Rock Zoo obtained an Australian wild boar. Named Big Red III, it served at games until it escaped from an animal exhibit near Eureka Springs, Arkansas, in the summer of 1977. An irate farmer shot and killed it when it broke into an animal pen. Ragnar, a wild hog captured in South Arkansas by a farmer, served as mascot in 1977. During that fall, it killed a coyote, a 450-pound hog, and seven rattlesnakes. Ragnar died in February 1978. Currently, Big Red VI serves as mascot.

Interesting Facts: In the 1920s, the famous "Whoo, Pig! Sooie!" yell was added to athletic cheers.

Arkansas won the national football championship in 1964 (according to the Football Writers' Association).

In 1954, guard Bill Brooks won the Outland Trophy award; in 1966 Loyd Phillips, a tackle, won it.

The University has been a leader in track events. The men's cross-country team won the national championship in 1984, 1986, 1987, and 1990. Since 1984, Arkansas has won the men's indoor track national championship each year. In 1985, the men's outdoor track and field team was national champions.

Arkansas-Little Rock

Nickname: Trojans
Mascot: None
Colors: Maroon, Gold, and White
Conference: Sun Belt
Location: Little Rock

Year founded: 1927

Nickname: Two explanations exist as to the origin of Trojans as the school nickname. According to the sports information director, UALR copied Southern California's nickname, which is the Trojans. Another source says that the 1931 basketball team was responsible for the name. Because they wanted an aggressive name, the players agreed on Trojans.

Arkansas-Monticello

Nickname: Boll Weevils
Mascot: Boll Weevil
Colors: Kelly Green and White
Conference: Arkansas Intercollegiate
Location: Monticello
Year founded: 1909

Nickname: When UAM was founded, cotton was the chief agricultural crop in Arkansas, and the boll weevil was the most dreaded pest. The boll weevil is a small gray beetle with a long snout whose larva is hatched in and destructive to young cotton bolls. UAM's early students, many who were sons and daughters of Delta cotton planters, chose the boll weevil as their mascot because of its perseverance and the fear it caused whenever its name was mentioned.

Mascot: A student dressed in a boll weevil suit performs at all home football and basketball games.

Interesting Facts: From 1938 through 1941, UAM (then known as Arkansas A&M College),was home to an unusual football team. Coached by Stewart Ferguson, a professor of medieval history whose contract stipulated that he didn't have to win a game, the A&M team traveled the country earning the nickname "Wandering Weevils."

During a four-year period, Ferguson's team lost 38 games and won only three. The players also only played six home games. Traveling everywhere from East Orange, New Jersey, to Reno, Nevada, the team won a reputation as the Harlem Globetrotters of college football.

Ferguson did little coaching during the games, allowing his players to make up plays in the huddle. Globetrotter antics also took place as Lawrence "The Stork" Lavender, a 6'7" end, would often come out for pre-game warm-ups dressed in a top hat, white tie, and tails.

Arkansas State

Nickname: Indians
Mascot: Indian family
Colors: Scarlet and Black
Conference: Big West; Sun Belt
Location: Jonesboro
Year founded: 1909

Nickname: The school's first nicknames, instituted in 1911, were the Aggies and Farmers, because it was the only agricultural school in eastern Arkansas. In 1925, Gorillas became the moniker; that nickname, however, did not gain popularity. Players became known as Warriors in 1930, but only a year later, the present nickname, Indians, came into use. The nickname is derived from the Osage tribe which once roamed northern Arkansas. In the 18th century, Osage tribes were at war with nearly all other plains and woodland tribes. ASU fans continue to take great pride in that fighting spirit!

Mascot: An Indian family consisting of Chief Big Track (named for the legendary Osage tribe chief), an unnamed princess, and an unnamed brave make up ASU's mascot. The costumed mascots which perform at school athletic events are modeled after the Arkansas band of the Osage tribe. Chief Big Track's uniform, valued at more than $1,000, consists of 495 parts.

Interesting Facts: The Indian Uprising is a tradition begun in the early 1980s at Indian Fieldhouse, the school's basketball coliseum. ASU fans attending home games stand for the opening tipoff.

ASU basketball players enter the court prior to each game on cue of Strauss' "Also Sprach Zarathustra" (also known as the theme to "2001: A Space Odyssey"). The tradition was promoted in 1987 by an assistant athletic director after he viewed a videotape of a similar occurrence at the South Carolina-Clemson football game.

Army

Nickname: Cadets; Black Knights
Mascot: Mules
Colors: Black, Gold, and Gray
Conference: Independent
Location: West Point, N.Y.
Year founded: 1802

Nickname: Students, as well as athletic teams at the U.S. Military Academy, are called Cadets.

Black Knights is sometimes used to refer to Army teams. In *Gridiron Grenadiers*, author Tim Cohane in 1948 explained how the nickname originated:

"Blaik's Black Knights. That's what Will Wedge, of the New York *Sun*, called them. Will was being alliterative, appropriate, and colorfully descriptive. In their golden helmets with the black band up the center and their dark jerseys with the golden numbers and arm bands, they galloped for all the world as if they were on chargers."

Army's sports information director believes Wedge's description dates to December 1, 1944.

Mascot: The choice of the mule as an army mascot reflects its long-standing usefulness in military operations hauling guns, supplies, and ammunition. Strong and robust, the mule is an appropriate symbol for the Cadets.

An ice-wagon mule became the first mascot when an officer at the Philadelphia Quartermaster Depot decided Army needed something to counter the Navy goat in the 1899 game between the two academies. The first officially designated mascot was Mr. Jackson, who became mascot in 1936, and fulfilled his duties until his retirement in 1948. Pancho, Hannibal, K.C. MO, Trotter, and Buckshot have also been mascots.

Four mules currently serve as mascots. The two oldest, both males, are Spartacus and Ranger. Traveller and Trooper came to Army in 1990. Traveller was named after General Robert E. Lee's horse.

Interesting Facts: Army's most famous football manager was probably General Douglas MacArthur who managed the 1902 football team that lost only one game. MacArthur returned to West Point on May 12, 1962, to receive the Academy's coveted Thayer Award. The award is named after Colonel Sylvanus Thayer, superintendent of the Academy from 1817 to 1833.

The Commander in Chief's Trophy, first presented in 1972, is awarded annually to the winner of the round-robin football competition among Army, Air Force, and Navy teams.

The Army-Navy rivalry is as fierce as any in college football. The first Army-Navy game was played at West Point in 1890. In its history, games been played at 12 different fields. Through 2002, the game will be played at Philadelphia at John F. Kennedy Stadium.

Army won the national championship in football in 1914, 1944, and 1945. The Academy has had three Heisman Trophy winners. Only three other schools have had more winners than Army—Notre Dame (7), Ohio State (5), and Southern California (3). Cadets who have won the honor are fullback Felix "Doc" Blanchard in 1945, halfback Glenn Davis in 1946, and halfback Pete Dawkins in 1958.

The Helms Foundation named Army's basketball team national champions in 1944.

Army was men's national fencing champion in 1949.

Auburn

Nickname: Tigers
Mascots: Aubie the Tiger; War Eagle
Colors: Orange and Blue
Conference: Southeastern
Location: Auburn, Ala.
Year Founded: 1856

Nickname: Oliver Goldsmith's poem, "The Deserted Village," begins with the line, "Sweet Auburn! loveliest village on the plain." The daughter-in-law of John J. Harper, the founder of the city of Auburn, Alabama, named the town from this line (although the poet was actually referring to Auburn, England). The school's nickname came from a later line in the poem, which describes Auburn as "where deadly tigers await their unsuspecting prey." Today, although some still refer to Auburn athletes as Plainsmen, the correct nickname is the tiger.

Mascot: Auburn University has two mascots: a student dressed up as Aubie the Tiger and a live eagle. The tiger mascot, obviously, comes from the school's nickname. The reasoning behind the eagle is somewhat more confusing. There are four stories behind the tradition, but one is thought to be the most credible. This most popular version hails from the 1913 football season, as the team prepared for a game against Georgia. At a pep rally, an Auburn cheerleader told the crowd, "If we are going to win this game, we'll have to get out there and fight, because this means war." During the excitement, a student, E.T. Enslen, dressed in his military uniform, lost the metal eagle emblem from his hat. When another student asked him what it was, he loudly answered, "It's a War Eagle!" Other students and fans heard him, and the cry, "Waaaaaar Eagle!" was used at the football game the next day. Today, War Eagle V (also known as Tiger) is the school's live mascot; he lives in a specially designed aviary next to Jordan-Hare Stadium.

Interesting Facts: Auburn won the national championship (AP) in football in 1957 under coach Shug Jordan.

Guard Zeke Smith won the Outland Trophy in 1958 as top interior lineman. Halfback Bo Jackson won the 1985 Heisman Trophy, and Tracy Rocker won the Lombardi Award for top lineman in 1988.

Augustana

Nickname: Vikings
Mascot: Viking
Colors: Blue and Gold
Conference: Conf. of Illinois and Wisconsin
Location: Rock Island, Ill.
Year founded: 1860

Nickname: Augustana College was founded by Swedish immigrants; therefore, the nickname Vikings was chosen.

Mascot: A student dresses in a Viking costume at athletic events.

Interesting Facts: Augustana won the NCAA Division III national football championship for four consecutive years, 1983-1986.

Austin College

Nickname: Kangaroos
Mascot: Kangaroo
Colors: Crimson and Gold
Conference: Texas Intercollegiate Athletic Assoc.

Location: Sherman, Tex.
Year founded: 1849

Nickname: During the early part of the 20th century, Austin College played Southwest Conference schools. During an early game against Rice University, Austin College was winning by a wide and growing margin. The Rice coach observed that his opponent's football team was "as quick as kangaroos."

Mascot: A student dresses in a Katy the Kangaroo costume for athletic events.

Interesting Facts: Football came to Austin College in the 1890s, making it one of the pioneers of the sport in the Southwest.

In 1981 the college was the national NAIA Division II champion in football.

Austin Peay State

Nickname: Governors
Mascot: Governor Peay
Colors: Red and White
Conference: Ohio Valley
Location: Clarksville, Tenn.
Year founded: 1927

Nickname: When intercollegiate athletics were first introduced on the Austin Peay campus in 1929, the basketball team members were often called Normalites (the school's original name was Austin Peay Normal School) or Warriors. Today, athletes at Austin Peay State University are known as Governors, a nickname that surfaced in 1937. The moniker was a tribute to Governor Austin Peay, for whom the school was named.

Mascot: A costumed mascot named Governor Peay appears at

school games.

Interesting Facts: Harold "Red" Roberts, a member of the 1969 Austin Peay football team, set an NCAA record for most receptions in a single game with 20 for 252 yards and four touchdowns against Murray State. The record has since been tied, but not beaten.

B

Baldwin-Wallace

Nickname: Yellow Jackets
Mascot: Jackie the Jacket
Colors: Brown and Gold
Conference: Ohio Athletic
Location: Berea, Ohio
Year founded: 1845

Nickname: In 1927, a newspaper account referred to the football team as Yellow Jackets. No one knows exactly why the nickname was used, but it was probably a reference to the players' uniforms, which were yellow and brown. At the time, athletic teams were called the Brown and Gold. In the spring of 1930, the baseball team was referred to as the Yellow Jackets in the yearbook; in the same publication that fall the football team was called Yellow Jackets.

One unofficial story that has been repeated many times about the origin of the nickname traces it to a coach. In the early 1930s, Coach Ray Watts remarked during an exciting football game that his team was "swarming like a bunch of yellow jackets."

Mascot: A student dressed as Jackie the Jacket entertains at sporting events.

Interesting Facts: The school colors of brown and gold were suggested by Philura Gould Baldwin, Class of 1886, who was the granddaughter of Baldwin University founder, John Baldwin. At the time, Baldwin University and German Wallace College were separate institutions. When they merged and became Baldwin-Wallace College in 1913, it was decided that the official colors would remain brown and gold.

Baldwin-Wallace won the NCAA Division III national championship in football in 1978.

Baylor

Nickname: Bears
Mascot: Bear
Colors: Green and Gold
Conference: Southwest
Location: Waco, Tex.
Year founded: 1845

Nickname: Although founded in 1845, Baylor athletic teams went without a nickname until 1914. In December of that year, Samuel Palmer, University president, held a vote of the student body, and Bears narrowly defeated Buffaloes. Other nominated nicknames were Antelopes, Frogs, and Ferrets.

Mascot: Baylor University received its first live mascot in the 1920s. The troops of the 107th Engineers, a unit of the 32nd Infantry Division stationed in Waco, gave a bear to the school. Named Ted, he made his first appearance at a Baylor-Texas A&M football game. When the unit got its order to move on, the bear was left in the hands of the Baylor Athletic Department.

Probably the best-known mascot was Joe College who came to Baylor through the work of Bill Boyd, a Baylor student. Boyd bought the bear from a zoo that went broke at the Cotton Palace in Waco. He then approached Baylor president Pat Neff and offered to take care of the bear in exchange for free tuition. Neff accepted the offer.

Every two years Baylor gets a new bear, and most come from Bear Country USA, a drive-thru wildlife park in South Dakota. All the bears are kept at the Hudson Plaza and are sponsored by the Baylor Chamber of Commerce, a service fraternity on campus.

Baylor also has a student mascot costumed as a bear.

Interesting Facts: Each year at the Baylor Homecoming, the freshmen men hear the tragic epic of the "Immortal Ten." On January 22, 1927, coach Ralph Wolf was taking his first Baylor basketball team to Austin for a game when one of America's first athletic tragedies occurred. A speeding train from the I&GA Railroad Co. rammed the side of the bus at a crossing. James Clyde, "Abe" Kelly, captain-elect of the team, saw the train just before impact and pushed his roommate out of the window. He lost his life saving his best friend. Kelly and nine other players died.

The Bobby Jones Award is presented prior to each Homecoming game. It is named in memory of the former Bear quarterback from 1954-56 who helped defeat Tennessee in the 1957 Sugar Bowl. The award was established by Mrs. Rosemary Jones after her husband was killed in an automobile-train wreck while a member of the Tennessee coaching staff.

The first Jim Thorpe Award honoring the top defensive back in football was given to Thomas Everett in 1986.

Bemidji State

Nickname: Beavers
Mascot: Beaver
Colors: Green and White
Conference: Northern Intercollegiate
Location: Bemidji, Minn.
Year founded: 1919

Nickname: The beaver was chosen for the nickname because the animal is native to the area.

Mascot: A student mascot, a member of the cheerleading squad, wears a beaver suit at sports events.

Interesting Facts: Bemidji State University has won nine national ice hockey championships.

Bloomsburg

Nickname: Huskies
Mascot: Husky
Colors: Maroon and Gold
Conference: Pennsylvania
Location: Bloomsburg, Pa.
Year founded: 1839

Nickname: Bloomsburg University's nickname was chosen on October 9, 1933, at the suggestion of arts instructor George J. Keller who thought that the husky would be a good selection because it was "the most stubborn fighter of the canine family."

Mascot: The first husky mascot was named Roongo, a name derived from a clever combination of the school colors, maroon and gold. Roongo was so popular that he was borrowed by the University of Washington Huskies and served as the school's mascot in a 1930s Bowl game. Currently, a student dressed in a husky costume represents the school.

Interesting Facts: Roongo II accompanied Admiral Byrd on his expedition to the South Pole.

Boston College

Nickname: Eagles
Mascot: Eagle

Colors: Maroon and Gold
Conference: Big East
Location: Chestnut Hill, Mass.
Year founded: 1863

Nickname: Even though Boston College participated in athletic events beginning in the 1880s, a nickname was not chosen until 1920. That year, after the Boston College track team won the Eastern Intercollegiates, a Boston newspaper ran a cartoon depicting Boston College as a large cat. Edward McLaughlin, S.J. (Society of Jesuits), petitioned the student body through *The Heights* (the student newspaper) suggesting the Eagle would be a more appropriate symbol of the school. His impassioned plea, "Proud would a B.C. man feel to see the B.C. Eagle snatching the trophy of victory from old opponents, their tattered banner clutched in his talons as he flies aloft," convinced school officials immediately to adopt the eagle as its mascot.

Mascot: After Boston College adopted the eagle as its nickname, a fishing boat skipper from Texas named Captain Welch immediately sent the school what he thought to be an eagle. The bird was actually a hawk. Students kept the bird in a cage in the tower of the administration building. Prophetically, the bird broke free and flew away the day before a 7-6 loss to Marquette in October 1923.

The first real eagle, nicknamed Herpy, was captured on a New Mexico ranch in the 1920s and sent to the college by John A. Risacher, S.J. Herpy was placed in a large cage, and in an effort to bite through the cage, injured his beak and was sent to a zoo. Risacher then sent the college a stuffed and mounted golden eagle which occupied the athletic department offices for almost forty years.

The University did not have another live eagle until 1961 when a golden eagle from Colorado named Margo became the official mascot. When the eagle died in 1966 of a virus, the college began using costumed student mascots because eagles were by then an endangered species.

Interesting Facts: The Catholic school's colors are the Papal colors of maroon and gold. In the 1880s, ladies of the New England Conservatory of Music sewed a banner representing the colors. The banner is exhibited in the Roberts Center trophy case in the main lobby.

Boston College has participated in six major football bowls with two victories—one at the Sugar Bowl against Tennessee and another at the Cotton Bowl against Houston.

The school has only retired two numbers in the history of its athletics—#22 worn by Doug Flutie who won the 1984 Heisman Trophy, the Maxwell Award, and the Davey O'Brien Award and #68 worn by the 1985 Outland Trophy winner, Mike Ruth.

Bowling Green State

Nickname: Falcons
Mascot: Freddie and Frieda Falcon
Colors: Burnt Orange and Seal Brown
Conference: Mid-American
Location: Bowling Green, Ohio
Year founded: 1910

Nickname: Before 1927, Bowling Green State University's teams were called the Normals or Teachers. Ivan Lake, Class of 1923, suggested the nickname, Falcons, after reading an article on falconry. Lake, managing editor and sports editor of the Bowling Green *Sentinel-Tribune*, proposed the name change because it fit headline space and because falcons were "the most powerful bird for their size and often attacked birds two or three times their size."

Mascot: A costumed mascot, Freddie Falcon, became the official mascot in 1950. Frieda Falcon was added in the 1979-80 school year. Tryouts are held each spring for the two mascots, and the winners remain anonymous to the student body until each is beheaded at the last home hockey and basketball games.

Interesting Facts: "Ay Ziggy Zoomba," Bowling Green's unofficial fight song (the official fight song is "Forward Falcons"), became famous when former Falcon All-American and Detroit Lion All-Pro halfback Mike Weger sang it in the film, *Paper Lion*. The Falcon football team traditionally sings it after each victory.

Burnt Orange and Seal Brown have been the school's official colors since 1914. Legend says that Leon Winslow, an industrial arts faculty member, got the idea from watching a woman's hat on a bus trip to nearby Toledo. He liked the brown and orange colors of the hat.

The only football jersey ever retired at the school is #29. It was worn by Paul Miles from 1971-73, a three-time All-Mid-American Conference running back who gained more than 1,000 yards in each of his three years on the varsity squad.

The Peace Pipe is a traveling award that goes to the winner of the annual gridiron battle between Bowling Green and Toledo. The tradition began during the 1947-48 basketball season. At that time, the teams exchanged a six-foot long wooden peace pipe. Today's peace pipe is a smaller version of the original pipe.

The Anniversary Award is also a traveling award started in 1985 that commemorates the founding of Bowling Green and Kent in 1910. It is presented annually to the winner of the BG-Kent football game.

Brandeis

Nickname: Judges
Mascot: Judge
Colors: Blue and White
Conference: University Athletic Association
Location: Waltham, Mass.
Year founded: 1948

Nickname: Brandeis University, founded by the American Jewish community, is named for former Supreme Court Justice Louis Brandeis (1856-1941). Brandeis served on the Court from 1916-1939. Athletic teams are appropriately named Judges.

Mascot: A student costumed as a judge is the school's mascot.

Interesting Facts: Brandeis won the NCAA Division III national championship in cross country in 1983.

The men's soccer team won the 1976 Division III national championship.

Brigham Young

Nickname: Cougars
Mascot: Cosmo the Cougar
Colors: Royal Blue and White
Conference: Western Athletic
Location: Provo, Utah
Year founded: 1875

Nickname: Cougars was chosen to be BYU's nickname on October 1, 1923, by coach Eugene L. Roberts. He thought the moniker described his athletes perfectly. The cougar was looked upon favorably because it was a native Utah animal that was powerful, agile, and wise.

Mascot: In 1925, Dave Rust, a BYU alumnus, contacted Roberts about a mother cougar and her three kittens that had been captured. Two of the kittens soon arrived at Provo. Named Cleo and Tarbo, they became school mascots. Because problems arose from keeping live cougars, the University came up with a new version of the cougar mascot in 1959. A cheerleader, trying to boost school spirit, created Cosmo the Cougar, a costumed mascot. Cosmo has represented the school ever since. Each spring during cheerleader tryouts student government leaders choose Cosmo.

Interesting Facts: BYU won the national football championship (AP and UPI polls) in 1984 under Coach LaVell Edwards.

Quarterback Ty Detmer won the 1990 Heisman Trophy as well as the Maxwell Award and the top quarterback award, the Davey O'Brien Award. In 1989 Moe Elewonibi won the Outland

Trophy; in 1986 Jason Buck won the same award. In 1989 Jim McMahon and in 1983 Steve Young won the Davey O'Brien Award as the top quarterbacks.

The Wagon Wheel Award goes to the winner of the BYU-Utah State football game each year. The Beehive Boot is awarded annually to the best football team in the state.

The Oquirrh Bucket goes annually to the best basketball team in the state.

BYU won the men's golf championship in 1981.

Brooklyn College

Nickname: Kingsmen
Mascot: None
Colors: Maroon and Gold
Conference: East Coast
Location: Brooklyn, N.Y.
Year founded: 1930

Nickname: The Borough of Brooklyn is also known as Kings Country; therefore, Kingsmen was chosen as the nickname.

Brown

Nickname: Bears
Mascot: Bear
Colors: Seal Brown, Cardinal Red, and White
Conference: Ivy League
Location: Providence, R.I.
Year founded: 1764

Nickname: The bear was introduced to Brown University on January 20, 1904, by United States Senator Theodore Francis Green, Class of 1887. Senator Green, a member of the committee in charge of erecting the recreation facility known as Brown Union, wrote in 1923 of his search for an identification to compliment the furnishings of the building and also to represent the school. "The Brown Bear is truly American and, most important of all, he embodies and suggests those qualities we want to emphasize," the Senator wrote. "While somewhat unsociable, he is good-natured and clean. While courageous and ready to fight, he does not look for trouble for its own sake, nor is he bloodthirsty. He is not one of a herd but acts independently. He is intelligent and capable of being educated (if caught young enough!). Remember, an athlete can make Phi Beta Kappa. Furthermore, the bear's color is brown; and its name is Brown."

The main feature of Brown Union was the trophy room with its great arch. Here, over the great arch, the central point of Brown student life, Senator Green placed the head of a real Brown Bear mounted on a shield, where it was discovered during the dedication ceremonies. Thus, the nickname was launched.

Mascot: The year after the nickname's inauguration students took a live brown bear to the Dartmouth game. Bear cub mascots appeared on the sidelines at Brown games for many years. Presented to the University by an animal farm, their care and feeding was entrusted to the Brown Key organization. The live bear mascot was replaced by a costumed bear in 1963.

Interesting Facts: Brown seeks to maintain a proper educational perspective by not holding spring practice, having athletic dorms, or offering athletically related financial aid to participants of its 31 varsity and 11 club sport programs. The school does, though, have the Brown University Sports Foundation which was founded in 1983 to guarantee Brown's financial support for athletics via endowment funds.

Bucknell

Nickname: Bison
Mascot: Bucky Bison

Colors: Orange and Blue
Conference: Patriot League
Location: Lewisburg, Pa.
Year founded: 1846

Nickname: Bison became the nickname of Bucknell University somewhere around the beginning of the century. Bison once roamed the central Pennsylvania area where Bucknell is located.

Mascot: Bucky Bison is the costumed mascot that performs at sporting events.

Interesting Facts: Bucknell played in the first Orange Bowl, beating Miami (Florida), 26-0.

The school's athletes have a reputation for academic excellence: the school had 61 athletes to achieve national or regional Academic All-America recognition from 1984-1991.

Butler

Nickname: Bulldogs
Mascot: Bulldog
Colors: Blue and White
Conference: Midwestern Collegiate
Location: Indianapolis, Ind.
Year founded: 1855

Nickname: Before 1919, Butler University's athletic teams were known as Christians. After a losing football season in 1919, Butler's followers tired of the nickname. During the week leading up to Butler's game with its rival, the Franklin Baptists, Butler *Collegian* editor Alex Cavins and a member of his staff, cartoonist George Dickson, decided something "hot" was needed for the weekly pep meeting. About that time, a Butler fraternity mascot, a bulldog named Shimmy—walked into the *Collegian* office. Cavins then had an idea. The next day's paper included a cartoon showing Shimmy the bulldog, labeled Butler, taking a big bite out of the pants seat of a figure called "John the Baptist." The caption was "Bring on That Platter, Salome!" which referred to the biblical account of Salome wanting the head of the John the Baptist. Even though Butler lost the game to Franklin, the nickname Bulldogs was born.

Mascot: A student costumed as a bulldog performs at sporting events.

C

California

Nickname: Golden Bears
Mascot: Oski
Colors: Blue and Gold
Conference: Pacific 10
Location: Berkeley
Year founded: 1868

Nickname: The nickname Golden Bears has been associated with the University of California since the spring of 1895, when the school's 12-man track team traveled east to the Western Intercollegiate Meet in Chicago. For the historic meet, the team took two blue silk banners emblazoned with the word "California" and an image of the grizzly bear, the state's emblem. The banners were later displayed at a homecoming celebration for the track team, which had easily won the Chicago meet. Inspired by the celebration, English professor Charles Mills Gayley wrote a song entitled "The Golden Bear." The song ended with these words: "Oh have you seen our banner blue? The Golden Bear is on it too. A Californian through and through. Our totem he, the Golden Bear!" The University's athletic teams have been known as the Golden Bears ever since.

Mascot: The University of California had a live mascot in its early years, but the idea was abandoned as the older bear cubs proved to be too dangerous. Those early live mascots were known affectionately as Oski, named from a team cheer which included the words, "Oski wow, wow!" Today, the team's costumed mascot is also known as Oski. The costumed mascot made its debut at a 1941 freshman pep rally—he wore a padded yellow sweater, blue trousers, oversized shoes, large white gloves, and a paper mache bear head. In 1946, Oski became the responsibility of a special spirit committee. Even today, the members of the committee are not known, and the identity of Oski is kept secret from the student body and fans.

Interesting Facts: Perhaps the school's most treasured tradition is its historic rivalry with Stanford University; each year, the winner of the game is awarded The Axe. The rivalry between Cal and Stanford began in 1899 when a group of Stanford students destroyed a straw man adorned in blue and gold, all the while chanting "Give em the axe." A group of Cal students stole the axe and carried it back to Berkeley, where it was kept safe in a city bank. Cal proudly owned the axe until the 1930s, when several attempts were made by Stanford students to retrieve their property. In 1930, they regained the axe when a group of student photographers claimed they wanted to take a picture of the axe. Instead, with the help of tear gas, they managed to wrest the axe from its owners. By 1933, each school decided to make the axe the official trophy for the game's winner.

California has won nine national championships in water polo since 1973.

California-Irvine

Nickname: Anteaters
Mascot: Peter the Anteater
Colors: Blue and Gold
Conference: Big West
Location: Irvine
Year founded: 1962

Nickname: The University of California-Irvine athletic program began its search for an official nickname in 1965. Two of the school's water polo players, Pat Glasgow and Bob Ernst, inspired by the comic strip "B.C.," began a campaign to institute the Anteater as their school's nickname. As election day drew near, only the Anteaters, Eagles, Unicorns, Golden Bears, and Seahawks had garnered the 100 petition signatures required to be put on the ballot. The Anteater won the election with 55.9 percent of the vote.

Mascot: A costumed Peter the Anteater mascot serves as school mascot. In addition, a stuffed anteater resides in a glass case in the administration building.

Interesting Facts: The Anteater nickname and mascot gave rise to UC Irvine's unique battle cry, "Give 'em the tongue...ZOT! ZOT!"

UCLA

Nickname: Bruins
Mascot: Joe and Josephine Bruin; Big Bear
Colors: Blue and Gold
Conference: Pacific 10
Location: Los Angeles
Year founded: 1919

Nickname: All of UCLA's nicknames have derived from bears. In 1919, UCLA (University of California at Los Angeles) was known as the Southern Branch of the University of California at Berkeley. The football team was referred to as the Cubs because of its younger relationship to the California Bears. The team finally won its first conference game, 34-9, against Redlands in 1922. The next year the Cubs, under a new coach, Jimmie Cline, won two games and went by a new name—Grizzlies. That name stuck until 1928 when the Grizzlies joined the Pacific Coast Conference. The University of Montana, also a member of the

PCC, was already known as the Grizzlies. Thus, UCLA, which had changed its name from the Southern Branch in 1927, became the Bruins.

Mascot: UCLA is one of few universities in the nation to have two costumed mascots, a male and a female—Joe and Josephine Bruin. The two were joined in 1979 by Big Bear, an eight-foot Disney-designed mascot created to work specifically with the band.

Live bears were popular at UCLA for years, but they are no longer used. In the 1930s, a live bear and his trainer were rented by the Associated Students to appear at all home football games. However, large wild animals proved too difficult to handle, and the Coliseum outlawed their appearances. Then, in the 1950s, Little Joe, a Himalayan bear cub from India, became the mascot. However, he grew too large and joined a circus. Finally, in 1961, Josephine was purchased by the alumni and was kept in the Rally Committee chairman's backyard. She also grew too large and was moved to the San Diego Zoo.

Interesting Facts: UCLA has won many national titles in men's athletics: a football championship in 1954; nine championships in basketball—1964, 1965, and 1967-1973; 15 tennis championships; 13 in volleyball; eight in track and field; three in water polo; two in gymnastics; and one in swimming. Women teams at UCLA have also been national winners in outdoor track and field, volleyball, softball, tennis, badminton, and basketball.

Legendary coach John Wooden was at UCLA from 1949-1975. He ranks as the fourth all-time winningest Division I coach in the nation.

California Polytechnic

Nickname: Mustangs
Mascot: Musty the Mustang
Colors: Green and Gold
Conference:CCAA; WFC; Pacific 10

Location: San Luis Obispo, Calif.

Nickname: Because cowboys rode mustangs in the Old West, the school chose Mustangs as its nickname.

Mascot: Musty the Mustang is the costumed mascot that entertains at sporting events.

Interesting Facts: California Polytechnic State University won the NCAA Division II national football championship in 1980.

Calif.-Santa Barbara

Nickname: Gauchos
Mascot: None
Colors: Blue and Gold
Conference: Big West
Location: Santa Barbara
Year founded: 1920

Nickname: The University of California-Santa Barbara was formerly known as the Roadrunners, but a 1940s movie starring Errol Flynn brought about a new nickname. *El Gaucho* was so popular that the student body voted to change the school's moniker to the Gauchos.

Because of the Spanish influence in the area, Gauchos is a suitable nickname for a California college. Gaucho refers to a cowboy of mixed Spanish and Indian descent.

Cal State Fullerton

Nickname: Titans
Mascot: Elephant

Colors: Blue, Orange, and White
Conference: Big West
Location: Fullerton
Year founded: 1951

Nickname: In 1959 the school that would become Cal State Fullerton was known as Orange County Community College. The 453 students that year decided to organize as a student body and to elect a student council. One of the council's jobs was to pick a nickname for the school. More than a hundred names were suggested, and after the student council narrowed the list down to just a few, the students chose Titans. The vote, however, was close; the Titans narrowly defeated the Aardvarks and Rebels. Even after the nickname was decided upon, there was much confusion as to what it actually represented. Some students pictured a mythological figure, not unlike a Trojan. Others pictured something more akin to the Titan missile.

Mascot: Because there was confusion to the real meaning of the Titan nickname, it is evident that a corresponding mascot would have been hard to create. The unlikely mascot—an elephant named Tuffy the Titan—was adopted in 1962 following the school's "First Intercollegiate Elephant Race in Human History." What started as a gag event attracted elephants from schools across the United States. More than 10,000 spectators attended the event, which was held in a pasture-turned-playing field. The place was affectionately dubbed "Dumbo Downs." To publicize the event, the school created Tuffy the Titan, a circus-like elephant. Soon its image found its way onto sweaters, jackets, and notebook covers all over campus. With no other mascot, the elephant was officially adopted.

Incidentally, the elephant race lasted only one more year—after an elephant charged the crowd and caused minor injuries among spectators in 1963, the unique tradition was squelched.

Today, Cal State does not have a live mascot. However, two costumed mascots are used—a male and his female counterpart.

Interesting Facts: When students voted on a school nickname, they also chose school colors of royal blue and white. Their selection, though, was vetoed by the athletic equipment manager. He thought that orange was a more appropriate color, since the school was still known as Orange County State College. He "adopted" the color, although it was not officially acknowledged until 1987. Today, all three colors—blue, orange, and white—are used.

Cal State won the Baseball College World Series in 1979 and 1984.

Cal State Northridge

Nickname: Matadors
Mascot: None
Colors: Red, White, and Black
Conference: Independent
Location: Northridge
Year founded: 1958

Nickname: According to Dr. James E. Sefton, Cal State Northridge professor of history, the school's student body in January 1958 submitted hundreds of suggestions for a nickname. Among the recommendations were Atom Splitters, Aeolians, Chmultapultapecs, Desert Rats, Fernandoes, Friars, Helians, Hustlers, Llamas, Minotaurs, Outcasts, Phaetons, Roughriders, Sundogs, Sunworshippers, Valkyries, and Yogis. A screening committee certified 158 names for a preferential ballot. This vote produced five finalists: Apollos, Falcons, Matadors, Rancheros, and Titans. On March 14, 1958, at a semi-formal dance called the Blarney Ball, school officials announced Matadors the winner.

Interesting Facts: Florence Griffith Joyner, one of the world's fastest females, was a member of the Matador women's track and field team in 1979 and 1980. Joyner won three Olympic gold medals in 1988.

Senior All-American Darcy Arreola won the 1500 meter run

at the 1991 NCAA Championship with a school-record time of 4:11.46.

NBC sportscaster Dick Enberg was an assistant baseball coach at CS Northridge in 1962 and 1963.

Pop singer Paula Abdul was a cheerleader at CS Northridge in 1981-82.

Canisius

Nickname: Golden Griffins
Mascot: The Golden Griffin
Colors: Blue and Gold
Conference: Metro Atlantic Athletic
Location: Buffalo, N.Y.
Year founded: 1870

Nickname: The Golden Griffin became the nickname of Canisius College in the 1930s. A Griffin in Greek mythology was a half-eagle, half-lion creature. The *Griffin,* the explorer LaSalle's ship, disappeared after navigating the Niagara River (where Canisius is now located) on its way to the Strait of Detroit.

Mascot: A student called The Golden Griffin is the mascot.

Interesting Facts: Basketball All-American Henry Nowak, Class of 1957, was a member of Congress for 22 years.

The men's basketball team competed in the NCAA Tournament three straight years, 1955-57.

In 1989, the Demske Sports Complex opened. The facility, the only one of its kind in the nation, houses the baseball, softball, lacrosse, men's and women's soccer, and football teams.

Carnegie Mellon

Nickname: Tartans
Mascot: Scottish Terrier

Colors: Cardinal, Grey, and White
Conference: University Athletic Ass.
Location: Pittsburgh, Pa.
Year founded: 1900

Nickname: Carnegie Mellon's nickname can be traced to the founder of the University. Industrialist Andrew Carnegie founded Carnegie Technical Schools in 1900; the schools became Carnegie Institute of Technology 12 years later. In 1967, Carnegie Tech merged with Mellon Institute of Research to form Carnegie Mellon University.

The son of a weaver, Carnegie was born in Dunfermline, Scotland, in 1835. A tartan is a plaid woolen cloth; each Scottish Highland clan has its own pattern of tartan. Thus, the nickname fittingly pays tribute to the University's founder whose weaver father must have been quite familiar with tartans.

Mascot: A student costumed as a Scottish Terrier is the school's mascot.

Interesting Facts: Carnegie Tech's stunning 19-0 upset of Knute Rockne's 1926 Notre Dame football team remains as one of the school's most memorable victories.

Under coach William "Spike" Kern, Carnegie Tech defeated TCU in the 1939 Sugar Bowl, 15-7. Kern won the Jacob Ruppert Trophy as the nation's outstanding coach, and Tech received the Lambert Trophy which was given to the best team in the East.

Carson-Newman

Nickname: Eagles
Mascot: Eagle
Colors: Orange and Blue
Conference: South Atlantic
Location: Jefferson City, Tenn.
Year founded: 1851

Nickname: Carson-Newman College, a Baptist school, originally went by the nickname of Fighting Parsons. Legendary football coach Frosty Holt suggested in 1931 a nickname contest be held to find a more suitable name. Tennessee Jenkins, a female history teacher, won the contest when she recommended Eagles. Because the birds are native to the mountain bluffs of East Tennessee, Eagles is an appropriate nickname.

Mascot: A student costumed as an eagle is the school mascot.

Interesting Facts: The school's football team has won five NAIA national championships (1983, 1984, 1986, 1988, and 1989).

In 1965 the baseball team won the NAIA title.

"It gets foggy at Mossy Creek" is a legendary phrase associated with former coach Frosty Holt. Located on the banks of Mossy Creek, the athletic complex is often shrouded by fog and provides an eerie setting for arriving athletic opponents. Coach Holt once told players complaining about a road trip that the opponent would soon have to come to "the Creek ...and it gets foggy at Mossy Creek."

Case Western Reserve

Nickname: Spartans
Mascot: None
Colors: Royal Blue, Gray, and White
Conference: North Coast; University Athletic
Location: Cleveland, Ohio
Year founded: 1826

Nickname: Spartans became the nickname for Case Western Reserve when Case Institute of Technology and Western Reserve University merged in 1967. It is believed, according to the sports information director, that the name was selected by alumni of both schools. Before the two schools merged, CIT was known as the Rough Riders, and WRU went by the Red Cats.

Interesting Facts: Before CIT and WRU consolidated, the two schools had an intense athletic rivalry, particularly in football and basketball. Although WRU dominated in football, the basketball series of the two ended tied, 55-55.

The Case Alumni Association, which marked the 100th anniversary of the first CIT and WRU football game on December 20, 1991, is the oldest autonomous science and engineering alumni organization in the nation.

Catawba

Nickname: Indians
Mascot: Indian
Colors: Royal Blue and White
Conference: South Atlantic
Location: Salisbury, N.C.
Year founded: 1851

Nickname: When Catawba College was founded, it was located in Newton, North Carolina, in Catawba County. The Catawba Indian tribe had a settlement near the Catawba River in that county; therefore, the nickname Indians was chosen. When the college moved to Salisbury, North Carolina, in 1925, the nickname remained.

Mascot: A student dressed in an Indian costume is the mascot.

Interesting Facts: Catawba's football team made appearances in the Tangerine Bowl in 1947 and 1948 beating both opponents, Maryville and Marshall.

Catholic University

Nickname: Cardinals
Mascot: Cardinal

Colors: Cardinal Red and Black
Conference: Capital Athletic
Location: Washington, D.C.
Year founded: 1887

Nickname: In December 1925, undergraduates of The Catholic University of America held a contest to select a nickname for athletic teams. The winner was Richard Tippett, who chose Cardinals because it was the name of the senior class yearbook and because it referred to Cardinals, the high officials in the Roman Catholic Church.

Mascot: The mascot of the school is the cardinal (bird). A costumed cardinal represents the school at sporting events.

Interesting Facts: The Catholic University of America defeated Ole Miss in the 1936 Orange Bowl, 20-19.

Central

Nickname: Flying Dutchmen
Mascot: None
Colors: Red and White
Conference: Iowa
Location: Pella, Iowa
Year founded: 1853

Nickname: Pella and Central College have a strong Dutch heritage. Immigrant farmers from the Netherlands migrated to Iowa, a rich agricultural region, in the mid-1850s. *The Flying Dutchmen* is a legendary Dutch ghost ship.

Interesting Facts: Central won the NCAA Division III national championship in football in 1974.
   "CBS This Morning" host Harry Smith and NCAA Executive Director Dick Shultz are former Central athletes.

Central Arkansas

Nickname: Bears
Mascot: Huggy Bear
Colors: Purple and Gray
Conference: Gulf South
Location: Conway
Year founded: 1907

Nickname: Bears is the only nickname that has been associated with University of Central Arkansas athletics. The name was chosen in 1908, the first year of sports competition.

Mascot: Huggy Bear represents the school at athletic events. Sigma Tau Gamma fraternity is responsible for the costumed mascot.

Interesting Facts: Central Arkansas won the NAIA Division I football championship in 1985 and 1991.
   Scottie Pippin, an alumnus of UCA's basketball program, plays for the NBA champion Chicago Bulls and was a member of the U.S.A.'s 1992 Olympic basketball team.
   In 1991, the University played for the NAIA men's basketball national title but lost to Oklahoma City, 77-74.

Central Conn. State

Nickname: Blue Devils
Mascot: Dr. Blue Devil
Colors: Blue and White
Conference: East Coast
Location: New Britain
Year founded: 1849

Nickname: Central Connecticut State University athletic teams were known as the Huskies until after World War II when the nickname was changed to Blue Devils. Dr. William Lee, a dean at the college, was responsible for the new moniker, which was modeled after Duke University Blue Devils.

Mascot: Dr. Blue Devil is the costumed school mascot.

Interesting Facts: The Governor's Trophy is given each year to the winner of the Central Connecticut-Southern Connecticut football game.

Central Florida

Nickname: Knights
Mascot: Galahad
Colors: Black and Gold
Conference: Independent
Location: Orlando
Year founded: 1963

Nickname: According to the school's sports information director, the University of Central Florida used the "Knights of Pegasus" as the basis of its nickname. In Greek mythology, Pegasus, the winged horse of the Muses, was caught by Bellerophon who mounted him and destroyed the monster Chimera.

Mascot: Galahad, a horse donated by actor Burt Reynolds, is the mascot. In Arthurian legend, Sir Galahad was the noblest knight of the Round Table.

Central Michigan

Nickname: Chippewas
Mascot: None

Colors: Maroon and Gold
Conference: Mid-American
Location: Mount Pleasant
Year founded: 1892

Nickname: The first football team at what is now known as Central Michigan University began play in 1896 under the unofficial moniker Normalites (for Central Michigan Normal School). The nickname changed several more times. The first official nickname was Dragons, which appeared in 1925. Three years later, reporters at the student newspaper began calling the athletes Bearcats. That name stuck until 1942, when students and faculty decided there needed to be a change. They, in turn, voted for the nickname Chippewas, a name which reflects the rich Indian heritage of the mid-Michigan region.

Interesting Facts: Before the rule was instituted which restricted retiring the jerseys of only interior linemen, CMU retired the jersey of a running back. Jim Podoley's #62 is the only uniform number retired in the school's football history. Podoley was a two-time All-American; he still owns 10 school records (including scoring 51 touchdowns in his four seasons).

Central Missouri State

Nickname: Mules
Mascot: Abbedale; Mo
Colors: Cardinal and Black
Conference: Mid-America Inter-collegiate
Location: Warrensburg
Year founded: 1871

Nickname: Central Missouri athletic teams were first called Normals and Teachers. When the 1921-22 school year began, college officials no longer thought the names appropriate. The school's athletic committee established a contest that promised the winner, upon graduation, a subscription to the school newspaper for three years. Out of 80 recommended suggestions, John Thomason, Class of 1924, submitted the winning entry.

Jennies became the nickname for the women's athletic teams in 1973. Since a female mule is known as a jenny, the name was a suitable one.

Mascot: The University has both a live mule and a costumed mule that serve as mascots.

Abbedale, the school's current mascot, was donated to Central Missouri by Sam Smiser, Class of 1938. Smiser owns the Smiser Mule Ranch in Newhall, California, and is known throughout the country for his expertise as a mule producer and promoter.

Mo the Mule is the costumed student mascot.

Interesting Facts: Central Missouri State University is the only school in NCAA Division II history to win the men's and women's basketball championship in the same season (1984).

Chaminade

Nickname: Silverswords
Mascot: None
Colors: Royal Blue and White
Conference: Pacific West
Location: Honolulu, Hawaii
Year founded: 1955

Nickname: The Silversword is a plant native only to Hawaii. It can be found only in Volcanoes National Park on the island of Hawaii, and on Mount Haleakala, a dormant volcano on the island of Maui. Its pointed leaves are said to resemble the cross, a symbol of the Christian faith.

Interesting Facts: Chaminade University is named for Father William Joseph Chaminade, a French Catholic priest who founded the Society of Mary. The society's members are known as Marianists; Chaminade University is one of 106 Marianist schools around the world.

Chaminade's basketball team pulled one of the greatest upsets in college basketball history in 1982, when they defeated #1 Virginia. In subsequent seasons, the team also defeated other NCAA Division I teams—Louisville, Southern Methodist, and Providence. Probably due to these victories, the team garnered its first national audience with a game against Arkansas in the Maui International Basketball Tournament in 1991.

Charleston

Nickname: Cougars
Mascot: Clyde the Cougar
Colors: Maroon and White
Conference: Trans America
Location: Charleston, S.C.
Year founded: 1770

Nickname: One of the nation's oldest schools, the College of Charleston appropriately chose Cougars as its nickname. In Colonial America, cougars were indigenous to the Charleston area.

Mascot: Clyde the Cougar is the school's costumed mascot.

Interesting Facts: The College of Charleston won the NAIA national championship in men's basketball in 1983 defeating Wesleyan (West Virginia), 57-53.

On September 1, 1991, the College of Charleston joined Division I of the NCAA.

Chicago State

Nickname: Cougars
Mascot: Cougar

Colors: Green and White
Conference: Independent
Location: Chicago, Ill.
Year founded: 1867

Nickname: No information exists, according to the sports information director at Chicago State University, about the origin of Cougars as a nickname.

Mascot: A student dressed in a cougar suit entertains crowds at sporting events.

Interesting Facts: Chicago State finished third in the 1984 NAIA men's basketball championship.

Cincinnati

Nickname: Bearcats
Mascot: Bearcat
Colors: Red and Black
Conference: Independent
Location: Cincinnati, Ohio
Year founded: 1819

Nickname: Three different stories exist about how the University of Cincinnati athletic teams earned the nickname Bearcats.

One version says that the nickname resulted from a picture or cartoon of Cincinnati lineman Leonard K. "Teddy" Baehr standing on the field next to a Stutz Bearcat automobile.

Another story dates to 1914 when a sports cartoon showing a bear-like, cat-like animal harassing a wildcat was printed following the Cincinnati-Kentucky football game.

A third account traces the nickname back to a 1912 newspaper account of a UC game in which Cincinnati *Enquirer* sports editor Jack Ryder said that "the team played like bearcats."

The bearcat is a native animal of Southeast Asia, a carnivorous animal that can be ferocious when provoked. Also known as a binturong, the bearcat is a relative of the mongoose. Mike Dulaney, supervisor of primates, cats, and small animals at the Cincinnati Zoo, says that "Native Southeast Asians call the binturong 'bearcats' because they have whiskers like a cat and sit up on the hind haunches like a bear."

Mascot: UC has both a live mascot and a costumed one. Alice, who strolls the sidelines during most UC home football games, appears courtesy of the Cincinnati Zoo. Student mascots have been performing at UC athletic events for three decades. The current mascot, dressed in black fur and wearing a red Cincinnati sports jersey, dates from the 1986 football season.

Interesting Facts: Cincinnati won the national championship in men's basketball in 1961 and 1962.

The winner of the UC-Miami football game gets the Victory Bell. The winner of the UC-Louisville football game receives the Keg of Nails.

Clemson

Nickname: Tigers
Mascot: The Tiger
Colors: Orange and Purple
Conference: Atlantic Coast
Location: Clemson, S. C.
Year founded: 1889

Nickname: The late William J. Latimer, Class of 1906, is responsible for what is known about the origin of the nickname. Professor Walter Merritt Riggs, who coached Clemson's first varsity football team in 1896 and who also served as head coach again in 1899, is said to have "planted the seed" for the school's nickname.

In referring to the players from that first team, Latimer said, "Due to the lack of helmets and head protection, they (the players) wore long hair. These long manes might have gained them the name of Lions had it not been for the orange and purple striped jerseys and stockings that resembled tigers. The latter nickname seemed to stick."

Latimer then said about John Heisman's 1900 Clemson team: "They had been called Tigers early in their career. And Clemson used the insignia of a Tiger's head with bared fangs, with the motto 'Eat Em Up Clemson' before Heisman's day."

Latimer's findings are substantiated by the fact that Riggs had played football at Auburn (whose nickname was Tigers) and that its colors were orange and blue.

Mascot: Clemson University's well-known mascot is the costumed one known simply as The Tiger, sometimes called the man in stripes. The mascot was first instituted 37 years ago. Today, students go through extensive try-outs and auditions to win the coveted job. The biggest Tiger tradition of all is the pushup tradition, which began in 1978 when mascot Zack Mills began doing pushups for every point Clemson scored.

Officially, the school does not have a live mascot. However, in 1991, a 600-pound Siberian Tiger named Alex posed with the Clemson defense for the cover of the football media guide. Head coach Ken Hatfield suggested that a live tiger would add something to the picture.

Interesting Facts: Clemson has one of the most celebrated entrances onto the playing field of all collegiate teams. Called "running down the hill," it consists of the Clemson team gathering at the east side of the stadium about ten minutes before kickoff. A cannon sounds, the team song ("Tiger Rag") is played, and the Clemson team charges down a hill on that side of the stadium and onto the field.

Clemson Memorial Stadium is affectionately known to Clemson players and fans as Death Valley. The stadium was dubbed this name by Lonnie McMillian, a coach at former rival Presbyterian. His team never beat Clemson, and he once told newspaper reporters that he was going to play Clemson at Death Valley. The name stuck, although it didn't gain true popularity until the 1950s. The stadium has been ranked as the second best place to attend a college football game (in the 1989 *Sporting News* pre-season issue).

John Heisman, the coach for which the trophy is named, led Clemson to its first undefeated season in 1900. He coached at Clemson for four years.

The school celebrated its first national football championship in 1981, with a 22-15 win over Nebraska in the Orange Bowl.

Cleveland State

Nickname: Vikings
Mascot: Hagar and Helga
Colors: Forest Green and White
Conference: Mid-Continent
Location: Cleveland, Ohio
Year founded: 1923

Nickname: The student body selected Vikings as the school's nickname when Cleveland State University was formed in 1966. The school was previously known as Fenn College, a private institution whose athletic teams were called Foxes. Since students didn't think the name Foxes went well with the school's new name, they decided to vote on a different one. Close seconds and thirds in the contest were Lakers and Foresters. Throughout the years, the rumor has persisted that Cleveland State students hailing from St. Joseph High School in Cleveland stuffed the ballot boxes; the high school's nickname was Vikings.

Mascot: Costumed mascots Hagar and Helga are based on the comic strip created by the late Dik Browne. Hagar debuted in 1983 (with the permission, of course, of Browne and King Features Syndicate, Inc.). Helga joined him in 1991.

Interesting Facts: The Henry J. Goodman Arena at Cleveland State is the largest college-owned basketball facility in Ohio with a seating capacity of 13,610.

Coastal Carolina

Nickname: Chanticleers
Mascot: Chanticleer
Colors: Scarlet and Black
Conference: Big South
Location: Conway, S.C.
Year founded: 1957

Nickname: No other college has the nickname Chanticleer. The name was first suggested by a class of Coastal Carolina English literature students and its professor who wanted a unique nickname but one that also acknowledged their college's relationship to the University of South Carolina, of which Coastal is the largest regional campus. An English professor's contribution was appropriate, for he and his students chose Chanticleer, the name of a rooster in Chaucer's *Canterbury Tales.* The name associated well with South Carolina's Gamecocks.

Several attempts have been made over the years to replace the nickname with a more "modern" one, but the student body and alumni have voted overwhelmingly to keep the nickname.

Mascot: A student dresses in a chanticleer costume.

Interesting Facts: Kimbel Gymnasium, the home of Coastal Carolina basketball, is affectionately called the "Chicken Coop."

Colgate

Nickname: Red Raiders
Mascot: None

Colors: Maroon, Gray, and White
Conference: Patriot League
Location: Hamilton, N.Y.
Year founded: 1819

Nickname: Dexter Hoyt Teed, director of sports publicity for Colgate University during the 1932 season, is given credit for coining the nickname Red Raiders. At the opening game against St. Lawrence, the football players appeared on the field dressed in new game uniforms featuring maroon pants and a white jersey trimmed in maroon; players still wore the traditional Colgate white helmet. Upon seeing his team, Teed called the players the Red Raiders. The name stuck immediately.

Interesting Facts: The 1932 Colgate football team (the same one that earned the nickname Red Raiders) finished the season unbeaten, untied, and unscored upon.

Colorado

Nickname: Buffaloes
Mascot: Ralphie; Chip and Chipette
Colors: Silver, Gold, and Black
Conference: Big Eight
Location: Boulder
Year founded: 1861

Nickname: Prior to 1934, University of Colorado athletic teams were referred to as the Silver and Gold. On November 10, 1934, at the final football game of the season, CU students rented a buffalo calf. Its presence at the 7-6 victory over Utah was an immediate hit with the fans; after that game, the teams gained the nickname Buffaloes.

Mascot: The University has both a live mascot and two costumed mascots. The first buffalo, Mr. Chips, was given to CU by Mahlon White. It was a regular at home games through the 1950s. For several years CU went without a mascot. Then in 1966, the first Ralphie made its appearance. At first, the six-month-old calf was called Ralph until it was discovered that it was in fact a girl; thus, the name Ralphie. Attending every CU home football game for 13 years, Ralphie retired at the end of the 1978 season. She died at the ripe old age of 16 in 1982. Ralphie II served from the final home game in 1978 until she passed away on September 19, 1987, following a 31-17 win over Stanford. On November 7, 1987, Ralphie III made her debut at the CU-Missouri game. The present buffalo weighs about 1200 pounds and is able to reach speeds of up to 25 miles per hour. She is owned by John and Sharon Parker and is kept at the Parker Ranch.

CU has two student mascots, Chip and Chipette, who perform at athletic events.

Interesting Facts: Colorado's only football national championship (AP poll) was in 1990 under Coach Bill McCartney. That year, linebacker Alfred Williams won the Butkus Award.

Colorado's halfback Byron "Whizzer" White's 1937 mark of 246.3 yards per game stood as the Division I-A season record for 51 years until Oklahoma State's Barry Sanders broke it with 295.5 yards in 1988.

The school has won 12 national championships in skiing.

Colorado won the NIT basketball championship in 1940.

Colorado State

Nickname: Rams
Mascot: Ram
Colors: Green and Gold
Conference: Western Athletic
Location: Fort Collins

Year founded: 1870

Nickname: The official nickname of Colorado State University was adopted in 1957. Rams was selected because of the geographical location and agricultural background of the school.

Mascot: An English bulldog named Peanuts was Colorado State's first live mascot.

It accompanied the football and basketball team to both home and road games. In 1919, Peanuts was replaced with a black bear cub who stayed a short time as mascot. It was not until 1946 that a Rocky Mountain bighorn sheep became the school's mascot. Donated to the athletic department by a student group, Cam I's name symbolized the school's former name, Colorado A & M.

The current mascot is Cam IX who debuted during the Rams' 1989 basketball season, the first year that Colorado State returned to the NCAA Tournament in two decades. Cam IX is a Rambouillet ram, the largest and strongest of the fine-wool sheep. Weighing about 275 pounds, Cam resides at the school's livestock farm.

Colorado State also has a costumed mascot, a student dressed in a ram costume who participates at athletic events.

Interesting Facts: One of the oldest traditions at Colorado State is the Aggie "A." Looming above the school's Hughes Stadium on the foothills west of Fort Collins, it stands as a landmark for the city and the University. The whitewashed rock formation measures 450 feet tall and 300 feet wide. It was created as an outgrowth of a planned "sneak day" from classes by male graduating students in 1923. The president then, Charles Lory, found out about the plan and summoned the students to his office where all parties agreed instead to build the "A." Civil engineering major Don Jones from Cody, Wyoming, designed the letter, and students began the project. Whitewashing the "A" soon became an annual school tradition for male freshmen.

Columbia

Nickname: Lions
Mascot: Lion
Colors: Columbia Blue and White
Conference: Ivy League
Location: New York, N.Y.
Year founded: 1754

Nickname: The Columbia University Student Board adopted the Lion as the sports symbol in 1910, following presentation of a blue and white banner bearing a Lion rampant with the motto, "Leo, Columbiae" (Lion of Columbia). George Brokaw, Class of 1909, suggested the nickname.

The Columbia Lion served as the basis for the MGM logo. It was suggested by Howard Dietz, Class of 1917, and was adopted by the movie studio soon after.

Prior to being called the Lions, Columbia athletic teams were labeled the Blue and White.

Mascot: A student costumed as a lion cheers on crowds at sporting events.

Interesting Facts: Columbia was the third college in the country to play intercollegiate football. Princeton and Rutgers played the first game in 1869. Columbia played Rutgers, with 20 men on a side, at New Brunswick, New Jersey, on November 12, 1870—Rutgers winning six games to three.

Columbia played in the first Ivy League game on November 16, 1872, losing to Yale, 3-0.

The only undefeated football team in Columbia history was the 1915 squad coached by T. Nelson Metcalf which went 5-0 in the first football season.

The two best gridiron records were compiled within the four -year span of 1931 and 1934. Lou Little's team won the 1934 Rose Bowl, beating Stanford, 6-0.

The men's basketball team won the national championship in 1904, 1905, and 1910.

Since 1951, Columbia has won the men's fencing national title 11 times.

Connecticut

Nickname: Huskies
Mascot: Husky
Colors: National Flag Blue and White
Conference: Yankee
Location: Storrs
Year founded: 1881

Nickname: On November 9, 1934, a group of fun-loving Connecticut students piled into a Model-T Ford just prior to the Connecticut-Rhode Island football game and traveled to the Rhode Island campus in Kingston and stole the school's beloved mascot ram named Ramesis II. The heist, dubbed "ram-knapping" by the media, made national news. Because of the incident and at the urging of the editor-in-chief of Connecticut's student newspaper, Connecticut students conducted a poll and elected to adopt a Husky dog as the school's first official mascot. Thus, the nickname Huskies was born.

Mascot: The University of Connecticut has a long tradition of live mascots. In December 1934 the first Husky was delivered to the campus. The beautiful white pup was named Jonathan I after Jonathan Trumbull, the governor of Connecticut during the Revolutionary War. Three months after his arrival, Jonathan I died. He was buried near the steps of Old Whitney Hall, and students contributed a bronze plaque to his memory.

Probably no Connecticut mascot was more well known than Jonathan III. He was with Admiral Byrd when the famed explorer undertook "Operation High Jump" to the Antarctic in

1946-47. After he arrived for the 1947 football season, he was known as the UConn Husky!

In the spring of 1969, in the midst of the student uprisings across the country, the Student Senate voted to sell Jonathan VII. The student body had other plans. After students gathered 2,500 signatures on a petition, a newly formed Student Senate in 1970 brought back Jonathan VII. He lived to be 14 years old.

In addition to the present Jonathan X, a costumed mascot also entertains at athletic events.

Interesting Facts: Connecticut won the national championship in soccer in 1981. The women's team played for the championship in 1984 and 1990 but lost to North Carolina both times.

The University won the 1988 NIT Championship in men's basketball.

The women's field hockey team won the national title in 1981 and 1985.

Connecticut College

Nickname: Camels
Mascot: Camel
Colors: Royal Blue and White
Conference: New England Small College Athletic
Location: New London
Year founded: 1911

Nickname: Camels became the college nickname in 1969. Selected by the men's basketball team, Camels was chosen because of its originality as well as for its symbol of endurance and fortitude.

Mascot: A student costumed as a camel is the school's mascot.

Interesting Facts: The women's rowing team at Connecticut College has won four New England titles in recent years. The College is constructing a new rowing tank facility which will feature a 5,000-square foot rowing/training room.

Coppin State

Nickname: Eagles
Mascot: Eagle
Colors: Blue and Gold
Conference: Mid-Eastern Athletic
Location: Baltimore, Md.
Year founded: 1900

Nickname: The Eagles nickname comes from the college's first yearbook, named *The Eagle* by students. The Eagle was chosen, as it was stated in that first publication, "because this great American bird characterizes courage, strength, and keenness of vision." It was, then, a natural choice for the school's nickname.

Mascot: A costumed eagle mascot performs for Coppin State athletic crowds.

Interesting Facts: CSC's 1976 basketball team won the NAIA national championship.

Larry Stewart, former Coppin State basketball player and now a player in the NBA, was 1991's Black College Player of the Year.

Coppin State College was named for Fanny Jackson Coppin, one of the leaders in black education in the late 19th century. A former slave, she attended Ohio's Oberlin College and earned her bachelor's degree in 1865. She was one of the first black women to earn a degree from a major American college.

Cornell

Nickname: The Big Red
Mascot: Bear
Colors: Red and White

Conference: Ivy League
Location: Ithaca, N.Y.
Year founded: 1865

Nickname: In 1905, Romeyn Berry, a recent Cornell University graduate and future graduate manager of athletics for the school, was writing the lyrics for the school's new football song. Cornell had no nickname; therefore, Berry simply referred to his alma mater as the "big red team," alluding to the school colors. The name caught on, and Cornell has been the Big Red ever since.

Mascot: Cornell's nickname and mascot have no true connection. The first live bear mascot simply appeared for the first time in 1915 during Cornell's undefeated national championship season. There have been three live bear mascots since, although today the mascot is a Cornell student in a costume who performs at all home football and hockey games.

Interesting Facts: Cornell has one of the largest intercollegiate programs in the country. The men's lacrosse team was the NCAA champion in 1971, 1976, and 1977. The women's crew team won the national championship in 1989. Cornell won the national championship in hockey in 1967 and 1970. The University has won the Intercollegiate Rowing Association Regatta 24 times, more than any other school.

Cornell is the only Ivy League school with an eight-lane indoor track.

In 1971 Ed Marinaro, now an actor, won the Maxwell Award, given by the Maxwell Football Club of Philadelphia, for the top player in college football.

Dartmouth

Nickname: Big Green
Mascot: None
Colors: Dartmouth Green and White
Conference: Ivy league
Location: Hanover, N.H.
Year founded: 1769

Nickname: Big Green was adopted in 1972 after Indians was dropped as Dartmouth College's nickname. Native American students had voiced concern over the use of the name. It is not known why Big Green was chosen, but there is speculation that the name could refer to the large pine tree found in the official College seal and also in the alma mater, "Men of Dartmouth."

Interesting Facts: Dartmouth won the national championship in football in 1925 with a 8-0 record. The College went undefeated in football in 1965 but was unranked; in 1970, it was 9-0 and #14 in the AP poll.

Dartmouth won the national championship in men and women's skiing in 1958 and 1977. The College has had skiers entered in every winter Olympics.

The men's golf team won the national championship in 1921.

Dartmouth won the national championship in hockey in 1941-42.

The College has also won national championships in gymnastics, rowing, heavyweight eights, four without cox, trap-shooting, sailing, cross cut saw, figure skating, fencing, kayaking, skeet shooting, speed skating, squash, tae kwon do, tennis, and track and field.

Davidson

Nickname: Wildcats
Mascot: Wildcat
Colors: Black and Red
Conference: Big South
Location: Davidson, N.C.
Year founded: 1837

Nickname: Several versions exist about the origin of Davidson College's nickname. Davidson, a small college, has historically played major colleges and has experienced considerable success. The nickname was adopted sometime between 1917 and 1920. Some sources say the name originated at a football game between Davidson and Georgia Tech when some Georgians commented that the Davidson team "fought like a bunch of wildcats."

Albert S. Potts, Class of 1919, wrote sports stories for Charlotte and Atlanta papers while a student. According to his accounts, he began using Wildcats in his stories because he didn't think the school's nickname at the time, Preachers, suited their fighting spirit.

However, Lacy McAlister, Class of 1920, feels the name was the result of Davidson's 21-7 win over Auburn in 1917. At that time the Atlanta *Constitution* headlined the game story "Wildcats Twist Tigers' Tail."

Mascot: A student dressed as a wildcat represents the athletic teams.

Interesting Facts: In 1984, the women's tennis team, led by coach Caroline Price, became the first and only Davidson team to win a national championship when it took home the Division III title.

Dayton

Nickname: Flyers
Mascot: Rudy Flyer
Colors: Red and Blue
Conference: Midwestern Collegiate
Location: Dayton, Ohio
Year founded: 1850

Nickname: Dayton's nickname, Flyers, was suggested by Bro. Charles Arns and accepted by the Catholic university in 1923. The city of Dayton is known as the birthplace of aviation.

Mascot: Rudy Flyer, an exaggeration of a 1920s barnstorming pilot, was adopted by the Student Association in 1980. A student dressed as Rudy Flyer entertains crowds at athletic events.

Interesting Facts: Dayton played for the NCAA Division III football championship in 1991, but lost to Ithaca College (N.Y.)

The University of Dayton Arena hosted what many consider the greatest college basketball game of all time. On March 22, 1975, Kentucky ended Bobby Knight's Indiana Hoosiers' dream of an undefeated season by defeating them 92-90 in the NCAA tournament Mideast Regional Final, handing IU its lone loss in 32 games that season.

Pittsburgh Steelers' coach Chuck Noll is a Dayton alumnus.

Delaware

Nickname: Fightin' Blue Hens
Mascot: Fightin' Blue Hen
Colors: Royal Blue and Gold

Conference: Yankee
Location: Newark
Year founded: 1833

Nickname: The unique nickname, Fightin' Blue Hens, is associated with the history of Delaware. Though there are conflicting stories as to the name's origin, the generally accepted story goes back to the Revolutionary War.

On December 9, 1775, the Continental Congress resolved that a military battalion was to be formed from the lower three counties along the Delaware River. One of the eight companies formed was composed of men from Kent County and was under the command of Captain Jonathan Caldwell, who was reported to be an avid fan of and owner of gamecocks. The militia is reported to have staged cock fights with these birds which were known as the Kent County Blue Hens because of their blue plumage. The renown of these chickens spread rapidly since cock fighting was a popular form of amusement then, and the Blue Hens quickly developed a reputation for ferocity and fighting success.

Captain Caldwell's company likewise acquired a reputation for its fighting prowess in engagements with the British and was soon known as "the Blue Hen Chicken" company. One story says that Caldwell's company rushed into battle screaming "We're sons of the Blue Hen, and we're game to the end."

Captain Caldwell's company was part of Colonel John Haslet's first Delaware regiment. Although referred to as "The Fighting Delawares," Haslet's regiment was also called "The Blue Hen's Chickens," which has become the accepted name for all Delawareans. The name was officially adopted by the Delaware General Assembly in April 1939 when the Blue Hen Chicken was named the state bird.

Mascot: The Agricultural School has a flock of actual birds which are game cocks.

A student costumed as a Fightin' Blue Hen represents the school at all athletic events.

Interesting Facts: Delaware won national championships in NCAA Division II football in 1946, 1963, 1971, 1972, and 1979.

The most celebrated game in Delaware history was probably the Delaware-Youngston State game in 1979. The Blue Hens, who trailed Youngstown State 31-7 at halftime, roared out of their locker room to score 44 second-half points after the Youngstown public address announcer had said, "Let's Hang The Chicken!" Delaware won 38-21 for the national title and the best record in college football, 13-1.

Delaware State

Nickname: Hornets
Mascot: The Hornet
Colors: Columbia Blue and Red
Conference: Mid-Eastern Athletic
Location: Dover
Year founded: 1891

Nickname: The nickname Hornets originated from a team bus called The Blue Hornet, used in the 1940s.

Mascot: The Hornet is the costumed mascot.

Interesting Facts: The 1934 football squad went 8-0, allowing just two points all season. Delaware State won the 1947 Flower Bowl in the school's only known post-season bowl game.

Delta State

Nickname: Statesmen
Mascot: Statesman
Conference: Gulf South
Colors: Forest Green and White
Location: Cleveland, Miss.

Year founded: 1924

Nickname: Delta State University's nickname was first used in the mid to late 1950s. According to the sports information director, the origin is believed to be that the school's athletes "performed and behaved like true statesmen."

Mascot: A student dressed as a statesman is the mascot.

Interesting Facts: The women's basketball team has won five national championships.

Margaret Wade, former coach, was inducted into the Basketball Hall of Fame in Springfield, Massachusetts, in June 1985.

Lusia Harris, three-time All-American in women's basketball, scored the first points ever in women's Olympic basketball in 1976.

DePaul

Nickname: Blue Demons
Mascot: Billy Blue Demon
Colors: Royal Blue and Scarlet
Conference: Great Midwest
Location: Chicago, Ill.
Year founded: 1898

Nickname: When the first athletic team to represent DePaul University organized in 1900, the uniforms proudly displayed a blue "D." The first nickname developed from this, as the first teams were called D-Men. This name evolved into Demons and, eventually, into Blue Demons. The color blue signifies loyalty. The student body chose the final nickname in 1901.

Mascot: A student dressed in costume appears at games as Billy

Blue Demon.

Interesting Facts: DePaul won the NIT men's basketball tournament in 1945.

The men's basketball team ranked first in the nation at the end of the regular season in both 1980 and 1981.

DePauw

Nickname: Tigers
Mascot: Tiger
Colors: Gold and Black
Conference: Indiana Collegiate Athletic
Location: Greencastle, Ind.
Year founded: 1837

Nickname: When students selected a nickname for their DePauw athletic teams in 1918, the five final suggestions were Tigers, Yellow Demons, Yellow Jackets, Wasps, and Fighting Parsons. The nicknames chosen, including the winning Tigers, were selected to work with the already established school colors of gold and black.

Mascot: A student dresses up in a tiger costume for football and basketball games.

Interesting Facts: The annual clash between DePauw University and Wabash College has been called "the oldest uninterrupted football rivalry west of the Alleghenies." The two schools have met each other without fail since 1910; no other rivalry has been played continuously for so many years. The winner of the game takes home the Monon Bell, a tradition started in 1932. The Bell has been stolen at least five times throughout the years, the most infamous "thefts" taking place in the mid-1960s. After several Wabash students stole the bell after a DePauw victory, a group of DePauw students stole it back and promptly buried it in the north end zone of their school's stadium. It remained buried there for 11 months, until the next Monon Bell Game. Prior to the game, however, the ground froze; the students were barely able to recover it in time for the game, which Wabash won.

Detroit

Nickname: Titans
Mascot: Tommy Titan
Colors: Red, White, and Blue
Conference: Midwestern Collegiate
Location: Detroit, Mich.
Year founded: 1877

Nickname: Prior to 1919, the University of Detroit athletic teams claimed the nickname Tigers. Because Detroit's professional baseball team went by the same name, things were often confusing. In the fall of 1919, sportswriter Stan Brink of the Detroit *Free Press* gave the school a new nickname. Because the members of the football squad were exceptionally large that year, Brink thought that Titans would be a good name.

Mascot: Tommy Titan is the school's costumed mascot.

Interesting Facts: The men's fencing team won the 1972 NCAA national title.
From 1974-1977, ABC's/ESPN's commentator Dick Vitale was head basketball coach.

Drake

Nickname: Bulldogs
Mascot: Spike and Spice Bulldog
Colors: Blue and White
Conference: Missouri Valley
Location: Des Moines, Iowa
Year founded: 1881

Nickname: Football coach John L. Griffith kept his pet bulldog on the sidelines during practices and games; therefore, the team became known as the Bulldogs.

Mascot: Two costumed student mascots—a male called Spike and a female named Spice—entertain at Drake University athletic events.

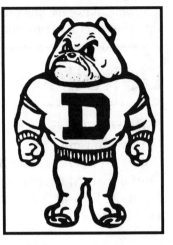

Interesting Facts: The Bulldogs have won seven Missouri Valley Conference championships and made four NCAA tournament appearances. Since 1962, Veterans Memorial Auditorium has been the home of Drake basketball. The Bulldogs have a lifetime winning percentage of over 70 percent at Veterans Auditorium and have had two perfect home seasons there, posting 13-0 marks during the 1963-64 and 1969-70 seasons.

Duke

Nickname: Blue Devils
Mascot: Blue Devil
Colors: Royal Blue and White
Conference: Atlantic Coast
Location: Durham, N.C.
Year founded: 1838

Nickname: In 1922, William H. Lander, assistant editor of the Duke *Chronicle,* suggested Blue Devils as the athletic nickname because of the growing dissatisfaction with the monikers Methodists and Blue and White. Beginning with the 1922-23 *Chronicle,* co-editors Lander and Mike Bradshaw insisted that all sports teams be referred to as Blue Devils in the paper. That year the name didn't catch on with the campus news bureau or the cheerleaders. Through sheer repetition, though, Blue Devils eventually became the nickname for all athletic teams.

Blue Devils originated from the French Blue Devils, an Alpine corps which wore a blue uniform with a blue beret.

Mascot: A student costumed as a Blue Devil performs at sporting events.

Interesting Facts: Duke University won the 1991 national championship in men's basketball with a 32-7 record and repeated as champ in 1992.

On November 29, 1888, Trinity College (which later became Duke University) defeated the University of North Carolina, 16-0, in the first game of intercollegiate football ever played below the Mason-Dixon line. Six hundred spectators attended the contest held at the fairgrounds in Raleigh on Thanksgiving Day. Men paid 25 cents to see the game, and women 15 cents.

Duke is the only site other than Pasadena, California, to have hosted the Rose Bowl; the school played Oregon State in the 1942 Rose Bowl in Durham. Duke coach Wallace Wade said of his 20-16 loss, "I think I had to pay too much attention to making arrangements for the playing of the game and not enough to the coaching of the team."

Duke has participated in all four of the major football bowl games. In 1939 Duke lost to Southern California in the Rose Bowl. In 1945 Duke beat Alabama in the Sugar Bowl. In 1955 Duke beat Nebraska in the Orange Bowl, and three years later Oklahoma beat Duke in the same bowl. In the 1961 Cotton Bowl, Duke defeated Arkansas.

Duquesne

Nickname: Dukes
Mascot: Duke
Colors: Red and Blue
Conference: Midwestern Collegiate
Location: Pittsburgh, Pa.
Year founded: 1878

Nickname: Contrary to popular opinion, Dukes was not chosen because it was a shortened version of Duquesne. The origin of the nickname goes back to 1911 when the University of the Holy Ghost was changed to Duquesne University of the Holy Ghost. (The shortened name, Duquesne University, became official in 1935.) Duquesne was chosen in honor of Marquis Duquesne who built Fort Duquesne at The Point in Pittsburgh in 1754. He was the first man to bring Catholic observances to the city. Since a marquis and a duke dress similarly, the unofficial symbol of the school's athletic teams became duke, a more recognizable name than marquis.

Mascot: The costumed mascot dresses in a top hat with tails and a sash of royalty across his chest.

Interesting Facts: Duquesne's football tradition began in 1927 when Elmer Layden joined the school as head coach and athletic director. He was one of the fabled "Four Horsemen" of Notre Dame lore. He coached the team until 1933 when he returned to Notre Dame as head coach and athletic director. His final game as coach at Duquesne was a historical one. It was at the first Festival of the Palms Bowl in Miami, Florida. Today, the bowl is known as the Orange Bowl. (By the way, Duquesne won the game against Miami convincingly, 32-7.) While at Duquesne, Layden instituted some of college football's more famous practices; he was the first coach to use home and away jerseys and devised the system of signal officials informing players and fans of penalties.

The 1939-40 Duquesne basketball team was the first to play in both the NIT and NCAA championships. The Dukes won the 1955 NIT basketball championship.

In 1950, All-American Chuck Cooper became the first black player drafted by the NBA; he was chosen by the Boston Celtics.

East Carolina

Nickname: Pirates
Mascot: Pirate
Colors: Purple and Gold
Conference: Independent
Location: Greenville, N.C.
Year founded: 1907

Nickname: East Carolina University's nickname can be traced back to 1934. That year the *Tecoan*, the yearbook for what was then East Carolina Teachers College, carried pirates as its theme. The pages were filled with paintings and sketches of patched-eye figures, tall ships, and buried treasure. The yearbook referred to tales of "Teachy the Pirate" often told by natives in the nearby historic town of Bath. Pirates was a natural choice because the school is located just a few miles from the Outer Banks of North Carolina where pirates hid out in the Colonial period.

Mascot: A student dressed in a pirate costume performs at athletic events.

Interesting Facts: The annual Great Pirate Purple/Gold Pigskin Pigout Party is the school's (and one of the state's) most popular springtime events. Festivities at the event include fireworks, concerts, golf and tennis tournaments, cooking contests, a baseball game, and, the big attraction, the spring football game. In 1990, the Party attracted 30,000 people to the pre-football game festivities and 10,000 to the football game—the largest spring game attendance ever in the state of North Carolina.

East Carolina has one of the youngest football programs in the country, only having played the sport for 56 years.

East Stroudsburg

Nickname: Warriors
Mascot: Warrior
Colors: Red and Black
Conference: Pennsylvania State Athletic
Location: East Stroudsburg, Pa.
Year founded: 1893

Nickname: East Stroudsburg University's athletic teams were known as the Red and Black until 1932. On April 8th of that year, a writer for the *Stroud Courier*, the campus newspaper, who signed her column, "Just Debs," wrote: "The majority of colleges have nicknames for their athletic teams. This writer in the future is going to refer to the local teams as the Warriors. We're in Indian territory, you know, and our men run wild on the sports field frequently." The new nickname was born.

Mascot: A student dressed like an Indian warrior is the school's costumed mascot.

Interesting Facts: The spot where East Stroudsburg's Eiler-Martin Stadium now stands was originally a swamp. The land was filled by East Stroudsburg State Teachers' College students working in federal work programs started after Franklin Roosevelt was elected president in 1932. Many football players at the time were members of the work crew.

East Tennessee State

Nickname: Buccaneers
Mascot: Bucky; Pepper
Colors: Navy Blue and Old Gold
Conference: Southern
Location: Johnson City
Year founded: 1911

Nickname: A 1936 vote of East Tennessee State University's student body decided the school's nickname, Buccaneers. A legendary explanation is that athletic teams got their names from a pirate (a buccaneer) named Jean Paul LeBucque. This tongue-in-cheek story says that LeBucque, looking for an inland hiding place for his treasure, sailed as far as Tennessee before he was killed.

Mascot: A buccaneer named Bucky and a parrot named Pepper serve as ETSU's costumed mascots at athletic events.

Interesting Facts: East Tennessee State's Memorial Center, which opened in 1977, is probably the only building in the world which contains a football field and a medical college. The entire second floor of the tri-level structure is home to the James H. Quillen College of Medicine.

East Texas State

Nickname: Lions
Mascot: Lucky the Lion
Colors: Blue and Gold
Conference: Lone Star
Location: Commerce
Year founded: 1889

Nickname: Two explanations exist as to the origin of East Texas State University's nickname. According to an early article in the school newspaper, *The East Texan,* player-coach Marion "Doc" Mayo, son of founder Dr. W.L. Mayo, named the first football team the Lions. However, an August 1970 doctoral dissertation by Marie Simpson Franks about the history of the ETSU Department of Health & P.E., quotes a personal letter from Mrs.  Roy Owens that disputes the Mayo claim. Mrs. Owens' letter says, "It is true that my husband Roy Clifton Owens walked the streets of Commerce and asked for money to buy football uniforms, and that he did nickname the team 'the Lions'."

Mascot: The costumed mascot, Lucky, is part of the ETSU cheerleader squad.

Interesting Facts: ETSU was the first school to win NAIA championships in both basketball (1955) and football (1972).

In past years, ETSU played the Livingston (Alabama) Tigers for the Chennault Cup which honors Lt. General Claire Chennault—a Commerce, Texas, native of Flying Tigers fame. Currently, East Texas is playing Texas A&I for the Cup.

Eastern Illinois

Nickname: Panthers
Mascot: Panther
Colors: Blue and Gray
Conference: Mid-Continent
Location: Charleston
Year founded: 1895

Nickname: The nickname Panthers was chosen in a vote of the

Eastern Illinois University student body. It is unsure when the nickname was actually selected, although it is generally believed that it occurred in the 1920s or 1930s.

Mascot: A costumed panther performs at EIU athletic events.

Interesting Facts: The Panthers won the NCAA Division II national championship in football in 1978 beating Delaware by the score of 10-9.

Eastern Kentucky

Nickname: Colonels
Mascot: Colonel
Colors: Maroon and White
Conference: Ohio Valley
Location: Richmond
Year founded: 1906

Nickname: In 1966, when University status became official for Eastern Kentucky, the nickname changed from Maroons to Colonels to allow for a visible, tangible mascot.

Mascot: A student is dressed up like an old Kentucky Colonel Southern gentleman, complete with white hair and beard wearing a maroon and gray colonel uniform.

Interesting Facts: The University won the the NCAA Division I-AA national football championships in 1979 and 1982.

Eastern New Mexico

Nickname: Greyhounds; Zias
Mascot: Greyhound

Colors: Silver and Green
Conference: Lone Star
Location: Portales
Year founded: 1934

Nickname: The origin of Greyhounds came about in 1934 when football center Carrol McCasland saw a passing Greyhound bus making its daily run through town. Five days prior to inaugurating the first president of the University, the entire student body and faculty, after a heated discussion, voted on Greyhounds as the nickname. The first logo resembled the dog on the side of the Greyhound bus. A variety of logos are used today. Only one other school in the nation—Yankton College of South Dakota—uses the nickname Greyhounds.

The name Zias was chosen for women's athletics through a contest to rename the team. The Zia, the symbol also of the New Mexico state flag, is an ancient sun symbol of the Zia Indians. The zia symbol is composed of a circle from which four points radiate signifying the earth with its four directions; the year with its four seasons; the day with its time of sunrise, noon, evening, and night; and life with its four divisions of childhood, youth, manhood, and old age.

Mascot: Two costumed greyhounds—a male, Ralph, and a female, Roxy—represent the university.

Interesting Facts: The Eastern New Mexico University football team made one of the greatest comebacks in college history on September 15, 1984, in Ada, Oklahoma, against East Central University. Trailing 46-14, with 1:51 to go in the third quarter, the Greyhounds erupted for 36 unanswered points to pull out a 50-46 victory.

The football team has played in several unusual games in its history. Two were in 1957. In one game playing Austin College in Sherman, Texas, the majority of the Greyhounds suffered with the Asiatic flu, and by game time, nine starters had not practiced all week. Eastern used the platoon system every first down throughout the game to rest the weakened players. Eastern won 28-14. In another game against Los Angeles State, a thick fog and mist rolled into Greyhound Stadium leaving visibility minimal. Thirty-six stadium lights went off to further hinder visibility. Eastern was able to find its way on its own turf to win, 27-0.

The basketball team won the NAIA National Championship in 1968-69.

Eastern Washington

Nickname: Eagles
Mascot: None
Colors: Red and White
Conference: Big Sky
Location: Cheney
Year founded: 1882

Nickname: Savages was the name used to refer to Eastern Washington University's athletic teams for 92 years. Then, in 1974, the student body voted to change the nickname to Eagles. The new name was a suitable one since eagles live in the Eastern Washington area.

Mascot: The school has no live or costumed mascot, but the University logo is the eagle.

Interesting Facts: Eastern Washington played for the NAIA Division I football championship in 1967 but lost to Fairmont State (W.V.).

Edinboro

Nickname: Fighting Scots
Mascot: None
Colors: Red and White
Conference: Pennsylvania
Location: Edinboro, Pa.
Year founded: 1857

Nickname: Until 1964, Edinboro University's primary nickname was the Red Raiders, but the school's teams were also called the Plaid, Clan, Tartans, Highlanders, and Scotties. In 1964, students were given three choices to vote for—Tartans, Highlanders, and Scotties. Highlanders won, but because the vote was not overwhelming, confusion continued as newspapers used the nickname Scots. The sports information director at the time, Paul Newman, felt the school's numerous nicknames were hurting the identity of the school. He talked to the coaches and school president about changing the name to Fighting Scots. Edinboro continued to have both nicknames—Fighting Scots and Highlanders—until the 1969-70 school year when a Fighting Scot logo was officially adopted. A Fighting Scot with a kilt, sword, and shield is still used as the official logo.

Interesting Facts: Edinboro has won six national championships in men's cross country.

Elon

Nickname: Fightin' Christians
Mascot: A Fightin' Christian
Colors: Maroon and Gold
Conference: South Atlantic
Location: Elon College, N.C.

Year founded: 1889

Nickname: Before 1921, Elon teams were referred to by various newspapers as the Elon Eleven, the Maroon and Gold Machine, and the Bearcats. The first reference to the school as Christians came on November 11, 1921, when Elon College, affiliated with the Christian Church (now the United Church of Christ) played Guilford, a small Quaker college nearby, in their traditional football game. The meeting was called the battle of the Christians and Quakers, names that stuck in both cases. "Fightin'" was tacked on years later.

The women's teams were named the Golden Girls in the early years of organized women's basketball (1975) after a fan, William D. Ellis, wrote a poem naming the Golden Girls. In recent years, women teams have started to use the title of Lady Fightin' Christians, a move that has all but eliminated the Golden Girls.

Mascot: The mascot did not come into being until the early 1970s. A student dressed in the costume of a bearded Puritan is the school's representative at athletic events.

Interesting Facts: Elon won the 1980 and 1981 NAIA national championships in football. In 1982, the golf team won the national title, and the men's tennis team was national champions in 1990.

Bobby Hedrick, a running back for Elon, set numerous rushing records during the late 1970s and early 1980s with his 5,605 career rushing yards.

Evansville

Nickname: Aces

Mascot: Ace Purple
Colors: Purple and White
Conference: Midwestern Collegiate
Location: Evansville, Ind.
Year founded: 1854

Nickname: Prior to 1926, University of Evansville athletic teams used the nickname Pioneers. Dan Scism, a sportswriter, is credited with first using the name Aces in headlines. Scism said that Coach John Harmon in 1926 "suggested I call them the Aces because he was told by Louisville's coach that he didn't have four aces up his sleeve, he had five!"

Mascot: In the late 1960s, Larry Hill, an artist for the *Evansville Press,* created the first mascot, Ace Purple, in the image of a turn-of-the-century riverboat gambler, which represented Evansville's location on the banks of the Ohio River. The first Ace was not very popular as he walked around brandishing a club with a spike through one end; he also possessed a penchant for pulling out a derringer pistol and blowing his enemies into the next card party. Ace Purple vanished soon.

In 1977, when Evansville moved to Division I basketball, sports information director Greg Knipping saw the need for a team mascot. He contacted Keith Butz, known for revamping the Purdue Boilermaker. The trustees of Evansville, which is a United Methodist institution, had to be sold on the idea of bringing back a gambler as the costumed mascot. Knipping quickly pointed out that qualities of the gambler are also widely used on the athletic field—cunning, daring, a quick wit, and shrewd judgment. The school's officials were pleased with Butz's new creation of Ace Purple. Football coach John Moses said, "Ace Purple is definitely needed. He can't run, throw, catch or tackle...but he's got class."

Interesting Facts: The Evansville University Band members wear riverboat gambler uniforms, which are unique to college athletics.

F

Fairfield

Nickname: Stags
Mascot: None
Colors: Cardinal Red
Conference: Metro Atlantic
Athletic
Location: Fairfield, Conn.
Year founded: 1942

Nickname: Fairfield University's wooded 200-acre campus provided the inspiration for the first school seal. Designed when the Catholic university first opened to students, the seal featured a deer leaping over a tumbling brook which represented the school's close ties to nature. After seeing the school seal, the University's Order of Jesuits selected Stags as the official athletic nickname.

Interesting Facts: Fairfield's Alumni Hall has earned a reputation as one of the toughest arenas to play in due to the loyalty and enthusiasm of fans. Alumni Hall's "Stagmania" is led by student sections known as the Red Sea and Sixth Man.

The school compiled a 26-game winning streak in Alumni Hall from 1976-78. Fans were listed among the nation's most vocal in *Sports Illustrated's* 1986-87 college basketball preview issue.

Fairleigh Dickinson

Nickname: Knights
Mascot: Knight
Colors: Columbia Blue, White, and Maroon
Conference: Northeast
Location: Rutherford, N.J.
Year founded: 1942

Nickname: Athletic teams at Fairleigh Dickinson University have been known as the Knights since 1948. Dr. Peter Samartino, founder and first president of the school, suggested the name. Dr. Samartino's office was located in the administration building known as the Castle. Inside the building was a statue of a knight in a suit of armor.

Mascot: A student dressed as a knight is the school's mascot.

Interesting Facts: Fairleigh Dickinson began a program called "Giants Back to School" in 1985. Since the program began, 14 degrees have been granted. Fifteen members of the 1991 Super Bowl Champion New York Giants enrolled at the University.

Ferris State

Nickname: Bulldogs
Mascot: Bulldog
Colors: Crimson and Gold
Conference: Midwest Intercollegiate
Location: Big Rapids, Mich.
Year founded: 1884

Nickname: Bulldogs was chosen as the Ferris State University nickname in 1930. The name was applied to the Ferris Institute basketball team because the players demonstrated the ability to guard the opposition doggedly and never let up. During an eight-game winning streak for the 1930 squad, Ferris held the opposition to an average of 17.1 points per game. The present logo was redesigned in 1979 by former Ferris State graphic artist Terry Davenport, the son of the athletic director Dean Davenport.

Mascot: A student costumed as a bulldog is the school mascot. Each year the identity of the student is kept secret.

Florida

Nickname: Gators
Mascot: Albert and Alberta Gator
Colors: Orange and Blue
Conference: Southeastern
Location: Gainesville
Year founded: 1853

Nickname: In 1907, Austin Miller, a native of Gainesville, was enrolled in the University of Virginia. His father, Phillip Miller, a Gainesville merchant, came to visit him. While in Charlottesville, Mr. Miller decided to order some pennants and banners for the University of Florida from the Michie Company. The Millers went to the firm where they were shown pennants of other colleges. When the manager asked for Florida's emblem, both father and son realized that Florida had none; Austin then suggested the name Alligators because the alligator was native to Florida. Unfortunately, the Michie manager had never seen an alligator, therefore, he couldn't design one. After Austin located a picture in the University of Virginia library, the Michie firm designed an emblem. In 1908, Philip Miller's store carried the blue banners measuring six by three feet, showing a large orange alligator. The pennants proved to be popular with Florida students, and the nickname was launched.

Mascot: Two costumed male and female students—Albert and Alberta Alligator—represent the school at sporting events.

Interesting Facts: Quarterback Steve Spurrier won the Heisman Trophy in 1966. Currently, he is Florida's head football coach.

The Florida football team was named national champions for the 1984 season by the New York *Times* and *The Sporting News.*

The 1990 football team posted a 9-2 overall record, and its 9-1 start was the best in school history. It finished with the best SEC record with a 6-1 mark, the first time in school history that a Gator team had six conference wins in a season. The 1990 team also was the first UF team since 1928 to defeat both Alabama and Auburn in the same year.

Florida won the men's swimming and diving national championship in 1983 and 1984. The men's golf team was national champions in 1968 and 1973.

Florida A&M

Nickname: Rattlers
Mascot: None
Colors: Orange and Green
Conference: Mid-Eastern Athletic
Location: Tallahassee
Year founded: 1887

Nickname: Two stories exist about the origin of Rattlers as Florida A&M University's nickname. One explanation is that the name was given to the school's fledgling athletic teams in the 1920s by President J.R.E. Lee, Sr., who wished to give his school's teams "a name which would strike fear into the hearts of their opponents." Another story says that when the site of the current campus was cleared nothing existed but rattlesnakes and palm trees. Thus, the name rattlers became associated with the school. In fact, some early school seals showed a palm tree and a rattler under the tree.

Mascot: Florida A&M doesn't have a live mascot today, but the school did have one briefly in the mid-1970s. A rattler was kept fat and feisty feeding on rats and mice in the basement of the pharmacy school.

Interesting Facts: Florida A&M won national titles in football in 1938, 1940, 1942, 1977, and 1978.

Perhaps the greatest athlete to play for the school was Robert "Bob" Hays. Labeled the "World's Fastest Human," Hayes won NCAA titles in 1963 and 1964 in the 200-meter dash. In 1964 he won two gold medals in the 100-meter dash and as a member of the 4-by-100 meter relay team in the Olympic Games in Tokyo. Hayes went on to play for the Dallas Cowboys winning the Super Bowl Ring in the 1972 NFL game between Dallas and Miami.

Althea Gibson, Florida A&M tennis player, went on to international stardom with success at Wimbeldon and other tournaments. In 1957-58, she won both the AP Woman Athlete of the Year and the prestigious Babe Zaharias Award for the top female athlete of the year.

Florida Atlantic

Nickname: Owls
Mascot: Owl
Colors: Blue and Gray
Conference: Independent
Location: Boca Raton
Year founded: 1961

Nickname: Owls is an appropriate nickname for Florida Atlantic University's athletic teams. The University is located on an old airfield that also serves today as a wildlife sanctuary for the burrowing owl.

Mascot: A student costumed as an owl is the mascot.

Florida Southern

Nickname: Moccasins;
Mocs
Mascot: None
Colors: Scarlet and White
Conference: Sunshine State
Location: Lakeland
Year founded: 1885

Nickname: Florida Southern College's athletic teams adopted Moccasins as their nickname in the mid-1930s. The school is located near several lakes where many water moccasins reside. Officials knew that the water moccasin is one of the most fierce snakes; therefore, they saw Moccasins as a fitting nickname.

One of the current logos incorporates a diamond background that Frank Loyd Wright designed. In addition to the logo, the famous architect designed the FSC campus and 12 structures on campus. FSU is the site of the world's largest concentration of Wright architecture.

Interesting Facts: Florida Southern has captured 14 NCAA Division II national championships. Seven have been in baseball, six in golf, and one in men's basketball.

Florida State

Nickname: Seminoles
Mascot: Chief Osceola; Renegade
Colors: Garnet and Gold
Conference: Atlantic Coast
Location: Tallahassee

Year founded: 1857

Nickname: When Florida State University played its first football game on October 18, 1947, the team didn't have a name. Immediately, students rallied together and submitted several potential nicknames to be voted on by the entire student body. A week after the first game, the list was narrowed to six names: Golden Falcons, Statesmen, Crackers, Senators, Indians, and Seminoles. Seminoles eventually beat out Statesmen by 110 votes.

Mascot: Chief Osceola and Renegade were the brain-child of head football coach Bobby Bowden's wife Anne. Chief Osceola is a student dressed in an authentic Seminole Indian costume. Renegade is an Appaloosa horse.

Interesting Facts: A school tradition is focused around Chief Osceola and Renegade as they lead the FSU football team onto the field prior to the start of all home football games. After the coin toss at midfield, Chief Osceola, holding a 10-foot flaming spear over his head, rides Renegade from the far end zone of the stadium to mid-field where the huge Seminole head is painted. Renegade rears up on his hind legs, and Chief Osceola plants the fiery spear into the turf.

Florida State won the men's gymnastics national title in 1951 and 1952.

The University won the women's outdoor track championship in 1984; the women's indoor track team won in 1985.

Fordham

Nickname: Rams
Mascot: Ram

Colors: Maroon and White
Conference: Patriot League
Location: Bronx, N.Y.
Year founded: 1859

Nickname: Fordham University's original nickname was Rose Hills after Rose Hill Manor where the school is located. In 1904, the name was changed to the Rams because of the farm area surrounding the school. The school also is located across the street from the Bronx Zoo.

Mascot: Live rams that were donated to the school lived on campus in a barn until the mid 1970s. The upkeep of the rams was maintained by the student body who would buy shares—much like stocks—in the animals. The tradition was stopped because of the city's health concerns about live rams kept in an urban environment.

Interesting Facts: A graduating senior rings the victory bell located outside the gym following every football win. The bell was taken off a Japanese battleship during World War II and presented to the University by President Harry Truman.

The Los Angeles Rams are named after the Fordham Rams. In 1934, team owner of the then Cleveland Rams, Homer Marchman, was looking for a nickname for his new team and was impressed by the Fordham tradition. Since he liked the nickname, he named his team after it.

Fort Hays State

Nickname: Tigers
Mascot: Tiger
Colors: Black and Gold
Conference: Rocky Mountain
Location: Hays, Kans.
Year founded: 1902

Nickname: According to the sports information director at Fort Hays State University, the school president from 1913 to 1933 was responsible for Tigers becoming the athletic moniker. When William A. Lewis came to Fort Hays, he began using the University of Missouri's nickname, Tigers. Lewis had taught in Missouri schools and colleges.

Mascot: A student costumed as a tiger is the school's mascot.

Interesting Facts: The school's football stadium also owes its name to William A. Lewis. Called Lewis Field Stadium, it was built in 1936.

Fort Hays State won the NAIA men's basketball national championship in 1984 and 1985.

The University also claimed the NAIA women's basketball championship in 1991.

Francis Marion

Nickname: Patriots
Mascot: Patriot
Colors: Red, White, and Blue
Conference: Peach Belt Athletic
Location: Florence, S.C.
Year founded: 1970

Nickname: Patriots was a logical choice for Francis Marion University's nickname, since the namesake for the school was a true patriot. General Francis Marion (also known as the "Swamp Fox") of Revolutionary War fame is remembered as one of South Carolina's greatest heroes.

Mascot: A student dressed in a Patriot costume—with an over-sized head—appears at athletic events.

Interesting Facts: Francis Marion's women's basketball team won the 1982 AIAW Division II national championship and the 1986 NAIA national championship.

Francis Marion received university status in 1992; prior to that, the school was known as Francis Marion College. Also in 1992, the school's athletic program moved from NAIA affiliation to NCAA Division II affiliation.

Fresno State

Nickname: Bulldogs
Mascot: Time-Out
Colors: Cardinal and Blue
Conference: Big West
Location: Fresno, Calif.
Year founded: 1911

Nickname: In Fresno State University's first year, student body president Warren Moody and friends were continually greeted outside the main campus building by a white bulldog. Because the dog adopted them, the students decided to make him their mascot. Ardis Walker made the motion to adopt Bulldogs as the official nickname in a student body meeting. On November 21, 1921, the *Morning Republican* first referred to Fresno State as the Bulldogs.

Mascot: A student dresses up in costume for home sporting events. The bulldog is known as Time-Out.

Interesting Facts: Fresno State University won the NIT basketball championship in 1983, defeating DePaul, 69-60.

G

Gardner-Webb

Nickname: Runnin' Bulldogs
Mascot: Bulldog
Colors: Scarlet and Black
Conference: South Atlantic
Location: Boiling Springs, N.C.
Year founded: 1905

Nickname: No one knows the origin of the nickname Bulldogs. However, according to the sports information director, Gardner-Webb College evolved from Boiling Springs Boarding High School. The high school's nickname was Bulldogs. Runnin' was attached to Bulldogs when the basketball team was a high scoring one in the 1960s.

Mascot: Two students dressed up as male and female bulldogs perform at sporting events.

George Mason

Nickname: Patriots
Mascot: Patriot
Colors: Green and Gold

Conference: Colonial Athletic
Location: Fairfax, Va.
Year founded: 1957

Nickname: George Mason University's nickname pays tribute to its namesake. George Mason (1725-1792), a Colonial patriot, was born in Fairfax County, Virginia. A wealthy planter, Mason was a member of the Virginia Convention in 1776. He wrote the Virginia Resolves which later became the first 10 amendments to the Constitution.

Mascot: A costumed patriot is the school's mascot.

Interesting Facts: George Mason's 1985 women's soccer team won the NCAA Division I national title.
   The school's trap and skeet team has won seven straight collegiate national titles.

George Washington

Nickname: Colonials
Mascot: Colonial
Colors: Buff and Blue
Conference: Atlantic 10
Location: Washington, D.C.
Year founded: 1821

Nickname: Colonials is an appropriate nickname for George Washington University, a school named for America's Revolutionary War general and first President who led the country after the Thirteen Colonies became a nation.

Mascot: A student dresses as a Colonial (a George Washington figure).

Interesting Facts: Joe Holup, Class of 1956, is George Washington's all-time leading basketball scorer with 2,226 points.

Georgetown

Nickname: Hoyas
Mascot: Jack the Bulldog
Colors: Blue and Gray
Conference: Big East
Location: Washington, D.C.
Year founded: 1789

Nickname: Years ago Georgetown University had a team called the Stonewalls. It is thought that a student applied the Greek and Latin terms to the nickname and came up with "hoia saxa," meaning "what rocks!"

Although no one knows when the name "Hoya Saxa" was first used at the University, there is an explanation of the derivation of the words. "Hoya" is from the Greek word "hoios" meaning "such a" or "what a." The neuter plural of this word is "hoia," which agrees with the neuter plural of the Latin word "saxa," meaning "rocks." "Hoya" substitutes the "y" for "i." Hoya eventually evolved into the official nickname, Hoyas.

Mascot: A costumed student called Jack the Bulldog entertains crowds at sporting events.

At one time, Georgetown had live bulldogs as mascots. In 1962, a student committee decided to bring a bulldog mascot to the school. The dog was to be a symbol of Georgetown's fighting spirit, and the committee decided to collect money from students for the dog. Funds were solicited door-to-door on campus. In 1963, stock certificates were sold, and in 1964, an alumni basketball game raised money to build accommodations for the bulldog. The first bulldog was named Lil-Nan's Royal Jacket or popularly called Jack I. He was replaced by Jack II. In the late 1960s, the era of the live bulldog came to an end. The tradition was temporarily reinstated in the 1982-83 basketball season when a Georgetown alumnus, Dr. Michael B. Meyers, brought his bulldogs, Rocky and Taffy, to the games.

Interesting Facts: The men's basketball team won the national championship in 1984 with a record of 34-3. Patrick Ewing was the outstanding player of the NCAA Tournament.

Georgia

Nickname: Bulldogs
Mascot: UGA
Colors: Red and Black
Conference: Southeastern
Location: Athens
Year founded: 1785

Nickname: Many oldtimers say that the origin of the University of Georgia's nickname goes back to ties with Yale University. Georgia's first president, Abraham Baldwin, was a graduate of Yale. Many of the school's early instructors were also Yale men. The early buildings on campus, including Old College, were designed from blueprints of Yale buildings. Also, Yale's nickname is Bulldogs.

On November 3, 1920, Morgan Blake of the Atlanta *Journal* wrote that "The Georgia 'Bulldogs' would sound good because there is a certain dignity about a bulldog, as well as ferocity." Atlanta *Constitution* writer Cliff Cheatley used the name Bulldogs in his story five times on November 6, 1920, after Georgia's 0-0 tie with Virginia.

Mascot: On February 22, 1892, in Atlanta, Georgia's mascot for its first football game against Auburn was a goat. (The game was the beginning of the oldest continuing football rivalry in the South.) Old newspaper reports say that the goat wore a black coat with red U.G. letters on each side. With the goat adorned with a hat with ribbons all down his high horns, the Auburn fans yelled "shoot the bill-goat" throughout the game. In 1894, Georgia's mascot was a white female bull terrier owned by a student.

The first bulldog mascot that represented the school was Butch, an English bulldog that was spotted by students at the

Georgia-Georgia Tech game in Athens in 1946. He served until 1951. Another English bulldog, Mike, served from 1951 until 1955.

Since 1956, Georgia's official mascot has been UGA. Originally named "Hood's Ole Dan," UGA I served from 1956-1966. His son, UGA II, represented Georgia from 1966-1972. UGA III served until he died in 1981. UGA IV, the winningest of the mascots, attended a bowl game every year during his reign which ended in 1989. UGA V began his reign in the first game of 1990. UGAs are buried on the grounds of Sanford Stadium.

Interesting Facts: Led by Herschel Walker, Georgia won the national championship in football in 1980. Walker won the Heisman Trophy in 1982, the first time a Georgia player had won the award since Frank Sinkwich did in 1942. Walker also won the Maxwell Award as did Charley Trippi in 1946.

Tackle Bill Stanfill won the Outland Trophy in football in 1968.

Georgia, having been to 29 football bowl games, is among the top five bowl teams in America.

The University won the women's national gymnastics title in 1987 and 1989.

Georgia Southern

Nickname: Eagles
Mascot: Eagle
Colors: College Blue, White , and Gold
Conference: Independent
Location: Statesboro
Year founded: 1906

Nickname: The Blue Tide served as Georgia Southern University's nickname from 1924-1941. The origin of the moniker is not known.

World War II had a dramatic effect on the school's athletic teams. When the U.S. declared war on Japan after the December

7, 1941, Pearl Harbor attack, the majority of the 1941 Blue Tide football team joined the war effort. After World War II, when all sports except football were revived, the nickname was changed to Professors to complement the name of the school then, Georgia Teachers College. When the school was renamed Georgia Southern College in 1959, Professors was dropped. The student body voted for a new name, and Eagles was selected in a narrow vote over Colonels.

Mascot: A student dressed as an eagle entertains at athletic events.

Interesting Facts: After World War II ended in 1945, basketball and baseball returned to Georgia Southern University, but not football. The school had no team until 1981. Erk Russell, long-time Georgia defensive coordinator, shocked many people when he accepted the head coaching position. Since then, Georgia Southern has not had a losing season. Since joining the NCAA Division I-AA in 1984, GSU has won more games and a higher percentage of its games than any other I-AA team. The school won the national championship in 1985, 1986, 1989, and 1990. The 1989 football squad became the first team this century to finish with a 15-0 mark.

Coach Erk Russell led the school to three of its four national championships before he retired from coaching in December 1989. Inducted into the Georgia Sports Hall of Fame in 1987, he received numerous awards including the Eddie Robinson Award (for top Division I-AA coach) in 1989.

Georgia State

Nickname: Panthers
Mascot: Pounce
Colors: Royal Blue, Crimson, and White
Conference: Trans America
Location: Atlanta

Year founded: 1913

Nickname: The student body chose Panthers as Georgia State University's nickname in 1956. The vote took place when the Atlanta Division of the University of Georgia became Georgia State College.

Mascot: Pounce the Panther is the costumed student mascot.

Georgia Tech

Nickname: Yellow Jackets
Mascot: Buzz; Rambling Wreck
Colors: Old Gold and White
Conference: Atlantic Coast
Location: Atlanta
Year founded: 1885

Nickname:: Many conflicting accounts exist as to the origin of the Yellow Jackets nickname. As far as can be determined, the first reference to the name appeared in the Atlanta *Constitution* in 1905 and came into common usage at that time. Historians say the name, spelled as one word, was first used to refer to supporters who attended Tech athletic events dressed in yellow coats and jackets.

Other nicknames that Georgia Tech University teams have been called include Engineers; the Techs, the first known nickname which was phased out somewhere around 1910; and the Blacksmiths, which was used between 1902 and 1904, and thought to be an invention of sportswriters at the time. Another nickname thought to be coined by sportswriters was The Golden Tornado. The designation was created when Coach John Heisman led Tech to its first national championship in football in 1917. Georgia Tech was the first team from the South to earn the title of national champion, and any team thereafter which approached the same level of excellence was referred to as The Golden Tornado. The name was used as late as 1929, when Tech defeated California in the Rose Bowl.

Mascot: A student costumed as a yellow jacket is the school mascot.

Another official mascot is the Rambling Wreck car. Unveiled at the September 30, 1961, Georgia Tech-Rice football game, it now appears at home games leading the team onto the field.

Before 1961, although there was no official Rambling Wreck, several fraternities took turns driving various such vehicles. The *Technique*, Tech's student newspaper, referred to a 1914 Ford as a "Rambling Wreck" in 1927.

Interesting Facts: The legendary John Heisman was Georgia Tech's football coach from 1904-1919. His record was 102-29-7.

Georgia Tech won the national championship in football in 1917, 1928, and 1991.

Gonzaga

Nickname: Bulldogs; Zags
Mascot: Spike
Colors: Blue, White, and Red
Conference: West Coast
Location: Spokane, Wash.
Year founded: 1887

Nickname: In the early 1900s, Gonzaga University athletic teams were known as the Fighting Irish. However, after Notre Dame's great 1921 season, Gonzaga changed its name in tribute to the Indiana squad. (The team, by the way, was coached by Gus Dorais, the coach credited along with Knute Rockne with inventing the forward pass.) A local reporter who praised the team's "bulldog-like tenacity," first coined the new nickname. It was first used officially in 1922 when the team played West Virginia in the East-West Classic (the school's only post-season football bowl game). Although football was discontinued in the 1941 season, seven men's teams and six women's teams still sport the Bulldogs nickname. Gonzaga teams are also often re-ferred to as Zags, a derivative of the school's unique name.

Mascot: After not having a mascot for many years, students voted in 1985 to support a costumed mascot. Spike became the official name of the bulldog mascot that year after a name-the-mascot contest.

Interesting Facts: John Stockton, All-star guard with the Utah Jazz, is perhaps Gonzaga's best known athlete alumnus; he was Gonzaga's first first-round draft pick in the NBA. A close second is probably Frank Burgess, who led the nation in scoring in the 1960-61 season and was named first-team All-American by the Associated Press; he still reigns as the all-time leading scorer at the school.

However, well-known Gonzaga graduates aren't limited to athletics. The most famous graduate is Bing Crosby. The Crosby House, where Bing was raised, serves today as the Alumni Center for the school.

Grambling State

Nickname: Tigers
Mascot: Tiger
Colors: Black and Gold
Conference: Southwestern Athletic
Location: Grambling, La.
Year founded: 1901

Nickname: The origin of the nickname Tigers is unknown.

Mascot: A student costumed as a tiger serves as Grambling State's mascot.

Interesting Facts: Coach Eddie Robinson holds the record for most college football wins. He broke Paul "Bear" Bryant's record on October 5, 1985, with his 324th victory. In 1991, Robinson coached his 500th collegiate football game. A legend in his lifetime, he has won nearly every award possible for a college football coach.

Grambling has become one of the most prolific training camps for professional football, having sent almost 300 players to pro camps.

The Grambling Tiger Marching Band, considered one of the nation's best show bands, has performed on three continents.

The Grambling Football Radio Network is the largest black collegiate sports network in the nation.

Grand Canyon

Nickname: Antelopes
Mascot: Antelope
Colors: Purple and White
Conference: Great Northwest
Location: Phoenix, Ariz.
Year founded: 1949

Nickname: The Antelope nickname was selected because of the location of Grand Canyon University (originally Grand Canyon College); the ranges surrounding the town were known for antelopes. In 1957, students selected two possible nicknames—the antelope and the donkey. The antelope was chosen soon after.

GCU's nickname is distinctive in that only one other school in the nation—the University of Nebraska at Kearney—is called the Antelopes; the Nebraska athletes, however, are called the Lopers. In 1978, the two schools competed for the NAIA national basketball championship. It was the first time a NAIA championship game was played by two schools with the same mascot (the Grand Canyon 'Lopes defeated the Lopers).

Mascot: A costumed mascot appears at all men's basketball games.

Interesting Facts: The school, founded in 1949 by Arizona Southern Baptists, has won eight NAIA national championships. The men's basketball team won the championship in 1975, 1978, and 1988. The school has also had 49 NAIA All-Americans and more than 30 NAIA Scholar-Athletes.

The women's tennis teams have a rich history. They have won four NAIA national championships.

Grand Canyon joined NCAA Division II in 1992. In that first year, four of the school's nine athletic programs advanced to post-season play.

Grand Valley State

Nickname: Lakers
Mascot: The Great Laker
Colors: Blue, Black, and White
Conference: Midwest Intercollegiate
Location: Allendale, Mich.
Year founded: 1960

Nickname: Lakers was selected and voted on by the Grand Valley student body. The nickname is an appropriate one since the school is about 20 miles from Lake Michigan.

Mascot: A student costumed as The Great Laker is the school's mascot.

Interesting Facts: Grand Valley is associated with the Midwest Intercollegiate Football Conference, but the school is also a member of the Great Lakes Intercollegiate Athletic Conference.

Guilford

Nickname: Quakers
Mascot: Quaker
Colors: Crimson and Gray
Conference: Old Dominion Athletic

Location: Greensboro, N.C.
Year founded: 1837

Nickname: Guilford College, the oldest coeducational institution in the South and the third oldest in the nation, was founded by the Society of Friends, known as the Quakers. Thus, it is appropriate that its nickname is Quakers. The school still maintains strong Quaker ties.

Mascot: A student dressed as a Quaker man represents the school at sporting events.

Interesting Facts: Guilford won the NAIA men's national basketball championship in 1973. The women's tennis team won the NAIA national championship in 1981. In 1989, the men's golf team won the NAIA national title.

Guilford joined the NCAA Division III in 1990.

Hampden-Sydney

Nickname: Tigers
Mascot: Yank the Tiger
Colors: Garnet and Grey
Conference: Old Dominion
Location: Hampden-Sydney, Va.
Year founded: 1776

Nickname: One of the oldest colleges in the nation, Hampden-Sydney has been referred to as the Tigers since intercollegiate sports were first started. The choice of a nickname may be linked to the fact that the first two school presidents were graduates of Princeton University, also the Tigers.

Mascot: Yank the Tiger is the costumed student mascot.

Interesting Facts: Hampden-Sydney played its first organized football game on Thanksgiving Day, 1892.

Hampden-Sydney and Randolph-Macon (Ashland, Va.) have a long football rivalry. The Tigers and Yellow Jackets have met 96 times, Hampden-Sydney holding a 49-36-11 advantage over Randolph-Macon. The Beat Macon bonfire has always been a high point in the school's football season.

Hampton

Nickname: Pirates
Mascot: Pirate
Colors: Royal Blue and White
Conference: Central Intercollegiate Athletic
Location: Hampton, Va.
Year founded: 1868

Nickname: Hampton University's student newspaper, *The Script*, conducted an election in May 1933 to choose an official nickname. Pirates won out over Seasiders, Ironmen, Buccaneers, and Wildcats. Pirates was a fitting selection since the school is surrounded by water and the Naval Shipyard.

Mascot: A student costumed as a pirate is the school's mascot.

Interesting Facts: Hampton teams have won CIAA championships in men's basketball, men's and women's cross country, volleyball, women's track and field, and tennis.

Harvard

Nickname: Crimson
Mascot: John Harvard
Colors: Crimson, Black, and White
Conference: Ivy League
Location: Cambridge, Mass.
Year founded: 1636

Nickname: On May 6, 1875, Harvard University undergraduates voted on the school's color and chose crimson. Had the vote gone the other way, Harvard athletic teams would be known as the Magenta, the student newspaper still would be called the

Magenta as it was then, and the fight song might be "The Magenta in Triumph Flashing." Instead, crimson was chosen as the school's official color, became the University's nickname, and was adopted as the name of the school newspaper. The color controversy developed because crimson had been used as the Harvard hue in crew, but magenta had been used by the baseball team since 1863. The vote of 1875 settled the color issue, and all teams used crimson.

Writers over the years have referred to Harvard athletic teams as the Johnnies (for John Harvard) and the Cantabrigians or Cantabs (from Cantabrigia, the Medieval Latin word for Cambridge). The school's official nickname, however, is Crimson.

Mascot: Harvard did not have a mascot until 1950. That year, a member of the cheerleading squad decked out in Puritan garb to represent John Harvard. The practice continues today. Also, the Puritan caricature by Vic Johnson of the former Boston *Herald Traveler* now is a recognized Harvard symbol used by the University's sports publications.

The mascot John Harvard honors the namesake of Harvard University. John Harvard was a young Puritan minister and graduate of Emmanuel College at Cambridge (England). When he died in 1638, he bequeathed 780 pounds—half his estate—and 260 books to the school founded two years earlier. In gratitude, the General Court named the college after him.

Interesting Facts: Harvard won the national football championship in 1890, 1898, 1899, 1910, 1912, 1913, and 1919.

The University won the men's National Collegiate Rowing Championships' Varsity Eights in 1983, 1985, 1987, 1988, and 1989.

The men's golf team won the national championship six times, all before 1905.

Harvard, as a member of the Ivy League, abides by the rules of the league's founding document, the Presidents' Agreement of 1954. No spring football practice is held; no freshman participation in varsity football and crew is allowed; and no athletic scholarships are given. Athletic programs are financed not by gate receipts but through the overall budget of the Faculty of Arts and Sciences.

Hawaii

Nickname: Rainbows
Mascot: Rainbow Warrior
Colors: Green and White
Conference: Western Athletic
Location: Honolulu
Year founded: 1907

Nickname: Rainbows is an appropriate nickname for the University of Hawaii because the rainbow is important in Hawaiian lore. Rainbows were sacred to high chiefs and appeared as signs of a chief's presence. For example, a rainbow hovering over a newborn child indicated that he was of god-like rank.

The tradition about not losing while a rainbow was over the campus seems to have started during the 1923 Oregon State game. Hawaii won that contest, 7-0, after a rainbow appeared over the campus in Manoa Valley.

Mascot: The Rainbow Warrior was chosen as the mascot in a school-wide contest in 1990.

Interesting Facts: The school colors of green and white were chosen in 1909. A group of faculty wives who were setting up the campus social calendar for the year found that it wasn't possible, because of slow shipping, to get all colors of paper or cloth they needed for decorations at college functions. The wives decided, that because of Hawaii's tropic location, there would always be green plants and white flowers available for decorations. Thus, green and white were chosen as the school colors. Green is also the color of Lono, the Hawaiian god of agriculture and harvest. White items in the old Hawaiian culture were always associated with royalty.

In 1923, the Rainbow football team made its first visit to the mainland—by ocean liner— for a game. The trip took five days and was very expensive. As a result, subsequent teams only traveled to the mainland every other year. In the late 1940s, the team began to travel by air for the first time; the journey to the West Coast was reached in an unheard of nine hours. In order to cut down on expenses, the team stayed on the mainland for three weeks to play three games before returning to the Islands.

Probably the biggest star of early UH football was Thomas Kaulukukui, a 140-pound back who silenced a Los Angeles Coliseum crowd in 1935 with an electrifying 103-yard kickoff return in a game against UCLA. Kaulukukui, who was dubbed "Grass Shack" by the great sports writer Grantland Rice, became Hawaii's first All-American.

Hawaii's women's volleyball teams captured national championships in 1982, 1983, and 1987.

Henderson State

Nickname: Reddies
Mascot: None
Colors: Red and Gray
Conference: Gulf South
Location: Arkadelphia, Ark.
Year founded: 1890

Nickname: Several stories exist about the origin of Reddies as Henderson State University's nickname. Intercollegiate football at the school began in 1905, and for the first three years the team was known simply as the Henderson football team. Then, in 1908, the student body held a contest to give the team a name. The October 6, 1908, edition of the Henderson newspaper, the *Oracle*, stated that Nellie Hartsgeld named the football team Red Jackets because of the color of their jerseys. Some writers of the day, though, began calling the team Redmen and Reds. The name Reddie first appeared in the 1913 *Star* yearbook in a feature story concerning the 1912 Red Jacket season. In 1914, Reddies was used interchangeably with Red Jackets in the *Star*. From 1915 on, Reddies replaced Red Jackets as the official name. A popular explanation for Reddies is that the name fit into pep songs and yells better than the shorter Reds.

Interesting Facts: The colors of red and gray are symbolic. Red represents loyalty and courage, and gray is a tribute to the Confederate States of America.

Many students and alumni feel "the Reddie Spirit" is something only Henderson students can truly understand. The old story goes that this Reddie Spirit was born in 1914 when the school's main building, Old Main, burned to the ground, and Henderson students gathered that night and decided they would rebuild and continue to have classes.

Hillsdale

Nickname: Chargers
Mascot: Horse
Colors: Royal Blue and White
Conference: Midwest
Intercollegiate
Location: Hillsdale, Mich.
Year founded: 1884

Nickname: The origin of the nickname Chargers is unknown. A charger refers to a horse used in battle.

Mascot: A student costumed as a horse is the school's mascot.

Interesting Facts: Hillsdale College ranks as the all-time winningest school in the nation in NCAA Division II football with 470 total victories.

The 1985 football team won the NAIA national championship, the first in the school's history.

Hofstra

Nickname: Flying Dutchmen
Mascot: Captain Spaulding; Katie Hofstra
Colors: Gold, White, and Blue

Conference: East Coast
Location: Hempstead, N.Y.
Year founded: 1935

Nickname: Many myths and rumors abound as to the designation of Hofstra University's nickname. Ironically, the name is said not to have originated from the athletics program but in a physical education class in 1937. Instructor R. Burr Smith is reported to have commented on watching student Robert Kreuger's sluggish progress across the basketball court, "Look at the Flying Dutchmen." The name Flying Dutchmen became popular and was the overwhelming favorite of several nickname proposals voted on by the student body in a 1937 issue of the campus newspaper. The name is fitting because Hofstra has a strong Dutch heritage; the school is named after William S. Hofstra. The school was started on his property, and the first building on campus was Hofstra's mansion, which he affectionately named "Netherlands" after his homeland.

Mascot: Hofstra may hold the record for the school with the most mascots. Several interesting characters, presented by the Screaming Dutchmen Booster Club—a student spirit organization—appear at athletic events. Four of the characters are closely connected to the school's Dutch heritage. Captain Spaulding and Katie Hofstra entertain crowds in full Dutch dress. Katie Hofstra dates back to 1955. Captain Spaulding is based on a Groucho Marx skit about the lovelorn ghost of the captain of the famed clipper ship, the *Flying Dutchmen*. Mascots Kate and Willie Pride, a lion and a lioness, represent the lions on the Hofstra seal. The Hofstra Duck has no link to the Dutch heritage. Some say it is Hofstra's answer to the San Diego Chicken. It is the official mascot of the booster club.

Interesting Facts: The school's alma mater, "The Netherlands," was written by a faculty member to the music of the Dutch national anthem.

The Hofstra fight flag was a new addition in 1991. Modeled after an actual Dutch privateer's flag which is flown by the Netherlands Royal Navy, it was presented to the school's president by a representative of Holland's Queen Beatriz. The history of the flag dates back to 1572, when Dutch loyalists in their opposition to Spanish rule, used the flag's mast to ram the gates of a Dutch city.

In 1990, the Hofstra football team, a NCAA Division III participant, set 16 school records.

Holy Cross

Nickname: Crusaders
Mascot: Crusader
Colors: Royal Purple
Conference: Patriot
Location: Worcester, Mass.
Year founded: 1843

Nickname: The student body of the College of the Holy Cross chose Crusader as a nickname on October 6, 1925. The campus newspaper, *The Tomahawk*, sponsored the contest. The nickname was first used at a banquet in 1884 and was revived in 1925 by Stanley Woodward of the Boston *Herald*.

The other two nicknames that were considered in the contest were Chiefs and Sagamores. Chiefs was used for a brief period, but it had limited appeal.

Mascot: A student dresses as a crusader and carries a sword.

Interesting Facts: Holy Cross won the men's national basketball championship in 1947. It won the College Baseball World Series in 1952, defeating Missouri, 8-4.

Houston

Nickname: Cougars
Mascot: Cougar
Colors: Scarlet and White

Conference: Southwest
Location: Houston, Tex.
Year founded: 1927

Nickname: The University of Houston's first coach, John R. Bender, named the athletic teams the Cougars. Bender, who came to Houston from Washington State, gave that school's nickname to UH teams in 1927 when Houston was still a junior college. The student newspaper used the name, and when Houston entered intercollegiate athletics in 1946, Cougars was adopted as the school's official nickname.

Mascot: A student costumed as a cougar is the school's mascot. A live cougar named Shasta served as Houston's official mascot from 1947 to 1989. Former interim President George Magner decided not to replace Shasta V after the cougar died prior to the 1989 football season.

Interesting Facts: The University of Houston did not play an intercollegiate football game until September 21, 1946, when the school played Southwestern Louisiana. The first major college football game ever played on astroturf was the September 23, 1966, contest between the University of Houston and Washington State at the Astrodome.

The highest-ranked football team in UH history was the 1976 team, which was ranked fourth in the nation in both the AP and UPI final polls following the bowl games.

The Bayou Bucket is the annual trophy that goes to the winner of the annual Houston-Rice football game. The idea for the trophy originated in 1974 when Fred Curry, a Rice guard, became president of the Touchdown Club. Curry wanted to do something to build interest in the Houston-Rice series. After buying a beat-up bronze bucket for $60 in a New Braunfels, Texas, antique shop, Curry had the bucket mounted on an ornate base.

Houston has been a national leader in men's golf, winning 16 championships.

Howard Payne

Nickname: Yellow Jackets
Mascot: Yellow Jacket
Colors: Old Gold and Navy Blue
Conference: Texas Intercollegiate Athletic
Location: Brownwood, Tex.
Year founded: 1889

Nickname: Because it was a Baptist school, Howard Payne University's football team was known as The Baptists until 1915. The name became too general because other Baptist schools in Texas such as Baylor University were also playing football. The school held a contest to come up with a new nickname. A student, Carrie Camp, won with her selection of Yellow Jackets. She thought the name would be perfect because the college was small, the team was strong and fighting, and yellow was part of the school's colors.

Mascot: A student dressed as a blue and gold yellow jacket represents the school at sporting events.

Interesting Facts: Howard Payne College was a senior college until 1900 when it changed to junior college status. In 1914, it again became a senior college. That year, it was the largest and best equipped college in West Texas with a seven-acre campus, four basketball courts, one volleyball court, and six tennis courts.

Idaho

Nickname: Vandals
Mascot: Joe Vandal
Colors: Silver and Gold
Conference: Big Sky
Location: Moscow
Year founded: 1889

Nickname: The University of Idaho became known as the Vandals in 1918, when the basketball team "made shambles" of all its opposing teams. Local journalists began calling the team a "wrecking crew," which eventually led to the nickname Vandals. In 1921, the name was officially adopted for University of Idaho athletic teams.

Mascot: A costumed mascot named Joe Vandal performs at athletic events. Joe Vandal looks like a Viking, with a long beard and a Viking hat. The mascot developed from the 1918 season, when the basketball players reminded Edward Hulme, dean of the College of Liberal Arts, of the Norsemen.

Idaho State

Nickname: Bengals
Mascot: Bengal Tiger
Colors: Orange and Black
Conference: Big Sky
Location: Pocatello
Year founded: 1901

Nickname: In 1921, Ralph H. Hutchinson became director of physical education and athletics at Idaho State University. A graduate of Princeton, Hutchinson immediately formed an organization of athletes called the "I Club." The group adopted Princeton's Bengal Tiger as its own. Formerly, athletic teams were known as the Bantams.

Mascot: A student costumed as a Bengal tiger cheers on fans at athletic events.

Interesting Facts: Idaho State won the NCAA Division I-AA championship in basketball in 1981.

Illinois

Nickname: Fighting Illini
Mascot: Chief Illiniwek
Colors: Orange and Blue
Conference: Big 10
Location: Champaign
Year founded: 1868

Nickname: Illini comes from the name of an Indian tribe known for its fighting spirit. The Illini's neighbors were the

Shawnees, the Iroquois, the Sioux, the Chippewas, and the Kickapoos.

Mascot: Illiniwek (pronounced "ill-EYE-nih-wek") was the name of the loose confederation of Algonquin tribes that once lived in northern Illinois. The French changed the ending to "ois" in naming what became the state of Illinois.

The dramatic war dance of Chief Illiniwek is one of the most colorful traditions associated with collegiate athletics. Chief Illiniwek has been the symbol of University of Illinois athletics since 1926. Former football coach Robert Zuppke is believed to have suggested the name. Ray Dvorak, assistant band director, conceived the idea of performing an American Indian dance during halftime of the Illinois-Pennsylvania football game in Philadelphia. Lester Leutwiler, dressed in a homemade costume, was the first Chief Illiniwek for the 1926-1928 season.

The second Chief Illiniwek, Webber Borchers, appeared in authentic American Indian regalia. In the summer of 1930, Borchers went to the Pine Ridge reservation in South Dakota and found Sioux women who made the suit for him. On November 8, 1930, Borchers appeared in his authentic Indian outfit at the Illinois-Army game in New York's Yankee Stadium. Since that game, five different authentic outfits have been used by Chief Illiniwek. The one used now was purchased in 1983 from Sioux Chief Frank Fools Crow and is topped by a headdress of turkey feathers.

Interesting Facts: Illinois won the national championship in football in 1923 and 1927 and the men's national basketball championship in 1915.

The men's gymnastics teams have won nine national titles.

The men's outdoor track and field team won the first national title in that sport in 1921. Illinois went on to win four other national titles.

Illinois-Chicago

Nickname: Flames

Mascot: D. Dragon
Colors: Indigo and Flame
Conference: Mid-Continent
Location: Chicago
Year founded: 1896

Nickname: On September 1, 1982, the Chicago Circle and Medical Center campuses of the University of Illinois consolidated to become the University of Illinois at Chicago (UIC). With a new name came a new moniker for athletic teams—the Flames. UIC students selected Flames in a special election in May 1982. The Great Chicago Fire of 1871, which began a short distance from the campus, inspired the name.

Mascot: A friendly, fire-breathing costumed dragon called D. Dragon is the mascot of the school.

Interesting Facts: The UIC Pavilion, which is home for basketball games, is the largest collegiate ice hockey facility in the nation.

Illinois State

Nickname: Redbirds
Mascot: Reggie Redbird
Colors: Red and White
Conference: Gateway Collegiate
Location: Normal
Year founded: 1857

Nickname: Prior to 1923, Illinois State University's athletes were known as the Teachers. That year, athletic director Clifford E. "Pop" Horton and *Daily Pantagraph* sports editor Fred Young collaborated to change the nickname. Horton immediately wanted the name Cardinals because the school colors were cardinal and white. Young, though, changed the nickname to the

Redbirds to avoid confusion with the St. Louis Cardinals baseball team. The colors were also later changed to red and white.

Horton served as director of health and physical education at ISU for 38 years, and Young worked at the *Pantagraph* for more than 50 years. Both are members of the ISU Athletic Hall of Fame.

Mascot: Reggie Redbird, a student dressed in a bird costume, is the current mascot. Reggie received his name in 1980 in a contest among Junior Redbird Club members who are elementary and junior high school students. (At the time the name was chosen, baseball player Reggie Jackson was a big hit among the students.) Reggie received a new suit with brighter colors at the December 20, 1990, basketball game against Bradley. The outfit was donated to the school by Rick Percy, the general manager of Clemens and Associates Insurance in Bloomington.

Indiana

Nickname: Hoosiers
Mascot: None
Colors: Cream and Crimson
Conference: Big 10
Location: Bloomington
Year founded: 1820

Nickname: Athletes at Indiana University and all Indianians are referred to by the nickname Hoosiers. Many theories exist as to the origin of the nickname.

One explanation which seems to have more validity than others involves a Samuel Hoosier, a contractor on the Louisville & Portland (Ohio Falls) Canal. In 1825, he found that men from the Indiana side of the river were better diggers and thus hired more of them for his work force. They were known as "the Hoosier men," and later on as "Hoosiers," a name they carried back to their homes.

Another story involves a Colonel Jacob Lehmanowski, a Polish officer who served with Napoleon before settling in Indiana. The colonel delivered a series of lectures in which he extolled the virtues of the Hussars, which he pronounced as "Hoosier." According to the story, native settlers adopted it for themselves. The whole problem with this story is that the colonel didn't arrive in Indiana until 1840, and the word Hoosiers was in common usage in the 1830s.

Among numerous explanations is the light-hearted one attributed to Indianian writer James Whitcomb Riley. According to Riley, Indiana had vicious fighters who not only gouged and scratched but frequently bit off noses and ears. This happened so frequently that a settler coming into a bar room on the morning after and seeing an ear on the floor would casually push it aside and inquire, "Whose ear?"

Interesting Facts: Indiana has won a number of national championships, including the following:
- Men's cross-country in 1938, 1940, and 1942
- Men's swimming and diving six times from 1968-1973.
- Men's outdoor track and field in 1932.
- Wrestling in 1932.
- Men's soccer in 1982, 1983, and 1988.

Indiana State

Nickname: Sycamores
Mascot: None
Colors: Royal Blue and White
Conference: Missouri Valley; Gateway
Location: Terre Haute
Year founded: 1865

Nickname: A contest was held at Indiana State University in 1921 to select a nickname. Names were submitted to a committee of four, with the group's top three choices being placed before the student body in a campus-wide election. Sycamores was among the three submitted finalists. Although the name was booed when placed on the ballot, the students, in an apparent joke, voted Sycamores their choice. (The winner of the entry received $3 as first prize.) The campus newspaper, the *Normal Advance*, predecessor of the present newspaper, *The Statesman*, first used the name on January 3, 1922.

Interesting Facts: Indiana State University won the 1950 NAIA basketball tournament defeating East Central (Oklahoma), 61-47. The school played in the NCAA national championship game in 1979, losing to Michigan State. Larry Bird, a former NBA All-Star, led the team.

The University won the men's gymnastics national championship in 1977.

Iona

Nickname: Gaels
Mascot: Gael
Colors: Maroon and Gold
Conference: Metro Atlantic Athletic
Location: New Rochelle, N.Y.
Year founded: 1940

Nickname: The nickname Gaels is appropriate for Iona College, a school founded by the Congregation of Christian Brothers, commonly known as the Irish Christian Brothers. A Gael is anyone of Irish-Gaelic ancestry. The Gael, which is portrayed as a spunky character, provides Iona with a nickname that is consistent with the school motto, "certa bonum certamen" ("fight a good fight").

Mascot: The costumed Gael mascot is popular at athletic games where he loves to get fans involved and make people laugh.

Interesting Facts: Iona has built a tradition as one of America's most successful small-college basketball programs. The Gaels, in the last dozen years, have won five conference championships and have gone to the NCAA tournament four times and the NIT twice.

Iowa

Nickname: Hawkeyes
Mascot: Herky the Hawk
Colors: Old Gold and Black
Conference: Big Ten
Location: Iowa City
Year founded: 1847

Nickname: The University of Iowa took its moniker from the state of Iowa's nickname. Hawkeye can be traced back to the hero in James Fenimore Cooper's book, *The Last of the Mohicans.* In the novel, the Delaware Indians bestow the name on a white scout who lived and hunted with them. In 1838, 12 years after Cooper's book was published, a newspaper editor, James Edwards, was urged by a lawyer, David Rorer, to suggest the name Hawkeyes for the residents of the state. Edwards did so in his paper, the Ft. Madison *Patriot*, on March 24, 1838, several months before the status of Iowa Territory became official. In the fall of 1838, territorial officials, including the governor, formally met and accepted the name. Appropriately, Edwards moved to Burlington in 1843 and renamed his newspaper the *Hawkeye*.

Mascot: The Hawkeye nickname gained a tangible symbol in 1948 when journalism instructor Richard Spencer III created a cartoon character in the form of an impish hawk. The athletic department held a statewide contest to name the character. John Franklin, an Iowa alumnus, suggested Herky. The name stuck and has symbolized Iowa athletics ever since. A popular university symbol, Herky donned a military uniform and became the insignia of the 124th Fighter Squadron during the Korean War.

Today's Herky wears an over-sized football helmet and uniform during football season. During basketball season, he wears a basketball uniform and a regular hawk head.

Interesting Facts: Iowa's Nile Kinnick won the Heisman Trophy as the nation's top player in football in 1939; Kinnick also won the Maxwell Award that year. Quarterback Chuck Long won the Maxwell Award and Davey O'Brien Award in 1985. The Outland Trophy was won by guard Calvin Jones in 1955 and tackle Alex Karras in 1957.

The winner of the annual Iowa-Minnesota football game gets possession of a statue of a pig named "Floyd of Rosedale." A bet in 1935 between the governors of the two states gave birth to the statue. Because tensions between the two state schools had been running high, a wager was made to alleviate difficulties. After Iowa lost the 1935 game, Governor Clyde Herring presented Minnesota Governor Floyd B. Olson with Floyd of Rosedale, a champion pig and a brother of Blue Boy of Will Rogers' movie *State Fair*. Olson gave the pig to the University of Minnesota and commissioned a sculptor to capture Floyd's image.

Since 1975, Iowa has dominated college wrestling; the school has won 12 national titles.

Iowa State

Nickname: Cyclones
Mascot: Cardinal
Colors: Cardinal and Gold
Conference: Big Eight
Location: Ames
Year founded: 1868

Nickname: Before 1895, Iowa State University's athletic teams were known as the Cardinals. The weather that year was responsible for a new nickname. In the summer and fall of 1895, a large number of tornadoes, or what were then popularly called cyclones, caused much damage to Iowa. That fall, underdog Iowa State (then called Iowa Agricultural College) played Northwestern. After a commanding 30-0 lead at halftime, Iowa went on to beat the highly-touted Northwestern team, 36-0. The next morning's Chicago *Tribune* ran the game story headline

"Iowa Cyclone Devastates Evanston." From that time on, Iowa State was known as the Cyclones.

Mascot: The origin of the cardinal as a mascot dates to the early 1950s. The president of the Collegiate Manufacturing Company of Ames, Iowa, one of the nation's largest makers of stuffed animals, approached the ISU sports information director, Harry Burrell, to have the school's nickname changed. The company's president, Chev Adams, had as his rationale that "We cannot make a stuffed Cyclone!"

In 1955 Burrell and Adams suggested to the pep council president that a contest be held to choose a mascot. The students chose a cardinal, and Adams' company donated a likeness of the bird.

Another student contest was held to name the cardinal. The entry Cy won. Cy was considered an appropriate choice since it was a short version of the school's nickname. A baby bird mascot named Clone was later added. Today both figures stand nearly nine feet tall and cost around $2,500.

Interesting Facts: The 1895 football squad that earned the Cyclone nickname had a legendary coach for a short time. Glenn S. "Pop" Warner, later to become famous as coach of the Carlisle Indians, was the squad's inspirational mentor. Coaching the team in the late summer of 1895 before going to Georgia where he had been named head coach, Warner returned each summer through the 1899 season to do pre-season coaching.

Iowa State's first game in 1895 was against the Silver Bowl Athletic Club of Butte, Montana. The team, complete with its own chef, traveled to Montana by train. The train became snowbound, and the people aboard ran out of food; the football squad had to subsist on raw berries. The game, however, was harder than the trip there. Butte scored two touchdowns in the first 15 minutes. Coach Warner even suited up for the second half, but Iowa State still lost.

Iowa State's 1959 "Dirty Thirty" football team was one of the school's most celebrated teams. Considered one of the great underdog teams in college football, the thirty players went to the Orange Bowl but lost 35-12 to the Oklahoma Sooners.

Since 1965, the school has won 8 national wrestling titles.

Iowa State won three national titles in men's gymnastics.

Ithaca

Nickname: Bombers
Mascot: None
Colors: Blue and Gold
Conference: Empire Athletic Association
Location: Ithaca, N.Y.
Year founded: 1892

Nickname: Information about the origin of the Ithaca College's nickname comes from *The Ithaca College Story* by John Harcourt. In 1937, Ithaca was elected for membership in the NCAA. That year the student newspaper *Ithacan* referred to the school as the Cayugans. The previous year the *Ithacan* had announced a contest for an appropriate nickname. Many suggestions were made, and by January 1937, the students had decided upon the Cayugan. However, the press had another idea. By 1940, the name Bombers had surfaced in sports releases and soon drove out Cayugans. Harold Jansen, a member of the publicity staff and sports writer for several newspapers, probably coined the name by using it repeatedly in his own stories.

Interesting Facts: Ithaca, representing the NCAA Division III, has captured several national championships The football team won in 1979, 1988, and 1991. The baseball team gained top honors in 1980 and 1988. Wrestling teams won in 1989 and 1990. Field hockey teams took honors in 1982, and women's soccer teams won in 1990 and 1991.

Jackson State

Nickname: Tigers
Mascot: Tiger
Colors: Blue and White
Conference: Southwestern Athletic
Location: Jackson, Miss.
Year founded: 1877

Nickname: Jackson State University selected Tigers as its nickname in 1923. The origin of the name is unknown.

Mascot: A student dressed in a tiger costume represents the school at athletic events.

Interesting Facts: In 1920, when football was a new sport at Jackson State University (then known as Jackson State College), the "Iron Thirteen" made a name for themselves. The season started with only five or six players and no coach. The players practiced daily until their number reached 13. They selected Ernest Richards, a French teacher who had never played football, to be their coach. The dedicated 13 men made their own plays and directed their own practice. In their first game against Tougaloo, they won, 13-0. The team went on to win every game that year, including a 63-0 victory over Utica. The famous "Iron Thirteen" went undefeated for three years.

Jacksonville

Nickname: Dolphins
Mascot: Duncan the Dolphin
Colors: Green and Gold
Conference: Sun Belt
Location: Jacksonville, Fla.
Year founded: 1934

Nickname: In 1947, a contest was held with the student body choosing the name Dolphins. Other nickname suggestions included Green Raiders, Buccaneers, Juggernauts, and Green Dragons. Because of Jacksonville University's close proximity to the Atlantic Ocean and since dolphins actually do swim in the St. Johns River that runs along the campus, Dolphins was adopted.

Mascot: A student contest also decided the mascot's name of Duncan the Dolphin. A phone call from the athletic department to Hanna-Barbera resulted in a caricature of Duncan the Dolphin who was unveiled on December 8, 1990, at a basketball game with Maryland.

Interesting Facts: Jacksonville has retired four basketball jerseys in its history. Roger Strickland, #52, played from 1960-63 and was the first college Division I player to make two major All-American teams. Artis Giomore, #53, was an All-American who played from 1969-71. All-American James Ray, #43, became the first-round draft choice of the Denver Nuggets after his 1976-80 years. All-American Otis Smith, #32, played from 1982-86.

Jacksonville State

Nickname: Gamecocks
Mascot: Gamecock

Colors: Red and White
Conference: Gulf South
Location: Jacksonville, Ala.
Year founded: 1883

Nickname: Jacksonville State University's athletic teams were once known as the Eagle-Owls. However, the 1946 team voted to change the nickname to Gamecocks.

Mascot: A costumed mascot named Cocky performs at JSU basketball games.

Interesting Facts: The school has won three NCAA Division II national championships—baseball titles in 1990 and 1991 and a basketball win in 1985. Football teams have also been runners-up to the national crown twice.

James Madison

Nickname: Dukes
Mascot: Bulldog
Colors: Purple and Gold
Conference: Yankee (1993)
Location: Harrisonburg, Va.
Year founded: 1908

Nickname: Contrary to what some people may believe, James Madison University's nickname Dukes is not associated with royalty or aristocracy. The nickname was selected as an honor to the school's second president, Dr. Samuel P. Duke, who served from 1919-1949. The men's athletic program originated during his tenure.

Mascot: The bulldog serves as school mascot because historically it was the pet of royalty—kings and dukes. A student dressed as a bulldog with a crown and purple cape performs at athletic events.

Interesting Facts: Under Duke's presidency, State Teachers College was renamed Madison College in honor of President James Madison, a Virginia native. In 1977, the institution became James Madison University.

In 1966, Madison College received full coeducational status and men enrolled as resident students for the first time. (In 1946, men were first enrolled, but only as day students.)

The college started its first football season in 1972. Playing five games its first year, the school didn't win a game until the 1973 season.

Johnson C. Smith

Nickname: Golden Bulls
Mascot: Golden Bull
Colors: Blue and Gold
Conference: Central Intercollegiate Athletic
Location: Charlotte, N.C.
Year founded: 1867

Nickname: Johnson C. Smith University's nickname comes from *The Bull*, the school's award-winning yearbook. "Golden" was added to the name because of the school's colors—gold (and blue).

Mascot: A student, dressed as a golden bull wearing a blue sweater, performs at sporting events.

Interesting Facts: The first college football game between two black colleges was played between Johnson C. Smith and Livingstone College of Salisbury, North Carolina. Before the historic game, the colleges spent a couple of years studying and practicing the game, and then JCSU issued a challenge to Livingstone. The dare was accepted, and the game was played on December 27, 1892, in a storm. JCSU won 5-0 (at that time, a touchdown was worth five points).

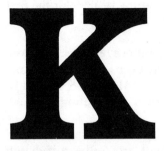

Kansas

Nickname: Jayhawks
Mascot: Jayhawk
Colors: Crimson and Blue
Conference: Big Eight
Location: Lawrence
Year founded: 1866

Nickname: The term Jayhawk dates back before the founding of the state of Kansas. In 1849, pioneers crossing what is today Nebraska called themselves The Jayhawkers of '49. The hawk and the bluejay, two familiar birds in the West, are believed to have been the source of the name.

Jayhawk was first used in present-day Kansas around 1858. Previously associated with robbing and looting, the term took on a new meaning during the Civil War. In 1861, Dr. Charles R. Jennison, a surgeon, used it. When commissioned as a colonel by Kansas governor Charles Robinson, he was charged with raising a calvary regiment. Jennison called his regiment the Independent Mounted Kansas Jayhawkers. Later, it was officially called the First Kansas Cavalry; the name was again changed to the Seventh Kansas Regiment. By the end of the Civil War, Jayhawks became associated with the spirit of comradeship and the courageous fighting qualities associated with keeping Kansas a free state.

By 1886, the University of Kansas had adopted the mythical

bird as part of the KU yell. It seemed natural in 1890 for the first football team to be called Jayhawks.

Mascot: Henry Maloy, a student from Eureka, Kansas, created a cartoon jayhawk in 1912. Different creations of the bird came along in 1920, 1923, 1929, the 1930s, and 1941. In 1946, Harold D. Sandy of Johnson County, Kansas, drew the smiling jayhawk which is used today.

In addition to the cartoon symbol of the University, Kansas also has a costumed mascot, a student dressed as a jayhawk who entertains at athletic events.

Interesting Facts: The Rock Chalk Chant is among the most famous of all college cheers, a yell that President Theodore Roosevelt said was the best that he had ever heard. The words "Rock Chalk" used in the cheer not only rhyme with Jayhawk, but are symbolic of the chalky limestone formations found on nearby Mount Oread.

Jayhawk fans "wave the wheat" following every Kansas scoring drive in football. The spectators waving their arms in the air resemble a breezy Kansas wheat field.

Kansas has won three men's indoor track national championships.

Kansas State

Nickname: Wildcats
Mascot: Willie the Wildcat
Colors: Purple and White
Conference: Big Eight
Location: Manhattan
Year founded: 1857

Nickname: Prior to 1915, Kansas State University athletic teams were known as the Aggies. That year, football coach Chief Bender gave the nickname Wildcats to his team because of the fighting spirit of the players. The nickname was changed to Farmers in

1916. Four years later, football coach Charles Bachman switched back to the Wildcat nickname.

Mascot: In 1922 Bachman helped introduce the first live mascot, Touchdown, to the campus. The present wildcat, named Touchdown XI, is kept at the Manhattan Sunset Zoo and doesn't attend Kansas State's athletic events.

A costumed mascot, Willie the Wildcat, who is dressed in a large life-like wildcat head, adds spirit and enthusiasm to sporting events.

Interesting Facts: Kansas State officially only has one color—royal purple, adopted in the fall of 1896. White, though, has been used as a complimentary color for many years. The term "Purple Pride" was first used during the Vince Gibson era, 1967-74.

The Governor's Trophy game between Kansas State University and the University of Kansas, which began in 1969, was the brainchild of Governor Robert Docking. The large traveling trophy is presented each year to the winning team and coaches immediately following the traditional rivalry.

Kent State

Nickname: Golden Flashes
Mascot: Golden Eagle
Colors: Blue and Gold
Conference: Mid-American
Location: Kent, Ohio
Year founded: 1910

Nickname: Two theories exist about the origin of Kent State University's nickname Golden Flashes. According to Philip Shriver's book, *The Years of Youth,* it is noted that in a letter to Linda Baughman, dated August 6, 1959, Merle Wagoner recalled that Kent State's athletic teams changed from Silver Foxes to Golden Flashes in 1926. The change occurred after the dismissal of President John E. McGilvrey for whose silver fox farm east of the campus the teams had first been named. With the impetus from T. Howard Winters, acting president of the school, a contest was held to select a new name, the winner to be given $25. No special significance was attached to the winning suggestion, Golden Flashes. After it had been approved by the student body and the faculty athletic committee, it was first used in 1927 by the basketball team.

Oliver Wolcott, a Kent center on the 1921 and 1922 football teams, also lays partial claim to the nickname. A sports editor of the local newspaper, the Kent *Courier Tribune*, Wolcott said that he referred to the 1927 football team as Golden Flashes because Silver Foxes seemed pretty frail to him.

Mascot: The golden eagle was designated as the Department of Intercollegiate Athletics' official mascot on October 12, 1985. The eagle was introduced at special halftime ceremonies during the football game between Kent State and the University of Texas-El Paso. The homecoming event marked the 75th anniversary of the founding of Kent State. The live golden eagle, Flash, is under the care and supervision of Earl Schriver of Baden, Pennsylvania, who transports the eagle to as many Kent State athletic events as possible.

A costumed golden eagle was also unveiled at the 1985 homecoming. Each spring the uniformed mascot (a member of the Kent State cheerleading squad) is chosen during tryouts.

Interesting Facts: Kent State's school colors of blue and gold came about by accident. In the 1910 state charter, Kent's school colors were designated as orange and purple. When some orange and purple basketball uniforms were sent to a local laundry and cleaned in hot water, they came back gold and blue-black. The story handed down is that the team and student body liked the new colors so well they adopted them.

Kentucky

Nickname: Wildcats
Mascot: Wildcat

Colors: Royal Blue and White
Conference: Southeastern
Location: Lexington
Year founded: 1865

Nickname: The University of Kentucky has had only one nickname, the Wildcats. The origin of the name dates back to 1909 to a speech made by Commandant Corbusier, head of the military department of State College (UK's former name). Speaking to a chapel audience of students about Kentucky's football team's 6-2 victory over Illinois, the Commandant declared that "they fought like Wildcats." The name began to be used by both students and the press and was soon adopted by the University.

Mascot: Several live mascots have served Kentucky. The first wildcat was given to the school in 1921. Called Tom, this Kentucky wildcat died quickly from being in captivity. Other wildcats followed—TNT, Whiskers, Hot Tamale, and Colonel —but they either died or were turned loose in the mountains because they didn't thrive out of their native habitat.

The school's costumed mascot originated during the 1976-77 school year. The student mascot serves as a friendly ambassador for the University not only at athletic events but also at academic functions.

Interesting Facts: Kentucky's colors have not always been blue and white. In 1891, prior to a football game against Centre, State College students held a meeting to choose both school colors and a yell. They decided on blue and light yellow—blue because it was symbolic of the bluegrass and yellow because it represented the rich land. In 1892, another meeting was held, and the colors blue and white were chosen. R.C. Stoll, a member of the 1891-95 football teams, said the color of blue was selected to match his blue necktie that he took off at the meeting and held up. Colors have ranged from navy blue in the early days to the now-familiar "Kentucky Blue," or royal blue.

In addition to the marching band, Kentucky's pep band of more than 100 members is the largest in the nation.

The UK cheerleading squad was the first to win three Universal Cheerleaders Association national championships. The honor went to the group in 1985, 1987, and 1990.

The 1898 UK football squad still remains as the only undefeated, untied, and unscored on Wildcat club in school history. Known as "The Immortals," the team outscored opponents, 180-0, in seven games.

Kentucky's men's basketball team won national championships in 1933, 1948, 1949, 1951, 1954, 1958, and 1978. UK won the NIT championship in 1946 and 1976.

On January 27, 1968, basketball coach Adolph Rupp became college basketball's all-time winningest coach.

Kentucky Wesleyan

Nickname: Panthers
Mascot: Panther
Colors: Purple and White
Conference: Independent
Location: Owensboro
Year founded: 1858

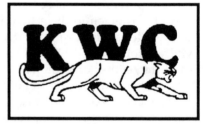

Nickname: The origin of the nickname Panthers is unknown.

Mascot: A costumed student dressed in a gray suit with a panther head represents the school at sporting events.

Interesting Facts: Kentucky Wesleyan has won six NCAA Division II men's basketball championships.

In 1928, in one of the first night games in the history of football, the Panthers upset the University of Cincinnati, one of the Top 20 teams in the country at that time, 6-0.

On January 1, 1931, football was discontinued at the school. In the fall of 1983, it was revived.

L

Lafayette

Nickname: Leopards
Mascot: Leopard
Colors: Maroon and White
Conference: Patriot
Location: Easton, Pa.
Year founded: 1832

Nickname: Prior to 1927, Lafayette College teams were referred to as The Maroon, based on the school colors of maroon and white. On October 7, 1927, the name Leopards was used in a sports story in the student newspaper. George Parkman, the sports editor of *The Lafayette*, recalled later that there was no real explanation as to why it was suddenly used. Parkman said that some of their opponents had animal nicknames, and someone decided that Lafayette should also have one.

Mascot: A student dressed as a costumed leopard entertains at sporting events.

La Salle

Nickname: Explorers

Mascot: Explorer
Colors: Blue and Gold
Conference: Metro Atlantic
Location: Philadelphia, Pa.
Year founded: 1863

Nickname: La Salle University, founded and sponsored by the Brothers of Christian Schools (Christian Brothers), is named after the founder of the Christian Brothers, St. John Baptist de la Salle.

The early media, believing that the school was named for La Salle, the explorer, used the nickname Explorers. Rather than challenge the name, school officials adopted it and have used it in all official athletic records since 1930.

Mascot: A student costumed as an explorer is the mascot.

Interesting Facts: La Salle won the national basketball championship in 1954 with a 26-4 record.

Lehigh

Nickname: Engineers
Mascot: None
Colors: Brown and White
Conference: Patriot League
Location: Bethlehem, Pa.
Year founded: 1865

Nickname: According to the school's athletic department, Lehigh University's nickname was used in honor of Asa Packer, an engineer who was a railroad builder and owner.

Lehigh has long had a reputation for its engineering excellence. One of its most famous engineers, Chrysler Chairman Lee Iacocca, Class of 1945, is on the Lehigh Board of Trustees.

Mascot: Lehigh has no official mascot. An engine, though, is pictured on the school logo.

Interesting Facts: Lehigh has won seven national championships in men's lacrosse. Winning outright championships in 1890, 1893, and 1922, the school shared titles with Cornell in 1914 and 1916, Stevens in 1917, and Syracuse in 1920.

Lehigh won the NCAA Division II national football championship in 1977.

Lenoir-Rhyne

Nickname: Bears
Mascot: Joe Bear
Colors: Red and Black
Conference: South Atlantic
Location: Hickory, N.C.
Year founded: 1891

Nickname: The origin of the nickname Bears dates back to 1924. A sports writer covering the baseball game between Lenoir-Rhyne and Wake Forest said Lenoir-Rhyne players were finally "turning in their tracks and growling like the bears that are said to infest their native highlands." The name caught on because in the fall of 1924 the *Hickory Daily Record*, the campus newspaper, and the school yearbook all contain references to Bears in conjunction with the football team. Lenoir-Rhyne became known as the Bears without any official action.

Mascot: Three years after the nickname was first used, a live bear called Joe Bear made his appearance as mascot. Three more bears followed, but the increasing problem of upkeep and safety made it difficult to keep a live bear on campus.

Since 1961, a student costumed as Joe Bear has performed at athletic events.

Interesting Facts: Lenoir-Rhyne College won the NAIA Divisional Championship in football, the college's only national title, in 1960 by defeating Humboldt State, 15-14, in St. Petersburg, Florida.

Liberty

Nickname: Flames
Mascot: Eagle
Colors: Red, White, and Blue
Conference: Independent
Location: Lynchburg, Va.
Year founded: 1971

Nickname: The nickname Flames is an augmentation of Liberty University's motto, "Knowledge Aflame." In 1974, the student body voted to retain this nickname over several other choices.

Mascot: The eagle was designated as the school mascot in 1980, the same year Liberty joined the NCAA as an associate member of Division II. (Liberty became a full member of the division in 1988). The eagle was chosen because of its patriotic symbolism and its connection with the school name, Liberty. The school logo was designed with the Flame nickname in mind.

Interesting Facts: In 1980, Liberty won the NCCA (National Christian Collegiate Association) national championship in basketball. It now is a member of NCAA Division I.

Linfield

Nickname: Wildcats
Mascot: Wildcat
Colors: Purple and Red
Conference: Columbia Football
Location: McMinnville, Ore.

Year founded: 1849

Nickname: The origin of Linfield College's nickname is unknown.

Mascot: The origin of the mascot is not known.

Interesting Facts: Linfield won the NAIA Division II national football championships in 1982, 1984, and 1986. In November 1990, Linfield clinched its 35th consecutive winning season. That meant that among all 669 colleges playing football in the United States (all NCAA and NAIA schools), Linfield was ranked #1 for most consecutive winning seasons.

Football at Linfield in the 1980s had come a long way from its beginnings in 1896. In that first year, the school only played two football games, but lost both of them—54-0 to Pacific College (now George Fox College) and 56-0 to Pacific University.

Long Beach State

Nickname: 49ers
Mascot: 49er
Colors: Brown and Gold
Conference: Big West
Location: Long Beach, Calif.
Year founded: 1949

Nickname: The 49ers was the nickname given to Long Beach State University when it opened its doors in 1949. The school's founding coincided with the the 100th anniversary of the California Gold Rush of 1849.

Mascot: A man dressed as an 1849 prospector has represented the school on and off during its history.

Interesting Facts: The men's volleyball team won the national championship in 1991; the women's team won in 1989.

The women's basketball team won third place honors at the NCAA Women's Final Four in 1987 and 1988.

Long Island

Nickname: Blackbirds
Mascot: None
Colors: Blue and White
Conference: Northeast
Location: Brooklyn, N.Y.
Year founded: 1926

Nickname: According to Dr. Elliott Gatner, an early historian of Long Island University, the school's athletic teams in the late 1920s and early 1930s were known as the Blue Devils because their uniforms were blue. Sometime between February and October 1935, the uniform color was changed to black, and athletes became known as the Blackbirds. School history says that a basketball reporter for the Brooklyn *Eagle*, who came to New York from the Midwest, observed that the LIU players, in their black uniforms, as they ran up and down the court dribbling the ball, reminded him of blackbirds bobbing up and down as they fed in the cornfields. The reporter used the nickname Blackbirds in one of his stories, and the name stuck.

In the school's early days, the basketball team was referred to as Beemen, after its legendary coach, Clair F. Bee, now in the Naismith Basketball Hall of Fame.

Mascot: The school no longer has a mascot. In years past, a costumed mascot did represent the school.

Interesting Facts: Long Island's basketball gymnasium may have as interesting a history as any court in the nation. The Arnold and Marie Schwartz Athletic Center was formerly the Brooklyn Paramount Theatre from 1928-1962. The 4,200-seat theatre for 34 years was the home of stage and screen stars such as Mae West, Bing Crosby, Rudy Vallee, and Ginger Rogers. The Mighty Wurlitzer pipe organ still produces marvelous sounds which rock the rafters.

Under Coach Bee, LIU was named the Helms Foundation national basketball champion in 1939. The Helms designation differed with the NCAA national champion and tournament winner, Oregon.

Louisiana State

Nickname: Tigers
Mascot: Mike the Tiger
Colors: Purple and Gold
Conference: Southeastern
Location: Baton Rouge
Year founded: 1860

Nickname: In the fall of 1896, when Coach A.W. Jeardeau's football team had a perfect 6-0-0 record, the school first adopted its nickname Tigers. Since most collegiate schools that year bore the names of ferocious animals, Tigers seemed a logical choice. The underlying reason, though, that Louisiana State University chose the nickname dates back to the Civil War.

A battalion of Confederate soldiers comprised of New Orleans Zouaves and Donaldsonville Cannoneers distinguished themselves at the Battle of Shenandoah. These rebels had been known as the fighting band of "Louisiana Tigers."

In 1955, the LSU Fourth-Quarter Ball Club called the Tigers the Fighting Tigers.

Mascot: Before a live tiger became a tradition for LSU athletic teams, a very realistic papier-mache tiger was used for more than a decade. Then in 1935, Mike the Tiger was purchased from the Little Rock Zoo by the student body for $750. Originally known as Sheik, his name was changed to Mike in honor of Mike Chambers, who served as LSU's athletic trainer when the mascot was purchased. Mike I reigned for 20 years before dying of pneumonia. Mike II served only one season, also dying of pneumonia. Mike III, purchased from the Seattle Zoo by the student body for $1,500, served 18 years as mascot. Mike IV, who hailed from Florida, served 14 years. A tiger from Alabama, Mike V began his reign on April 30, 1990, when he moved into the tiger cage across from Tiger Stadium.

Interesting Facts: Tradition says that for every growl by Mike the Tiger before a football game, the Tigers will score a touchdown that night.

The Tigers won the national football championship in 1958 with an 11-0 season. Halfback Billy Cannon won the Heisman Trophy that year. Cannon's performance against Ole Miss on Halloween night in 1959 is probably the most famous play in Tiger gridiron records, and, some say, clinched the Heisman Trophy for him. That night, the Rebels took a 3-0 lead into the final quarter, threatening to end an 18-game LSU winning streak, when Cannon made a 89-yard punt return to win the game.

LSU was the first college team to ever play on foreign soil. On Christmas Day in 1907, the football team traveled to Cuba where it stomped the University of Havana team, 56-0.

The school won the women's national indoor track title in 1987, 1989, and 1991; the women's outdoor track and field team has won five titles since 1987.

The men's outdoor track and field team has claimed three national titles.

Louisiana Tech

Nickname: Bulldogs
Mascot: Bulldog
Colors: Columbia Blue and Red
Conference: Independent
Location: Ruston
Year founded: 1894

Nickname: The origin of the school's

nickname can be traced to a legendary story that is said to have occurred five years after the founding of Louisiana Tech. In 1899, five students were returning home from school one day when they discovered an old, hungry bulldog sitting under a tree. After feeding the dog, they continued their journey. When they had reached their destination, however, they found to their surprise that the bulldog had followed them. They kept the dog after the landlord agreed to the bulldog staying in the kitchen.

That night their house caught on fire, and the bulldog ran from room to room arousing all occupants. After everyone but one boy had made his way to safety, the bulldog re-entered the house to rescue him. After the fire was extinguished, the students went inside to search for the dog. They found him lying in an unburned corner of one room, dead from smoke and heat inhalation. The shaken students took the bulldog back to the place they had found him the previous day. They dug a grave, wrapped him in two jackets—one red, the other blue—and buried him. After the boys told their story to other students, the whole campus was soon mourning the death of the homeless bulldog. Two years later, Tech organized a football team. A unanimous decision was reached that the first hero of Tech, a bulldog, would be the mascot.

Mascot: Tech has two mascots—a live bulldog and a costumed one named Champ.

Interesting Facts: Louisiana Tech won the NCAA Division I women's basketball championship in 1981, 1982, and 1988.

Tech is the all-time winningest Division I team in women's basketball. Several players have won national awards over the years. In 1982, Janice Lawrence won the most outstanding player of the NCAA tournament; Erica Westbrooks won the award in 1988.

Tech won the NCAA Division II national football championship in 1973.

Louisville

Nickname: Cardinals

Mascot: Cardinal
Colors: Cardinal Red, Black, and White
Conference: Independent
Location: Louisville, Ky.
Year founded: 1798

Nickname: The University of Louisville's nickname emerged sometime after 1913. Since the cardinal is the state bird of Kentucky, it was selected to give the school statewide identification.

Mascot: A student dressed in a cardinal costume performs at sporting events.

Interesting Facts: Louisville won the men's NCAA basketball championship in 1980 and 1986, both under coach Denny Crum.

Through 1991, Louisville had appeared 21 times at the NCAA basketball tournament.

Loyola College

Nickname: Greyhounds
Mascot: Greyhound
Colors: Green and Gray
Conference: Metro Atlantic; Colonial
Location: Baltimore, Md.
Year founded: 1852

Nickname: Prior to the 1927-28 academic year, Loyola College athletic teams were designated the Green and Grey, the Loyola's, or the Jesuits. Before suggestions for a nickname were made in 1927, it was stipulated that recommendations had to somehow incorporate Loyola's colors of green and gray. Some students suggested parrots or grey squirrels. The most serious recommendation, though, came from Edward W. Tribbe who suggested the greyhound. Because the greyhound at the time was believed to be the world's fastest animal (this was before the cheetah had been timed), it was voted the official nickname.

Mascot: Loyola College has both a live mascot and a costumed greyhound.

A pedigree greyhound named Alexandra, a former racing dog who was forced to retire because of an injury, is the current school representative. In the mid-1930s, Loyola had two pedigree greyounds on campus, but the noisy atmosphere at the basketball games proved to be taxing to their nerves.

Loyola Marymount

Nickname: Lions
Mascot: Lion
Colors: Crimson, Gray, and Columbia Blue
Conference: West Coast Athletic
Location: Los Angeles, Calif.
Year founded: 1914

Nickname: The origin of Loyola Marymount's nickname was not known until sports information director Barry Zepel did some research. Zepel discovered, after talking to Jesuit priests in the school's infirmary, that when the campus was moved to its present location on a bluff in 1927, many mountain lions roamed the unsettled area. When school officials broke ground for the school's new building, they adopted the Lions as their official nickname.

Mascot: A student in a lion costume represents the school at athletic events.

Interesting Facts: Loyola won the NAIA men's basketball championship in 1945.

Loyola University

Nickname: Ramblers
Mascot: Wolf
Colors: Maroon and Gold
Conference: Midwestern
Collegiate
Location: Chicago, Ill.
Year founded: 1870

Nickname: Loyola University is the nation's only college that has the nickname Ramblers. The origin of the moniker goes back to when football was king at Loyola. Prior to the 1920s, all athletic teams were known as the Maroon and Gold. In 1925, the football coach, along with the student newspaper, held a contest to choose a nickname. The winning entry was Grandees, which tied into the Spanish origins of St. Ignatious of Loyola. However, the name did not catch on. In 1926 the football team traveled so much across the United States, "rambling from state to state," that the press referred to Loyola as the Ramblers. Despite the fact that football was dropped as a varsity sport in 1930, the nickname remained.

Mascot: Lu, the Loyola Rambler mascot, made its debut in 1990 as the official mascot of the athletic program.
    A student costumed as a wolf wears a maroon and gold jersey with the word "Ramblers" on it.

Interesting Facts: Loyola won the NCAA men's basketball championship in 1963 with a record, 29-2.

Maine

Nickname: Black Bears
Mascot: Bananas the Black Bear
Colors: Blue and White
Conference: North Atlantic; Yankee
Location: Orono
Year founded: 1865

Nickname: In 1914, a Penobscot Indian guide gave the University of Maine a small bear cub, and the nickname Black Bears was born.

Mascot: Maine's mascot also goes back to 1914. The cub presented to the school was a favorite with the fans. As legend has it, the crowd went "bananas" at the sight of the new mascot and started the tradition of Bananas the Bear. Having bears on the sidelines ended in 1966 when a Maine court outlawed the practice of using a live animal as a mascot. For three years, the school had no mascot. In 1969, the service fraternity Alpha Phi Omega took on the task of providing a student mascot. With the help of Gamma Sigma Sigma, a service sorority, a costume was made, and Bananas was back. Although the mascot has since undergone many changes, its presence remains constant.

Interesting Facts: The football program at the University of Maine began in 1892. The heyday of football at the school was under coach Harold Westerman (1951-66). The Black Bears posted 15 consecutive winning seasons; the 1951 and 1961 teams went undefeated. The 1965 team, perhaps the most celebrated squad in school history, won the Yankee Conference, received the Lambert Cup trophy, and competed in the Tangerine Bowl.

Jack Zollo was perhaps the most astonishing competitor ever to wear a Black Bear uniform. Leaving the University to fight with the 82nd Airborne Division in Italy and Belgium during World War II, he suffered severe wounds. In 1947, though, he returned to UM and led the Black Bears to a 6-1 record while being named an All-American offensive guard.

Manhattan

Nickname: Jaspers
Mascot: None
Colors: Kelly Green and White
Conference: Metro Atlantic
Location: New York, N.Y.
Year founded: 1853

Nickname: As the school's first athletic director, Brother Jasper of Mary brought the then little-known sport of baseball to Manhattan College in the late 1800s. He then served as the school's baseball coach. Today, athletic teams honor his legacy with their official nickname.

Interesting Facts: Brother Jasper is credited with inventing the seventh inning stretch. When Manhattan College played a semi-pro baseball team, he noticed that his team's players and fans were becoming restless as the team came to bat in the closely contested seventh inning. He called time-out and told the students to stand up and stretch for a few minutes until the game was resumed.

Manhattan College played in the first Orange Bowl football game.

The school won the 1973 NCAA Indoor Track and Field national championship.

Mankato State

Nickname: Mavericks
Mascot: Maverick
Colors: Purple and Gold
Conference: Northern
Intercollegiate
Location: Mankato, Minn.
Year founded: 1867

Nickname: Prior to 1977, athletic teams at Mankato State University were called Indians. The nickname was dropped because of objections by Native Americans and also because Mankato had switched conferences.

Douglas Moore, president of Mankato State, asked John Hodowanic, director of University Relations, to begin working on a new name. A group composed of students, faculty, and alumni came up with a list of nearly 75 names. Mavericks, suggested by MSU sociology professor Roy Cook, was chosen over names such as Muskies and Lightning.

The first design of the nickname was a horse, but Moore maintained that the design too closely resembled the Golden Mustang used by another NIC school, Southwest State. Moore, a native Texan, recommended that a steer be used for the design. His suggestion may have originated from the maverick longhorn steer in Texas. His idea was accepted. Artist-illustrator Barbara Howell-Furan of Lake Crystal, Minnesota, designed the new logo that featured the Maverick name in the shape of a steer.

Mascot: Mankato has both a live maverick and a student costumed as a maverick.

Interesting Facts: The Mavericks share Blackeslee Field with the

Minnesota Vikings each summer as the pro team uses the natural grass field for three weeks.

Mansfield

Nickname: Mountaineers
Mascot: Mountie the Mountaineer
Colors: Red and Black
Conference: Pennsylvania State Ath.
Location: Mansfield, Pa.
Year founded: 1857

Nickname: Because Mansfield is located in the Allegheny Mountains of northern Pennsylvania, athletic teams have always been known as Mountaineers. The name is also appropriate to the area because soldiers who fought in the Civil War from Mansfield and the surrounding area were called Mountaineers.

Mascot: Mountie the Mountaineer is the costumed student mascot.

Interesting Facts: On May 17, 1891, Mansfield State Normal School played its first football game. Over a year later on September 28, 1892, Mansfield made football history when the school played the first ever night game.

Marist

Nickname: Red Foxes
Mascot: Red Fox
Colors: Red, White, and Black
Conference: Northeast
Location: Poughkeepsie, N.Y.

Year founded: 1929

Nickname: The athletic teams at Marist College have been known as the Red Foxes since the founding of the school by the Marist Brothers. The red fox is the prominent animal in the province of France, the birthplace of the Marist Brothers.

Mascot: A student costumed as a red fox performs at sporting events.

Mars Hill

Nickname: Lions
Mascot: Cosmo the Lion
Colors: Blue and Gold
Conference: South Atlantic
Location: Mars Hill, N.C.
Year founded: 1856

Nickname: Athletic teams at Mars Hill were originally called Mountain Lions due to the mountain location of the college. In the early 1980s, the name was shortened to Lions.

Mascot: Cosmo is the costumed lion mascot who performs at sporting events.

Marshall

Nickname: Thundering Herd
Mascot: Marco
Colors: Green and White

Conference: Southern
Location: Huntington, W. Va.
Year founded: 1837

Nickname: The Thundering Herd is one of the most unique nick- names in collegiate athletics. The name refers to the buffalo which once roamed the western plains of the United States as well as the Appalachian area (including the hills of what is now West Virginia). The Thundering Herd provided food, clothing, tools, and weapons for the early inhabitants. In the early 1920s, Duke Ridgley, sports editor and columnist of the Huntington *Herald-Dispatch*, took the name from the title of one of Zane Gray's Old West novels.

Marshall's teams in its early years were better known as the Big Green. In 1958, the school's student body held a contest to choose a nickname and selected Big Green. Despite the vote, the Thundering Herd refused to disappear. In 1964, Dr. Stewart Smith, president of the school, appointed a faculty-student committee to suggest a nickname that denoted more action. The Thundering Herd won out over Big Green and Rams. On January 5, 1964, the Thundering Herd became the official nickname of Marshall University.

Mascot: Marco is the costumed buffalo mascot who performs at athletic events.

Interesting Facts: Marshall played for the Division I-AA football title in 1991 but lost to Youngstown State, 25-17.

The men's basketball team won the NAIA tournament in 1947.

Maryland

Nickname: Terrapins (Terps)
Mascot: Terrapin
Colors: Red, White, Black, and Gold

Conference: Atlanta Coast
Location: College Park
Year founded: 1807

MARYLAND TERRAPINS

Nickname: University of Maryland president H.C. Byrd recommended Terrapins for the school nickname in 1922 as a result of the student newspaper's search for an official name. Some people resisted Byrd's choice opting for the older and historically entrenched term, Old-Liners. A label derived from the Revolutionary War when Maryland soldiers earned accolades for bravery and perseverance against British soldiers, Old-Liners had a vocal following. By 1935, though, the University yearbook had changed its name from *Reveille* to *Terrapin* by a vote of the student body. Although it took years, Terrapins finally won out as the official athletic nickname.

Mascot: Testudo, a Diamondback turtle whose name is derived from the scientific classification for turtle, is Maryland's official mascot. Samuel P. Gorham of Providence, Rhode Island, cast Testudo in bronze by request of the Class of 1933. Testudo was modeled after a feisty Diamondback that came from Dr. Byrd's hometown of Crisfield. The 500-pound Diamondback has peered at generations of Maryland students entering the Theodore R. McKeldin Library in the heart of the College Park campus.

A student costumed as a terrapin performs at athletic events.

Interesting Facts: According to Dick Lamb, a historian of the Football Writers Association, the first regularly scheduled college football game to be televised was the Maryland-Penn game of October 5, 1940. Penn defeated Maryland, 51-0, before a crowd of 40,000. The game was televised to some 200 homes by WPTZ in Philadelphia.

Maryland's football team improved from that 1940 game and won the national championship in 1953 with a 10-1-0 record.

Maryland won the 1987 women's field hockey championship and in 1968 the national championship in men's soccer.

Maryland-Baltimore

Nickname: Retrievers
Mascot: Retriever
Colors: Old Gold and Black
Conference: East Coast
Location: Baltimore
Year founded: 1966

Nickname: Retrievers, the nickname of the University of Maryland at Baltimore, is derived from the Chesapeake Bay Retriever, the official mascot of the state of Maryland. (A retriever is a dog trained to find killed or wounded game and bring it to a hunter.)

Mascot: A student dressed as a retriever entertains crowds at athletic events.

Interesting Facts: In 1980, the school won the Division II national championship in men's lacrosse.

Massachusetts

Nickname: Minutemen
Mascot: Minuteman
Colors: Maroon and White
Conference: Yankee
Location: Amherst
Year founded: 1863

Nickname: Years ago athletic teams at the University of Massachusetts went by the nickname Redmen. In the spring of 1972, a group of American Indians from New York wrote the school's administration asking them to curtail the use of the word. The Native Americans referred in the letter to "undesirable racial connotations of the Redmen nickname." The administration's reply was to ask all University staff and media, including athletic personnel, to refrain from using the word Redmen as much as possible.

Because the University's Student Senate thought the name created a "false picture of American history," it polled the student body for a new name. Minutemen was the consensus of students. The name Massachusetts Minutemen also had an alliterative and rhythmic quality that made it popular.

The name has an historical and patriotic relationship with the state. The Minutemen were Revolutionary patriots who pledged themselves to answer a call to arms at a minute's notice. Originally, these men met in scattered groups throughout New England to plan for the possible defense of their homes. They were formally organized in Massachusetts in November 1774 when the provincial congress authorized their enlistment in the militia. They were the men whom Paul Revere called from their homes and their work when he made his famous ride. At the Battles of Lexington and Concord in Massachusetts on April 19, 1775, Minutemen defeated British forces.

Mascot: A minuteman costumed in colonial dress is the student mascot.

Interesting Facts: The University won the women's lacrosse championship in 1982.

McMurry

Nickname: Indians
Mascot: Indian
Colors: Maroon and White
Conference: Texas Intercollegiate Ath. Assoc.

Location: Abilene, Tex.
Year founded: 1923

Nickname: Indians was the nickname adopted by McMurry University founder and first president Dr. J.W. Hunt. His parents were missionaries to the Indian tribes in the Oklahoma Territory. McMurry was founded and is still operated by the Northwest Texas and New Mexico Conferences of the United Methodist Church.

Mascot: A student costumed as an Indian represents the school at sporting events.

Interesting Facts: Homecoming at McMurry focuses on its Indian heritage. Social clubs build Tipi Village, a reconstruction of authentic Indian dwellings, which are judged by Native Americans. Approximately 8,000-10,000 school children from across the region visit each year.

Memphis State

Nickname: Tigers
Mascot: Tom II; Pouncer; Bouncer
Colors: Blue and Gray
Conference: Great Midwest
Location: Memphis, Tenn.
Year founded: 1912

Nickname: The earliest nicknames for Memphis State were the Teachers, the Normals, or the Blue and Gray (when the school was known as State Normal School). After the final game of the

1915 football season, however, a spontaneous student parade created shouts of "we fight like Tigers." The nickname began to be used by students and by campus publications. The name didn't make it outside the campus, though, until the 1924 season when Memphis newspapers began using the moniker. After the 1929 season, when West Tennessee State Normal became West Tennessee Teachers College and the players were called the Teachers, the Tigers nickname became even more popular. In 1957, when the school received University status, the Tigers became the official nickname of the school teams.

Mascot: Memphis State has three different mascots. Tom II is a live Bengal tiger; he recently replaced Tom I, who had lived for 19 years.

Two costumed mascots also attend athletic events. One is a large tiger named Pouncer; Bouncer is a smaller one.

Interesting Facts: The only national championship in school history belongs to golf. Hillman Robbins won the NCAA golf championship in 1953.

The basketball team has been to the NCAA Final Four competition twice.

Mercer

Nickname: Bears
Mascot: Bear
Colors: Orange and Black
Conference: Trans America
Location: Macon, Ga.
Year founded: 1833

Nickname: Mercer received its nickname during the early 1900s during a football game with the University of Georgia. A Mercer player with long hair (players did not wear helmets at the time) came running through with the ball. A Georgia player responded, "From whence came that bear?"

Mascot: A student costumed as a bear performs at sporting events.

Interesting Facts: Mercer was one of the charter members of the Trans America Athletic Conference formed in 1978. The other two original members are Samford University and Centenary College.

Merrimack

Nickname: Warriors
Mascot: None
Colors: Navy Blue, Gold, and White
Conference: Northeast-10; Hockey East
Location: North Andover, Mass.
Year founded: 1947

Nickname: Merrimack is taken from the name of an area Indian tribe. Warriors is used as a nickname in the tribe's honor.

Interesting Facts: Merrimack won the 1978 NCAA Division II championship in hockey.

Miami

Nickname: Hurricanes
Mascot: Sebastian the Ibis; The Miami Maniac
Colors: Orange, Green, and White
Conference: Big East
Location: Miami, Fla.
Year founded: 1925

Nickname: Two stories exist as to the origin of the University of Miami's nickname. One says that the 1927 football squad held a team meeting to select the name Hurricanes, hoping they would sweep away opponents just as the devastating hurricane did on September 16, 1926. Another version says that Miami *News* columnist Jack Bell asked end Porter Norris of the 1926 squad what the team should be called. Norris, after being told  that both local dignitaries and University officials wanted to name the team for a local flora or fauna, said the players wouldn't stand for it and suggested Hurricanes since the opening game had been postponed by such a storm.

Mascot: Sebastian the Ibis is the student mascot for Miami's football team. The selection of an ibis as mascot goes back to folklore. The ibis, a symbol of knowledge found in the Everglades and Egypt, is the last sign of wildlife to take shelter before a hurricane and the first to reappear after the storm. The ibis was considered Miami's first unofficial mascot when the school yearbook adopted the name *Ibis* in 1926. During the 1950s, the popularity of the name grew.

In 1957, San Sebastian Hall, a residence hall on campus, sponsored an ibis entry in the homecoming celebration. Then in 1958, John Stormont, a Miami student, performed at games in an ibis costume. Currently, the person inside the costume is John Routh who also portrays The Miami Maniac, the official mascot of Hurricane basketball and baseball. Routh, the only professional mascot in college sports, began as Cocky, the mascot of the University of South Carolina.

Interesting Facts: Miami has won four national championships in football: in 1983, beating Nebraska in the Orange Bowl; in 1987, defeating Oklahoma in the Orange Bowl and completing its first 12-0 season; in 1989, beating Alabama in the Sugar Bowl; and in 1991, beating Nebraska, 22-0, in the Orange Bowl.

In 1986, quarterback Vinny Testaverde won the Heisman Trophy, the Maxwell Award, and the Davey O'Brien Award.

Miami played in the first Orange Bowl game in 1935, losing to Bucknell, 26-0.

On March 24, 1980, Hurricane diver Greg Louganis won both the one-and three-meter events at the NCAA Championships. Louganis went on to win the gold in the 1984 and 1988 Olympic Games.

In September 1988 at the Seoul Olympic Games, Mike Fiore won a gold medal in baseball, and Wendy Williams won a bronze in diving.

Miami won the College Baseball World Series in 1982 and 1985.

Michigan

Nickname: Wolverines
Mascot: None
Colors: Maize and Blue
Conference: Big 10
Location: Ann Arbor
Year founded: 1817

Nickname: Mystery surrounds the origin of the nickname Wolverines. The term has long been used to refer to residents of the state. The wolverine is a member of the weasel family with short legs, large feet, and a thick bushy tail. A ferocious fighter, it was highly prized by early trappers. Football coach Felding H. Yost in 1942 said that the nickname may have come into use because of extensive trading in wolverine pelts in the Sault St. Marie area of Michigan. Researcher Albert H. Marckwardt discovered that the term Wolverines was being used as early as 1833, four years before Michigan statehood. Concerning the wolverine, he wrote: "Zoologists inform us that wolverines are now extinct in the state and indicate some doubt about their having been here at all in any considerable number. Historians have researched in vain among early fur inventories and bills of sale for similar evidence."

Mascot: The University of Michigan currently has no mascot although live wolverines were once used. Coach Yost conducted an extensive research for a wolverine, alive or dead. In 1923 and 1924 he assigned two former football players, Bruce Shorts and "Dad" Gregory, to see if a wolverine could be obtained from the Hudson's Bay Fur Company in British Columbia. The search resulted in a mounted wolverine, three feet long and weighing 26 pounds, plus four wolverine pelt rugs.

In 1927, ten live wolverines were obtained from Alaska and placed on exhibition at the Detroit Zoo. Two of the wolverines were brought out in cages for big football games, especially the Ohio State contest. As the animals grew larger and more ferocious, their outings to the football games ended.

Interesting Facts: Michigan won the national football championship in 1901, 1902, 1932, 1933, 1947, and 1948.

Bennie Oosterbaan, Michigan's most celebrated athlete, led the Big Ten in touchdowns in 1925, led the basketball conference in scoring in 1928, and led the Big Ten in hitting on the baseball diamond in 1928. He coached the football team for 11 years, leading the Wolverines to the national championship in 1948, his first season.

In 1940, halfback Tom Harmon won the Heisman Trophy as well as the Maxwell Award.

The school won the College Baseball World Series in 1953 and 1962.

Michigan won the national championship in men's gymnastics in 1963, 1969, and 1970.

Since 1937, Michigan has won 10 national championships in men's swimming and diving.

Michigan State

Nickname: Spartans
Mascot: Sparty
Colors: Green and White
Conference: Big 10
Location: East Lansing

Year founded: 1855

Nickname: In 1925, Michigan State College replaced the name Michigan Agricultural College. The changing of the school's name resulted in a contest to select a nickname to replace Aggies. The Michigan Staters was chosen. George S. Alderton, sports editor of the Lansing *State Journal*, and Dale Stafford, sportswriter for the Lansing *Capitol News*, decided the new nickname was too cumbersome for newspaper writing and vowed to find a new one. Among the nicknames rejected in the college contest had been Spartans, the nomination of former athlete Perry J. Fremont. (In ancient Greece, Spartans were citizens of Sparta, a Greek city-state. Known for their military discipline, the Spartans defeated the Athenians in the Peloponnesian War in 404 B.C.)

In 1926, Michigan State went on its first southern baseball training tour. Rewriting game leads sent from Fort Benning, Georgia, Alderton began to use Spartans sparingly and then ventured into headlines with the name. No one complained about the new name. Other newspapers began using it, and when the student publication used the name, it caught on.

Mascot: A student dressed as a military Spartan entertains at athletic events.

A huge statue, popularly known as Sparty, symbolizes Michigan State's athletic teams. Standing at the entrance to the school's athletic establishment, it stands ten feet-six inches in height and is mounted on a brick and concrete base five feet-four inches high. The statue weighs three tons and is one of the largest free-standing ceramic figures in the world.

Interesting Facts: Michigan State won the national championship in football in 1952.

In 1949, Ed Bagdon won the Outland Trophy for best interior lineman. Brad Van Pelt won the Maxwell Award for top football player in 1972. Percy Snow won both the Butkus Award and Lombardi Award for top linebacker in 1989.

Michigan State won the men's national basketball championship in 1979. Guard Magic Johnson was the outstanding player.

The winner of the Michigan State-Notre Dame game receives a megaphone sponsored jointly by the Detroit alumni clubs of Notre Dame and Michigan State. The award has been presented since 1949.

The school won the national championship in hockey in 1966 and 1986.

Middle Tennessee

Nickname: Blue Raiders
Mascot: Ole Blue
Colors: Blue and White
Conference: Ohio Valley
Location: Murfreesboro
Year founded: 1911

Nickname: In the early days, Middle Tennessee football teams went by several nicknames such as Teachers, Normalites, and Pedagogues. In 1934, students decided that the school needed a specific nickname. During the football season that year, the Murfreesboro *Daily News Journal* held a contest to choose a nickname. Charles Sarver, a football player, won a $5 prize for his contribution of Blue Raiders. (Sarver later said that he had borrowed the Colgate Red Raiders nickname and substituted MTSU Blue for Colgate Red.) The name caught on fast, and ever since athletic teams have been known as the Blue Raiders.

Mascot: Ole Blue, a costumed student who represents a Blue Tick Hound, is the mascot. According to the sports information director at Middle Tennessee State University, no one knows why Ole Blue was chosen as the mascot. It may have been because of the school colors.

The school mascot originally depicted Confederate General Nathan Bedford Forrest on a horse. This cavalryman was first used about 1945. In 1965, the Student Government Association established strict specifications as to what size the student must be who would emulate Forrest. This was done supposedly because there was only one uniform available and a "good fit" was desired. A few years later, though, the Forrest figure was dropped because students protested its use. Many students thought Forrest was an inappropriate symbol because of his link with the Ku Klux Klan and the Confederacy.

Interesting Facts: Middle Tennessee's football arch rival is Tennessee Tech. The two teams play each year for an authentic totem pole called "Harvey" by MTSU students and "Shin-a-ninny" by Tech students. The tradition of the trophy was started when it was donated by Nashville businessman Fred Harvey in the early 1960s. The totem pole disappeared for a number of years; it was thought to be taken by Tech students. The trophy resurfaced in 1991.

Millersville

Nickname: Marauders
Mascot: Marauder
Colors: Black and Gold
Conference: Pennsylvania State Athletic
Location: Millersvile, Pa.
Year founded: 1855

Nickname: A sportswriter in the mid-1920s was the first to refer to Millersville University teams as Marauders. A marauder is one who goes about in search of plunder.

Mascot: A student dresses as a marauder.

Interesting Facts: Baseball and football both originated at Millersville in 1889. Men's basketball, founded in 1900, is on its way to its 1,000 victory. At the end of the 1991-92 season, the school had 982 wins.

Minnesota

Nickname: Golden Gophers
Mascot: Goldie the Gopher
Colors: Maroon and Gold
Conference: Big 10
Location: Minneapolis
Year founded: 1851

Nickname: The history of Golden Gophers goes all the way back to 1857. Minnesota was labeled the Gopher State as the result of a cartoon satirizing the "Five Million Loan Bill" which appeared in the legislature on February 24, 1858. That bill, which provided a loan for the building of railroads in Minnesota, was bitterly opposed. In order to bring the subject into perspective, a cartoon was circulated showing the "Gopher Train" drawn by nine striped Gophers with human heads. The cartoon permanently affixed upon Minnesota the nickname Gopher State.

In the early 1930s, Minnesota football teams, under the direction of Bernie Bierman, established themselves as national champions. The local press described the Gopher teams as the "golden-shirted horde" and the "golden swarm." These descriptions, simultaneous with the team's change to golden-colored jerseys, brought about the name Golden Gophers.

Mascot: Goldie the Gopher is the costumed mascot who entertains at athletic events.

Interesting Facts: Minnesota won national championships in football in 1934, 1935, 1936, 1940, 1941, and 1960. Minnesota teams were also co-champions with SMU in 1935 and with Mississippi in 1960.

Halfback Bruce Smith won the Heisman Trophy in 1941. Tom Brown in 1960 and Bobby Bell in 1962 were Outland Trophy winners.

Minnesota's cherished football traditions include the Little Brown Jug, the Floyd of Rosedale, and Paul Bunyan's Ax.

The Little Brown Jug is given to the winner of the annual Minnesota and Michigan game. The "trophy" was created by accident when, following the 1903 game in Minneapolis, the Wolverine trainer left his team's water jug behind. Once the discovery was made in Ann Arbor of the missing jug, Michigan coach Fielding H. Yost requested Minnesota to return it. However, he was told, in effect, to "come and get it." Thus, the battle for the jug began

Back in 1935, Floyd of Rosedale was a national championship hog who became the object of a wager between the governors of Minnesota and Iowa as to the outcome of a football game. The prize of every Gopher-Hawkeye football game is the bronze statue of a hog.

Until 1948, the Gophers and the Wisconsin Badgers played for the Slab of Bacon Trophy. Then the National "W" Club from the University of Wisconsin introduced Paul Bunyan's Ax to the winner of the two schools.

Minnesota won the national championship in men's basketball in 1902 and in 1919. Louis Cooke coached both teams.

Minnesota won the Baseball College World Series three times.

Mississippi

Nickname: Rebels
Mascot: Colonel Rebel; Johnny Rebel
Colors: Cardinal Red and Navy Blue
Conference: Southeastern
Location: Oxford
Year founded: 1848

Nickname: The student newspaper, *The Mississippian*, sponsored a contest in 1936 to choose a nickname. Rebels, suggested by Judge Ben Guider of Vicksburg, was one of five entries submitted to Southern sports writers for final selection from a list of more than 200 proposed nicknames. Eighteen of the 21 sports writers who responded chose Rebels. The University Athletic Committee made the name official. Judge William Hemingway, chairman of the committee, said of the decision, "If 18 sportswriters wish to use 'Rebels', I shall not rebel, so let it go Old Miss Rebels."

Mississippi's other nickname, Ole Miss, became part of University life in 1896. It was selected in a contest held to identify the new yearbook. Suggested by Elma Meek of Oxford, each succeeding issue of the annual has been given this copyright identity.

Mascot: Colonel Rebel first made his appearance in school publications in 1938 when he appeared in *The Rebel Number*, the Ole Miss yearbook. Colonel Rebel has since become the official University insignia.

Mississippi's costumed mascot goes by the name Johnny Rebel. Making his debut in the Liberty Bowl at the Memphis State game in 1979, Johnny Rebel performs at both football and basketball games. Wearing a red and blue tuxedo and carrying a walking cane, he plays the part of a Southern gentleman.

Interesting Facts: Mississippi's school colors were chosen in 1893. That year, while in training for a five-game season, the players discussed colors for the team. The manager suggested the union of the crimson of Harvard and the navy blue of Yale. These colors were chosen for the football team and later were adopted as the school's athletic colors.

From 1957 to 1972, Ole Miss made 15 straight bowl appearances participating in six Sugar Bowls, one Cotton, two Gators, two Bluebonnets, two Liberties, one Sun, and one Peach. The University did not return to a bowl game until 1983.

Mississippi College

Nickname: Choctaws
Mascot: Chief Choc

Colors: Navy Blue and Old Gold
Conference: Gulf South
Location: Clinton
Year founded: 1826

Nickname: Prior to 1921, the Mississippi College football team was known as the Collegians. That year students got together and decided that Collegians just didn't fit the 7-2-1 team. A contest was held to choose a new nickname. Montie A. Davis of Pascagoula, who would later become a World War I hero and then a long-time Baptist minister, suggested Choctaws. He later wrote, "I looked around me and I found that one of the old Choctaw trails actually crossed the college campus and there was even a marker on campus marking the site. It was part of the original Natchez Trace."

Davis' suggestion and three others—Yellowjackets, Dutchies, and Warriors—were among the final four. Davis was quick to point out why three of the names would not be acceptable. "Yellowjackets," he said, "were good only in dry weather and just the week before the football team had played on a muddy and wet field. Dutchies was in honor of the president of the College, Dr. J.W. Provine, and wouldn't mean anything to people outside the school. Warriors? What Warriors?" Davis also said, "I studied up on the Choctaws and knew what they could do. I let the students know that Choctaws were noted for their bravery and fair play and they had speed to burn and could run like a deer. They could also swim like a fish, if necessary." His research paid off because Choctaws won by a clear majority. The Indian connection became popular with the college. The yearbook is the *Tribesman*; the literary magazine, the *Arrowhead*; the student handbook, the *Tomahawk*; and the student grill is the Wigwam.

Mascot: Chief Choc is the popular student mascot who entertains at sporting events.

Interesting Facts: Mississippi College, a Baptist school, won the

NCAA Division II football championship in 1989. The win marked the first time that a Mississippi team—public or private—had won a national championship in football. The #16 seed Mississippi College won the title, 3-0, over Jacksonville State.

Mississippi College's 1921 team was led by the legendary Edwin "Goat" Hale, now a member of the National Football Foundation Hall of Fame and the greatest running back to play at the school. Hale led Mississippi College to wins over Tulane University (14-0), Louisiana College (68-0), Union University (35-0), Birmingham Southern (27-6), University of Mississippi (27-7), Millsaps (56-0), and a 7-7 tie with the University of Florida.

Mississippi State

Nickname: Bulldogs
Mascot: Bully XVI
Colors: Maroon and White
Conference: Southeastern
Location: Starkville
Year founded: 1878

Nickname: Mississippi State's athletic teams have officially been known as the Bulldogs since 1961, but reference to the nickname can be traced back to the beginning of the century. On November 30, 1905, students at Mississippi A&M, celebrating a 11-0 football win over in-state rival Mississippi, displayed a bulldog pup in a parade through downtown Jackson. For several years after, the school's athletic teams were referred to as Bulldogs and Aggies. When Mississippi A&M became Mississippi State College in 1932, the Aggie moniker was dropped. From 1935-1960, State's teams were often called the Maroons in reference to the school colors, although Bulldogs was also used. The origin of the movement to make Bulldogs the official nickname in 1961 is unclear.

Mascot: Bully XVI, a registered English bulldog, is State's current mascot. The first mascot was brought to campus in 1935 by Major Ralph Sasse, football coach at State from 1935-1937. Ptolemy was a gift from the Edgar Webster family of Memphis. Ptolemy's successor was Bully I, who died in 1939 when a campus bus ran over him. The bulldog lay in state in a glass top casket and, following a half-mile funeral procession, was buried under the player's bench on the 50-yard line at Scott Field. Even *Life* magazine covered the event.

Interesting Facts: The Mississippi State Cowbell is a tradition first introduced at athletic events during the late 1930s. Although it is banned from SEC football and basketball games, the cowbell can often be heard at non-conference games.

    Coach Allyn McKeen, a 1991 inductee in the National Football Foundation's Hall of Fame, led the Bulldogs to their first bowl victory, a 14-7 win over Georgetown in the 1941 Orange Bowl.

    Coach Emory Bellard's teams made back-to-back post-season bowl appearances for the first time in school history. The 1980 team lost to Nebraska in the Sun Bowl while the 1981 team defeated Kansas, 10-0.

    The 1991 season saw the inauguration of football coach Jackie Sherrill's all-volunteer student kickoff coverage team called the Mad Dawgs.

Mississippi Valley State

Nickname: Delta Devils
Mascot: Red Devil
Colors: Green, White, and Red
Conference: Southwestern Athletic
Location: Itta Bena
Year founded: 1950

Nickname: Cleotha Hatcher, athletic director and head football coach, was responsible for Mississippi Valley's nickname. Hatcher, who coached from 1950-53, recorded how the nickname originated: "Dr. J. H. White (Mississippi Vocational College's President) told me on a very hot day to come up with a mascot and a nickname for MVC. I said to him, 'It's hot as the devil today.' That's where the Devil came into the picture. Because of Mississippi Vocational's Delta location, the Devils got the prefix Delta; and besides, Delta Devils had a good ring to it."

Mascot: A costumed mascot called the Red Devil entertains at sporting events.

Interesting Facts: Deacon Jones, who went on to play for the Los Angeles Rams and was inducted into the National Football League Hall of Fame, played for Mississippi Valley in 1959-60.

Archie "Gunslinger" Cooley was Mississippi Valley's legendary coach from 1980-86. One of his standouts was Jerry Rice who later played for the San Francisco 49ers.

Missouri

Nickname: Tigers
Mascot: Truman the Tiger
Colors: Old Gold and Black
Conference: Big 8
Location: Columbia
Year founded: 1839

Nickname: The origin of Missouri's nickname can be traced back to the 1860s. Before the Civil War, plundering guerilla bands habitually raided small towns, and people in Columbia constantly feared attacks. Temporary "home guards" and vigilance companies banded together to fight off any possible forays. Because the protecting organizations discouraged any guerilla activity, the groups began to disband in 1854. Later, during the Civil War, it was rumored that a guerilla band led by the notorious Bill Anderson planned to sack the town. An armed guard of Columbia citizens quickly built a blockhouse and fortified the old courthouse in the center of town. They were called The Missouri Tigers. The marauders never came. Presumably, the reputation of the intrepid Tigers had spread, and Anderson's gang detoured around Columbia.

When Missouri's first football team was organized in 1890, the athletic committee adopted the nickname Tigers in official recognition of those Civil War defenders.

Mascot: A student dressed as Truman the Tiger performs at Missouri athletic events.

Interesting Facts: Missouri is referred to as Mizzou.

Missouri's most celebrated rivalry is with the University of Kansas. This historic contest began in 1935. Each year the winner of the Missouri-Kansas game is given the Indian War Drum. The drum is a symbol of the Osage Indians who once roamed the plains of Kansas and Missouri.

The winner of the Missouri-Nebraska game is given the Missouri-Nebraska Bell.

The Tiger-Sooner Peace Pipe is smoked during half-time of the Missouri-Oklahoma game. Inaugurated in 1929, the ceremony takes place between the Mystical Seven, a University of Missouri honorary group, and a similar organization representing Oklahoma.

The Telephone Trophy is presented to the winner of the Missouri-Iowa State game. The idea for the trophy came as a result of a Missouri assistant coach, prior to the 1959 game at Iowa State, putting on his headset in the press box and getting a big surprise—he could hear the Iowa State coaches chatting. The wires were crossed, and each side could hear the other one.

Missouri-Kansas City

Nickname: Kangaroos
Mascot: Kangaroo
Colors: Blue and Gold
Conference: Independent

Location: Kansas City
Year founded: 1933
Conference: Independent

Nickname: The editors of the campus newspaper decided in 1936 that it was time the school (then called Kansas City University) had a mascot to represent the debate team. (No organized athletic teams existed at the time.) Later that year an article appeared in the Kansas City *Star* titled "Kangaroo May Go to KCU...Student Editors Believe University Should Have a Symbol." At this time, interest already existed in a kangaroo mascot since the Kansas City Zoo had purchased two baby kangaroos.

In 1937, though, the editors of the University yearbook *The Crataegus* decided that a kangaroo was not an appropriate symbol for the school. They opted to delete the proposed kangaroo emblem from the yearbook, but supporters then mounted an attack. As criticism continued, famed cartoonist Walt Disney came to the rescue. In April 1937, a leading KCU political group, the CO-OP Party, had won a decisive election with Casey the Kangaroo as its insignia. The same month, the KCU humor magazine, *The Kangaroo,* was published. Six months after the first kangaroo appeared on its cover, another one was featured, along with Mickey Mouse. The artist this time, though, was a famous name—Walt Disney. Support for the kangaroo mounted, and in a few years, the *Crataegus* folded, and the *Kangaroo* became the school's yearbook and the official nickname.

Mascot: Kasey the Kangaroo is the costumed student mascot.

Interesting Facts: UMKC basketball games are played at Municipal Auditorium, "The Roo Pit," in downtown Kansas City, the site of more NCAA Final Fours than any other building.

Monmouth

Nickname: Hawks

Mascot: Hawk
Colors: Royal Blue and White
Conference: Northeast
Location: West Long Branch, N.J.
Year founded: 1933

Nickname: The Press Club at Monmouth College held a student campaign in 1939 to pick an athletic nickname. A long list of entrants was cut to 15; suggestions included Bearcats, Bees, Bisons, Commuters, Orange Fliers, Trojans, MaJiCians, EmJaCees, and Nighthawks. Through a ballot in the college newspaper, *The Outlook*, Monmouth students nominated Nighthawks, EmJaCees, and MaJiCians. Monmouth athletic teams became Nighthawks by a margin of six votes. The sports information director explained, "Upon the school's entry into daytime ranks in 1956, the name was shortened to the present Hawks."

Mascot: A live hawk is the school's mascot.

Montana

Nickname: Grizzlies
Mascot: Grizzly
Colors: Copper, Silver, and Gold
Conference: Big Sky
Location: Missoula
Year founded: 1893

Nickname: Montana's first football team was organized in 1897 and dubbed "the varsity." The title was used for the team until 1909. That year someone suggested the nickname Bruins, and it began to be used. Then when Montana played Utah in 1912, a Salt Lake sportswriter coined the name Grizzlies for the marauding Montanans. Until the school joined the Pacific Coast

Conference in the 1920s, Montana teams were known as Grizzlies, Bruins, or Bears. It became confusing because the University of California was known as the Bears, and UCLA's nickname was the Bruins. The University of Montana was content to use only the name Grizzlies. The nickname is appropriate because Montana has more grizzly bears than any other state.

Mascot: A costumed student named Grizzly is the mascot.

Montevallo

Nickname: Falcons
Mascot: Freddie Falcon
Colors: Purple and Gold
Conference: Southern States
Location: Montevallo, Ala.
Year founded: 1896

Nickname: The origin of the nickname is unknown.

Mascot: The costumed mascot, Freddie Falcon, originated from a name-the-mascot contest.

Interesting Facts: The women's volleyball team at Montevallo owns the NAIA record for national tournament appearances, having played 10 consecutive years.
     The school's baseball coach, Bob Riesener, has won over 700 games.

Moorhead State

Nickname: Dragons
Mascot: Dragon
Colors: Scarlet and White
Conference: Northern Sun Intercollegiate

Location: Moorhead, Minn.
Year founded: 1887

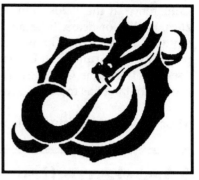

Nickname: Years ago Moorhead State University's athletic teams were called the Pedagogues and commonly referred to as Peds. (A pedagogue is a schoolteacher.) Legend says that after a fire destroyed Old Main on February 9, 1930, Flora Frick, a physical education instructor, suggested the nickname Dragons. Miss Frick had seen the football team roar out onto the field from their temporary hole-in-the-ground dressing room and said, "They look just like dragons."

Clarence "Soc" Gasrud, an MSU alumni and professor emeritus, says that the Frick story is not true. Gasrud, who has written a book on the history of Moorhead, says that a student body election chose Dragons in the spring of 1930.

Mascot: A student dressed as a red dragon with spiked tail is the school mascot.

Mount Senario

Nickname: Fighting Saints
Mascot: Fighting Saint
Colors: Blue and Gold
Conference: Upper Midwest Athletic
Location: Ladysmith,Wis.
Year founded: 1962

Nickname: A Catholic college, Mount Senario's athletic teams are appropriately named Fighting Saints. The sports information director does not know the origin of the name.

Mascot: A student costumed as a Fighting Saint is the school's mascot.

Interesting Facts: The Fighting Saints won the 1991 NSCAA (National Small College Athletic Association) National Championship.

Murray State

Nickname: Racers
Mascot: Dunker
Colors: Blue and Gold
Conference: Ohio Valley
Location: Murray, Ky.
Year founded: 1922

Nickname: In the early 1920s, some local fans commented on the "thoroughbred spirit" that Murray State University's athletic teams seemed to possess. Since Kentucky is horse country, that helped popularize the nickname Thoroughbreds. Since the name was long for newspaper headlines, many editors shortened the nickname to Racers. By the 1950s, Racers had replaced Thoroughbreds as the commonly accepted term for Murray State's athletic teams.

Thoroughbreds is used today only by the baseball team.

Mascot: Dunker originated out of a logo created in the 1970s by a Murray State alumnus. Today a costumed mascot named Dunker entertains crowds at sporting events.

Racer I, a thoroughbred horse, is Murray State's live mascot. The horse circles the track around the football field after every MSU football score.

Interesting Facts: The winner of the Murray State-Western Kentucky football game receives the Red Belt Trophy. The traveling trophy kept in the winner's training room originated in 1978 when Murray State trainer Tom Simmons forgot his belt at a district trainers' meeting. Simmons borrowed a red belt from Western Kentucky trainer Bill Edwards. When Edwards asked for the belt back, Simmons said, "You'll get it back when Western beats us in football." Simmons mounted the belt on wood, and the Battle for the Red Belt began.

Murray State won the national championship in rifle in 1978, 1985, and 1987.

N

Navy

Nickname: Midshipmen
Mascot: Bill the Goat
Colors: Navy Blue and Gold
Conference: Independent
Location: Annapolis, Md.
Year founded:1845

Nickname: Students at the U.S. Naval Academy are called midshipmen; therefore, it is an appropriate nickname for athletic teams.

Mascot: The first goat mascot used by Navy athletic teams was in 1893 when an animal named El Cid (The Chief) was given to the Brigade by officers of the *U.S.S. New York.* El Cid helped Navy to a 6-4 triumph over Army that year. Two cats, a dog, and a carrier pigeon have also been Navy mascots, but goats have served since 1904. Angora goats named Bill have served for years. The current mascot is Bill XXVI.

Interesting Facts: The familiar Indian figurehead facing Bancroft Hall and Tecumseh Court has been on the Annapolis campus since 1866. Midshipmen once referred to the figurehead of the *U.S.S. Delaware* as Tamenend, the great chief of the Delawares, Powhatan, and King Philip. Midshipmen finally settled on

Tecumseh, the fierce Shawnee chieftain who lived from 1768-1813. The original wooden Indian was replaced by a durable bronze replica presented by the Class of 1891. Before each Army-Navy competition in any sport, Tecumseh gets a fresh coat of war paint.

The Japanese Bell came from Okinawa, where its ancient purpose was to repel barbarian invasion. Commodore Matthew C. Perry brought it to America following his expedition to Japan in 1854. His widow donated it to the Naval Academy in 1858. The Bell, believed cast in 1456, rings when the Midshipmen score a football victory over Army or when Navy has an edge in the five spring sports.

The Enterprise Bell, which came from the bridge of the famed World War II aircraft carrier *The Enterprise*, arrived at the Naval Academy in 1950. Admiral Harry W. Hill, then Superintendent, brought the "E" Bell to the Academy. It rings when Navy scores a major victory over Army in any sports competition.

The Commander-in-Chief's Trophy is presented annually to the winner of the football competition among Army, Navy, and Air Force—and is named for the President of the United States. The three-sided trophy stands two and a half feet tall and is engraved with the schools' seals. Reproductions of the three mascots—the Army Mule, the Navy Goat, and the Air Force Falcon—are ensconced on the sides.

The men's fencing team has won three national championships.

Nebraska

Nickname: Cornhuskers
Mascot: Herbie Husker
Colors: Scarlet and Cream
Conference: Big 8
Location: Lincoln
Year founded: 1869

Nickname: University of Nebraska

football teams were formerly called the Old Gold Knights, Antelopes, and the Bugeaters. Lincoln sportswriter Charles S. "Cy" Sherman disliked referring to the Nebraska teams with such an unglamorous name as Bugeaters. Sherman, who later gained national renown as the sports editor of the Lincoln *Star* and helped to originate the Associated Press Poll, started referring to the Nebraska team as Cornhuskers in 1900. (Iowa, at times, had been called the Cornhuskers, but seemed to prefer being called the Hawkeyes.) The name caught on and eventually became the official nickname for the state and University.

Mascot: A student called Herbie Husker entertains at sporting events.

Herbie Husker is also the registered logo of the Cornhusker Athletic Department. The cartoon character evolved out of Nebraska's 1974 trip to the Cotton Bowl. Artist Dirk West of Lubbock, Texas, designed a Cornhusker cartoon for the Cotton Bowl press headquarters that caught the attention of Nebraska sports information director Don Bryant. Later, Bryant contacted West for permission to use the cartoon. Since West expressed a desire to refine his original cartoon, he was commissioned to draw an original Cornhusker cartoon character to serve as a mascot for all men's teams at Nebraska. Herbie is a burly, rugged, and confident character who represents the athletic and the agricultural traditions of the school.

Interesting Facts: Nebraska won the national championship in football in 1970 and in 1971.

Going into the 1991 school year, Nebraska's football team held the following records: an NCAA-record string of 29 consecutive winning seasons; an NCAA-record string of 22 consecutive seasons with at least nine wins; an NCAA-record string of 175-consecutive home sellouts since November 3, 1962; and a nation-leading string of 22 consecutive bowl appearances.

Coach Tom Osbourne is currently the winningest active football coach at a major college.

Every time Nebraska plays football at home, Memorial Stadium becomes the third most populous area in the state (behind Omaha and Lincoln).

Nebraska-Omaha

Nickname: Mavericks
Mascot: None
Colors: Crimson and Black
Conference: North Central
Location: Omaha
Year founded: 1908

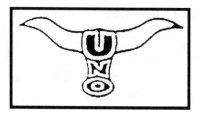

Nickname: The University of Nebraska at Omaha has been known by three nicknames. In its earliest days, teams were called Cardinals. In 1947, when athletics resumed after World War II, Indians became the new nickname. Student opposition brought an end to Indians in 1973, and a schoolwide election was held to choose a new name. Mavericks was selected.

Mascot: The University has no mascot. In the 1940s, though, a mascot called Ouampi accompanied the teams, who at that time were known as the Indians.

Interesting Facts: In the 1930s, the school's football team became the first ever to use a plane to travel to a game.

Nebraska-Omaha owns three national championships—softball winner in 1975, NAIA wrestling champion in 1970, and NCAA Division II wrestling champion in 1991.

Nevada-Las Vegas

Nickname: Rebels
Mascot: Hey Reb
Colors: Scarlet and Gray
Conference: Big West
Location: Las Vegas
Year founded: 1957

Nickname: When the University of Nevada-Las Vegas began competing in athletics in 1958, the school was known as Nevada Southern University. To most citizens of Nevada, it was viewed as the southern branch of the University of Nevada at Reno. Because the school was located in the south, and because Nevada became a state during the Civil War (1864), Rebels was adopted as the nickname. NSU's mascot was a wolf who wore a Confederate hat and full length general's coat.

The University of Nevada Board of Regents changed the two state schools' names in 1970 to UNLV and UNR. Immediately, students complained about what they considered the discriminatory nickname, Rebels. In 1974, a decision was made to drop the wolf and Confederate aspects of Rebel in favor of a Revolutionary War-era patriot.

Mascot: Hey Reb is a student mascot dressed as a Colonial Rebel.

Interesting Facts: UNLV won the 1990 national championship in men's basketball. The Rebels' score of 103-73 against Duke was the largest victory margin in the history of the national championship game.

Former basketball coach Jerry Tarkanian was the nation's winningest active collegiate basketball coach (by percentage). Tarkanian's trademark, "Tark's Towel," dated back to his coaching days at Redlands High School in 1960. During a league championship game, the coach sought a simpler way to quench his thirst. Rather than trips to the water fountain for a drink, he soaked a towel with water and chewed on it whenever he needed a drink. Tarkanian said, "We won the game and the championship, and since I'm not one to change when something works, I've stuck with the towel ever since. I guess I believe in lucky charms." Tarkanian now coaches in the NBA.

Nevada-Reno

Nickname: Wolf Pack
Mascot: Wolf

Colors: Silver and Blue
Conference: Big Sky
Location: Reno
Year founded:1874

Nickname: The University of Nevada-Reno's nickname originated in the 1920s. North Carolina State is the only other college in the nation with the Wolf Pack moniker, although NCS spells its mascot as one word.

Mascot: A student dressed as a wolf performs at athletic events.

New Hampshire

Nickname: Wildcats
Mascot: Wildcat
Colors: Blue and White
Conference: Yankee
Location: Durham
Year founded: 1866

Nickname: The University of New Hampshire acquired the nickname Wildcats in 1926. That fall a farmer in Meredith, New Hampshire, captured a wildcat and kept it in a small cage. Three Durham townspeople found out about the animal's capture, and after acquiring the wildcat from the farmer, brought it to campus. It was kept in a cage behind Thompson Hall, the school's administration building. The caged wildcat attended home football games. It was said that the animal didn't like the band because it would put its paws up to its ears when the band played. In the fall of 1927, the animal was put on a double leash because the governor's wife had protested about a caged animal at the Homecoming game.

Mascot: A student wears a wildcat costume.

Interesting Facts: The University of New Hampshire has won three national championships in men's field hockey, two in women's basketball, and two in men's indoor track.

New Hampshire College

Nickname: Penmen
Mascot: None
Colors: Blue, Gold, and White
Conference: New England Collegiate
Location: Manchester
Year founded: 1932

Nickname: New Hampshire College's nickname Penmen derives from the school's original name, New Hampshire College of Accounting and Commerce. The quill, or pen, used by colonial accountants became synonymous with the school. Today, the Penmen logo shows a man in colonial garb holding a large quill, or pen, as a staff. The character on the logo with his muscular arms, legs, and torso also represents the ruggedness of New England's original settlers. Although the logo was relatively unpopular when introduced in 1969, it has since become accepted and well-liked.

Interesting Facts: New Hampshire College won the 1989 NCAA Division II national championship in men's soccer.

New Mexico

Nickname: Lobos
Mascot: Lobo Louie; Lobo Lucy

Colors: Cherry and Silver
Conference: Western Athletic
Location: Albuquerque
Year founded: 1889

Nickname: In 1921, a government trapper caught a wolf pup on the Floyd Lee Ranch in western New Mexico. A man named Jim Young gave the wolf to the University of New Mexico as a mascot. Until that time, New Mexico teams had been called the University Boys. Now that they had a mascot, they had to also have a name. Lobo, the Spanish name for wolf, was adopted. New Mexico cheerleaders took responsibility for the cub, and it appeared in harness at every game. Although it grew tame, a child teased it and was bitten at one of the games. University officials disposed of the cub, as one historian put it, "for fear other ill-bred brats might become tempted to play with the wolf and bring on a damage suit."

Mascot: Two students dressed as Lobo Louie and Lobo Lucy serve as mascots.

In the late 1970s and early 1980s, a live wolf made a comeback, but its career was short-lived because of safety precautions.

Interesting Facts: University Arena or "The Pit," as it is affectionately called, was built in 1966 in a 37-foot hole on Albuquerque's Southeast mesa. First, the roof was constructed, then the hole was dug, and finally the Arena built. The Lobo basketball team that plays in The Pit averaged an astounding 15,993 fans in the past 25 years, an amazing 97% of capacity.

The Pit was the site of the 1983 NCAA Championships.

Toby Roybal is the only Lobo basketball player ever to have his jersey retired. A three-year letterman from 1954-56, Roybal was New Mexico's first roundball superstar. Roybal's biggest moment came on January 11, 1956, in Carlisle Gym. He tossed in 45 points against Montana, shattering the single game scoring record, one which stood for 21 years. In the same game, Roybal went to the freethrow line 25 times and made 19. Both remain school records.

Luc Longley is the only Lobo to be selected in the first round of the NBA Draft. He was drafted by the Minnesota Timberwolves in 1990. Longley led New Mexico in career scoring (1,769), rebounding (922), and blocked shots (336).

New Mexico State

Nickname: Aggies
Mascot: Pistol Pete
Colors: Crimson and White
Conference: Big West
Location: Las Cruces
Year founded: 1888

Nickname: When New Mexico State University was founded, it was a land-grant agricultural school. Its first name was New Mexico A&M. Thus, the nickname Aggies is an appropriate label for the school.

Mascot: The school's mascot, Pistol Pete, was named after Frank Eaton, an early 20th century western gunfighter. Eaton's nickname was Pistol Pete.

Interesting Facts: New Mexico State won the Sun Bowl in 1959 and 1960.

New Orleans

Nickname: Privateers
Mascot: Lafitte the Insti-gator

Colors: Royal Blue and Silver
Conference: American South
Location: New Orleans, La.
Year founded: 1958

Nickname: During the 1964-65 school year, the University of New Orleans—known then as Louisiana State University in New Orleans— had four student elections before it adopted Privateers as its nickname. When a student referendum narrowed a list of mascot proposals (which included Cajuns, Mariners, Marlins, Ospreys, Pelicans, Seagulls, and Tigers) from ten to five, Panthers (27%) led Dolphins (26%) and Privateers (25%) in a run-off election in December 1964. The school's student council approved a third election after it received a petition containing more than 1,000 signatures protesting the selection of Panthers. Students reasoned that the winner had a slim plurality and that its name had nothing to do with New Orleans history or the school's location on Lake Ponchartrain. In the third election in March, Dolphins received 40.6% of the vote, Privateers 40.5%, and Panthers 18.9%. In the final election, Privateers defeated Dolphins.

The nickname selected was appropriate for a New Orleans school. A privateer is a member of a crew of an armed private ship commissioned to cruise against the commerce or war ships of an enemy. One of the most famous privateers in U.S. history was Jean Lafitte, who carried letters of marque (commissions) from several governments to prey upon the shipping of other countries. Lafitte's hideaway was located on Barataria Bay south of New Orleans. Lafitte's cannoneers were instrumental in helping to defeat the British forces in the Battle of New Orleans in 1815.

Ironically, when Joey Favaloro, the school's new women's basketball coach in the 1980-81 season, suggested a change to Buc-kettes for the women's teams, no student vote was taken. His proposal was approved with no fanfare by the school's athletic and academic administration.

Mascot: Lafitte the Insti-gator is a student costumed as an alligator wearing a blue pirate's outfit.

Interesting Facts: New Orleans won Division II national championships in men's golf in 1971 and 1972.

The UNO women's basketball team won the 1983 NIT.

Former UNO baseball players Joe Slusarski and Ted Wood were members of the 1988 U.S. Olympic team which won the gold medal.

Lakefront Arena—home to basketball, volleyball, and swimming teams—is the site where Larry Bird scored a Boston Celtics' record of 60 points against the Atlanta Hawks on March 12, 1985.

New York

Nickname: Violets
Mascot: Bobcat
Colors: Purple and White
Conference: University Athletic
Location: New York City
Year founded: 1831

Nickname: Violets is one of the more unique nicknames among the nation's colleges. The name was chosen because the area of New York City—Greenwich Village—where New York University is located was very fertile for growing violets. They were planted all around the school's buildings at Washington Square Park during the late 1800s.

Mascot: New York's mascot has an unusual origin. The school library is named after Elmer Holmes Bobst. The card catalog is computerized and is called the Bobst Catalog System. Shortening Bobst and Catalog to Bob and Cat, the name Bobcat was created.

A student dressed as a bobcat performs at sporting events.

Interesting Facts: Basketball teams, which now play in the Coles

Sports Center, played in Madison Square Garden in the 1940s, 1950s, and early 1960s.

The school torch is handed down from the oldest faculty member to the youngest graduate each year during graduation ceremonies. The torch is the athletic emblem.

NYU has won 12 national championships in men's fencing.

Newberry

Nickname: Indians
Mascot: Ugh
Colors: Scarlet and Gray
Conference: Independent
Location: Newberry, S.C.
Year founded: 1856

Nickname: In the early years of Newberry College's sports program, students wanted to form an athletic association. Needing money and a field to play on, they cut down trees and sold the wood. They found a store which had dazzling red uniforms—that had gone unpaid by a major league team—and bought the uniforms at a low cost. Sports writers, impressed by the uniforms, began to call the players red men and then Indians.

Mascot: The costumed mascot, Ugh, is a popular cartoon-looking character. Ugh entertains crowds at every football and basketball game and also appears at other athletic functions such as banquets and fund raisers.

Interesting Facts: The Bronze Derby, the symbol of the Newberry College-Presbyterian College athletic rivalry, originated during the basketball season of 1946-47. Presbyterian, located only twenty miles away, played Newberry in a basketball game on January 3, 1947. Presbyterian won a close 51-47 victory. In a heated scuffle after the game, a Newberry student snatched a derby from a PC scholar. Presbyterian made efforts to get the derby returned. Charles MacDonald, PC athletic publicity director, suggested that the derby become a symbol of rivalry between the Indians and the Blue Hose. The derby was returned and bronzed by a local jewelry firm. In its early years, the Bronze Derby was exchanged during all athletic events; now the trophy is only interchanged at the annual football rivalry.

Niagara

Nickname: Purple Eagles
Mascot: Purple Eagle
Colors: Purple, White, and Gold
Conference: Metro Atlantic
Location: Niagara University, N.Y.
Year founded: 1856

Nickname: The name Purple Eagles resulted from combining one of the school's colors, purple, shown on the university seal, and the eagle, also displayed on the seal. The eagle is indicative of Niagara University's location on Monteagle Ridge.

Mascot: A student costumed as a purple eagle performs at athletic events.

Interesting Facts: Niagara's sports tradition is associated with basketball today, but football was the pre-eminent sport until it was stopped in 1950. Niagara's famous coaches included two of Knute Rockne's players—Edward Hunsinger and Joe Bach.

In the 1950s, Niagara's men's basketball teams went to the NIT six times, including four consecutive appearances from 1953-56.

All-American Calvin Murphy, Class of 1970, is the leading scorer in Niagara basketball history, with 2,548 points. Murphy, who went on to a long career in the NBA, had a single-game scoring record of 68 points set against Syracuse on December 7, 1968.

Nicholls State

Nickname: Colonels
Mascot: Colonel
Colors: Red and Grey
Conference: Southland
Location: Thibodaux, La.
Year founded: 1948

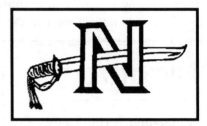

Nickname: Nicholls State University is named for Francis T. Nicholls, a Confederate colonel. Although Nicholls rose to the rank of general, the school chose colonel for its nickname. Nicholls later became governor of Louisiana.

Mascot: One of the cheerleaders wears a colonel costume for sporting events.

Interesting Facts: The school logo does not use a colonel but a sword interlocked in the letter "N."

North Alabama

Nickname: Lions
Mascot: Leo the Lion
Colors: Purple and Gold
Conference: Gulf South
Location: Florence
Year founded: 1872

Nickname: Lions has been the official nickname of the University of North Alabama for more than 40 years.

Mascot: In 1974, UNA President Robert M. Guillot established a new tradition by making the school the only one in the country to have a live lion mascot living on campus. Leo, a 35-pound cub at the time, was acquired by the school's president on July 22 and spent the next 14 years "roaring" UNA teams to victory. Leo, who grew to a weight of 540 pounds, died on January 20, 1988. In memory of the impact that Leo had on the school and the community, a bronze monument was placed near the compound that served as his home.

Leo II, an orphaned lion cub, arrived at UNA in July 1988 from a Texas ranch after his mother died giving birth. The mascot, who grew to a weight of more than 500 pounds by his third birthday, lives near the center of the campus in a renovated compound that once housed Leo I.

Interesting Facts: UNA won the NCAA Division II men's basketball championship in 1991, defeating the University of Bridgeport (Conn.), 79-72.

With that victory, athletics at UNA had come a long way since its beginnings in 1912. That year the then Florence State Normal School's football team lost 101-0 to Sewanee. Over the next 16 years, Florence State Normal suffered similar fates. After losing twice to Marion Institute, 86-0 and 85-0, in 1928 the program was dropped. On March 30, 1949, President Dr. E.B. Norton called for a student assembly to announce that football would be renewed the following fall.

In 1986, a group of area residents, with the sponsorship of Coca-Cola and Herff-Jones, Inc., worked to establish the Harlon Hill Trophy which would be presented each year to the top player in the NCAA Division II. Since that year, the "best" player is chosen by sports information directors at the 100-plus Division II schools and is presented during the week of the NCAA Division II Football Championship Game in north Alabama.

The Harlon Hill Trophy is named after an All-American receiver at Florence State Teachers College. Hill, drafted in the 15th round of the NFL draft by the Chicago Bears, was named National Football League Rookie of the Year in 1954. The next year he received the Jim Thorpe Trophy as the NFL's most valuable player.

Besides Harlon Hill, "Goober" is one of the most highly regarded graduates of UNA. George "Goober" Lindsey, star of television's "Andy Griffith Show" is a former Lion football player. Quarterback and two-year letterman for the Lions in 1950-51, he is a member of the Alabama Sports Hall of Fame.

North Carolina

Nickname: Tar Heels
Mascot: Rameses
Colors: Carolina Blue and White
Conference: Atlantic Coast
Location: Chapel Hill
Year founded: 1793

Nickname: Athletic teams at the University of North Carolina are called Tar Heels because North Carolina is known as the Tar Heel State. Two different stories exist about the origin of the nickname. A key element in both stories is the fact that the production of tar, pitch, and turpentine was for many years the state's principal industry.

One account goes back to the Revolutionary War. According to this story, troops of British General Cornwallis were crossing what is now known as the Tar River between Rocky Mount and Battleboro when they discovered that tar had been dumped into the stream to impede their crossing. When they finally got across the river, they found their feet completely black with tar. Their observation that anyone who waded North Carolina rivers would get tar heels led to the nickname.

The other popular theory can be traced back to the Civil War. During one of the war's fiercest battles, a column supporting North Carolina troops was driven from the field. After the battle, the North Carolinians who had successfully fought it out alone, met the regiment which had fled to safety and were greeted with the question, "Any more tar down in the Old North State, boys?"

"No, not a bit," shot back one of the North Carolina soldiers. "Old Jeff's bought it all up," he said, referring to Confederate President Jefferson Davis.

"Is that so? What's he going to do with it?"

"He's going to put it on you'ns heels to make you stick better in the next fight."

Upon hearing of the incident, Robert E. Lee smiled and said to a fellow officer, "God bless the Tar Heel boys."

Mascot: A white ram named Rameses is the Tar Heel mascot. In 1924, cheerleader Vic Huggins thought of a ram as a mascot by linking it with the nickname of Tar Heel star Jack Merritt, a fullback known as "The Battering Ram." In 1922, Merritt had acquired the nickname for the way he plunged into lines.

Prior to the Duke game, Rameses tries to outwit Blue Devil students trying to ramnap him. An old story that Richard Nixon, while a law student at Duke, was involved in an attempt to heist Rameses was denied by the White House during his presidency.

Interesting Facts: North Carolina has been given credit for throwing the first forward pass in a football game. John Heisman gave the Tar Heels that distinction in a 1928 edition of *Collier's Weekly*.

UNC-Charlotte

Nickname: 49ers
Mascot: 49er
Colors: Green and White
Conference: Metro
Location: Charlotte
Year founded: 1946

Nickname: The nickname of the University of North Carolina-Charlotte has an interesting origin. Many people erroneously believe that 49ers was chosen because the campus is located on N.C. Highway 49 (which it is) or because UNC Charlotte is located atop an abandoned gold mine (which it is not). The real reason involves the beginning of the school.

In 1946, the North Carolina legislature established an extension center of UNC-Chapel Hill at Charlotte as an educational service for returning World War II veterans. Thinking that the extension center had served its purpose, funds for the Charlotte campus were to be cut off. A group of concerned Charlotteans successfully dissuaded the lawmakers, and after a long legislative battle, the center became Charlotte College in 1949. Because the Charlotte group had the pioneer "we will not be defeated" spirit of 1849, the students adopted the nickname 49ers. The name was also appropriate because the birth of the school occurred exactly 100 years after the 1849 Gold Rush.

In 1963, Charlotte College became a four-year college, and in July 1965, the school became a member of the greater UNC system.

Mascot: A student costumed as an old bearded 49er entertains at sporting events.

Interesting Facts: UNC Charlotte's women's basketball team plays in the "Mine Shaft Gym," a 3000-seat facility. The men's team plays most of their games in the Charlotte Coliseum. The Shaft is where the men's team won 59 straight games from December 16, 1972, to November 28, 1983.

UNC-Greensboro

Nickname: Spartans
Mascot: Spartan
Colors: Gold, White, and Navy
Conference: Big South
Location: Greensboro
Year founded: 1891

Nickname: In 1967, when the men's sports program became formalized at UNC-Greensboro, the athletic department selected Spartans as the nickname. Women's athletics had existed for 20 years but without a formal nickname. Coincidentally, the University's logo pictures the head of the Greek goddess Athena, which resembles a Spartan.

The term Spartans is derived from the name of the inhabitants of Sparta, a city state in ancient Greece. Appropriately, Athena, the goddess of wisdom, played an important role in Greek life.

Mascot: A student costumed as a Spartan represents the school at athletic events.

Interesting Facts: North Carolina-Greensboro has won five NCAA men's soccer championships.

The University won the national title in women's golf in 1973.

UNC-Wilmington

Nickname: Seahawks
Mascot: Seahawk
Colors: Green, Gold, and Navy Blue
Conference: Colonial Athletic
Location: Wilmington
Year founded: 1947

Nickname: Seahawks became the school's nickname soon after its founding. Gene and James Warren, brothers and members of the first student council at Wilmington College (the University of North Carolina-Wilmington's former name), have taken responsibility for telling of its origin. A five-man student council, they said, convened to select a nickname. Seahawks was chosen because of the popularity of the Iowa Seahawks, a pre-flight service team coached by former University of Minnesota head coach Bernie Berman. Iowa was known for its excellent athletic teams at that time. The moniker also fit Wilmington College well because of its location near the ocean.

Mascot: A student dressed as a seahawk entertains crowds at sporting events.

Interesting Facts: Green and gold were adopted as the school colors also in 1947. Green was selected because of the color of the ocean, and gold because of the aura of the sandy beaches.

North Carolina State

Nickname: Wolfpack
Mascot: The Struttin' Wolf
Colors: Wolfpack Red and White
Conference: Atlantic Coast
Location: Raleigh
Year founded: 1887

Nickname: In the early days of North Carolina State University, varsity teams were called the Aggies, the Farmers and Mechanics, the Techs, or, most often, the Red Terrors. In 1922, though, they got a new name. A fan, disgruntled with the poor season (3-3-3), complained to athletics officials that the school could never have a winning record as long as the players behaved—both on and off the field—like a wolfpack. Students adopted Wolfpack as the football team's nickname, but continued to call other varsity teams the Red Terrors.

In 1946, Chancellor J.W. Harrelson called for a new mascot. He didn't like the Wolfpack label at all. "The only thing lower than a wolf is a snake in the grass," he said. He also reminded World War II veterans on campus that Nazi submarines had been called the wolfpack. The chancellor announced a contest to select a new nickname with the winner receiving sports tickets as the prize. Letters poured into his office suggesting new names—North Staters, Cardinals, Hornets, Cultivators, Cotton Pickers, Pinerooters, Auctioneers, and Calumets. Most letter-writers, though, wanted to keep Wolfpack. One alumnus wrote, "the Wolf is a scrappy, tough animal—the spittin' image of our team." Thus, the nickname remained—despite Harrelson's objection—and in 1947, all varsity teams were called the Wolfpack.

Mascot: The Struttin' Wolf, sometimes known as Toughie, is the mascot logo for NC State teams. It was designed by a student in the early 1970s and has become the trademarked logo of the school.

Interesting Facts: With a record of 28-8, North Carolina State's men's basketball team won the national championship in 1983. Outstanding player for the game was guard Sidney Lowe.

Football All-American Roman Gabriel played quarterback for Wolf Pack football teams from 1959-61. Gabriel played professionally with the Los Angeles Rams (1962-72) and with the Philadelphia Eagles (1973-77).

All-American Ted Brown is considered by many as the school's best running back. Playing from 1975-78, he joined the Minnesota Vikings in 1979 and played until 1985.

North Dakota State

Nickname: Bison; Thundering Herd
Mascot: Thundar
Colors: Yellow and Green
Conference: North Central
Location: Fargo
Year founded: 1890

Nickname: In the early 1890s, North Dakota State University's athletic teams were known as the Farmers. Teams were called Aggies in the early 1900s. Football coach Stan Borleske and his players didn't like being known as the Aggies; therefore, in 1919 they changed their name to Bison. The new nickname was appropriate since bison once roamed the North Dakota prairie in vast numbers. Over the years, Bison athletic teams added an additional name, Thundering Herd.

Mascot: Thundar is the costumed mascot of the athletic teams.

Interesting Facts: North Dakota State has claimed eight national football championships on the NCAA Division II level. The winning years were 1965, 1968, 1969, 1983, 1985, 1986, 1988, and 1990.

The school holds the record for having the most successful bowl and playoff teams on the Division II level.

The Nickel Trophy, inaugurated in 1938, is presented each fall to the winner of the North Dakota-North Dakota State football contest. Two inches thick, 22 inches in diameter, and weighing 75 pounds, the trophy is an exact replica of the once-minted U.S. coin. The five-cent piece was an appropriate symbol of NDS because of the engraved bison. The Nickel Trophy has been the object of many intercampus raids, recoveries, and thefts. Blue Key, honorary service fraternity on each campus, awards the trophy each year.

Jeff Bentrim, North Dakota State quarterback, received the first Harlon Hill Trophy in 1986. Bentrim led the Bison in four national championship games for three victories. He set a NCAA career record for rushing touchdowns (64) and led the nation in scoring for three consecutive years—the only player in any division to accomplish that feat.

Chris Simdorn won the Harlon Hill Trophy in 1990. Simdorn quarterbacked the Bison to two national titles, including a stunning 51-11 win over Indiana (Pa.) when he ran for two TDs and passed for three more.

A time-honored tradition at NDS is "Slap the Bison." A picture of a snorting bison sits above the football team's dressing room door at Dakotah Field. On game day, each Bison football player slaps the bison on the way out of the room prior to taking the field. The emblem of the bison travels with the team to road games.

Northeast Louisiana

Nickname: Indians

Mascot: Indian
Colors: Maroon and Gold
Conference: Southland
Location: Monroe
Year founded: 1931

Nickname: Athletic teams at Northeast Louisiana University have been known as the Indians since the school began as Ouachita Parish Junior College in 1931. It is believed that the nickname was used in reference to the Ouachita Indians, a sub-tribe of the Caddo Indians. The Ouachitas once roamed and raided along the Ouachita River near the present location of the University.

Over the years, some discontent has been voiced about the choice of the nickname. Woody Boyles, a former assistant football coach and the school's first baseball coach, remembered during his early days with Northeast at least one unhappy athlete. The captain of one of the first football teams made a plea to the student body at a pep rally to change the nickname because he was being called a "big fat squaw." No action was taken.

Mascot: In 1971, the logo for Northeast athletics was created as part of the observance of the 40th anniversary of the University.

A student costumed as an Indian is the school mascot.

Interesting Facts: NLU has won two national football championships. The Indians were national junior college champions in 1935. They won the NCAA Division I-AA title in 1987, making the school the only Southland Conference one to win the title.

Northeastern

Nickname: Huskies
Mascot: Mr. and Mrs. Husky
Colors: Red and Black

Conference: Yankee; North Atlantic
Location: Boston, Mass.
Year founded: 1898

Nickname: Northeastern adopted the nickname Huskies in 1927.

Mascot: The first live Husky appeared on campus on March 4, 1927. Coming to Boston's Station by train from Alaska, he was greeted by more than 1,000 students and the school band. Classes had been cancelled for the afternoon, and a police escort traveled the four miles to the campus. Originally named Sapsut, the dog became King Husky to the University. King Husky came from sled dog royalty. His father was the famous Noonok of Marly, the lead dog on Leonard Seppalla's team that rushed a diphtheria vaccine 645 miles from Nenna to Nome, Alaska.

For 14 years, King Husky I was mascot. His successors appeared at thousands of athletic events. King Husky VII died in 1989, and presently there is no live mascot.

Students wearing Mr. and Mrs. Husky costumes are now the official mascots who cheer on Northeastern teams at sporting events.

Interesting Facts: Northeastern's Matthews Arena is the oldest ice hockey arena in the world. Perhaps more widely known as the Boston Arena, Matthews Arena is home to the school's hockey and basketball teams.

Matthews Arena has as colorful a history as any sporting arena in the nation. Its chronology reads like a Who's Who in American Sports since its ground breaking on October 11, 1909. Legendary pugilists Jack Dempsey, Gene Tunney, and Joe Louis boxed there. The Boston Bruins played their first home game at the Arena on December 1, 1924. Chuck Connors, alias The Rifleman, jumped center and smashed the glass backboard in the Boston Celtics' first game on November 5, 1946. Presidents Teddy Roosevelt, Franklin D. Roosevelt, and John F. Kennedy spoke there as well as Charles Lindbergh, Amelia Earhart, Billy

Graham, and Dwight Eisenhower.

Northeastern is a member of the Eastern College Athletic Conference, the North Atlantic Conference, the Yankee Conference, and the Hockey East Association.

In recent years, the men's crew team competed in the Henly Royal Regatta in England.

Northeastern Illinois

Nickname: Golden Eagles
Mascot: Golden Eagle
Colors: Royal Blue and Gold
Conference: Independent
Location: Chicago
Year founded: 1961

Nickname: One explanation about the origin of Golden Eagles is that the nickname was chosen in 1965. When the school newspaper, *The Interim*, held a contest to select a nickname, students suggested many names. None of the names, though, appealed to athletic department personnel; therefore, Coach Gerald Butler suggested Eagles, and athletic director Chuck Kane added Golden. The two men submitted their recommendation to the newspaper which added the name to its list. In the student election, Golden Eagles won and became the official nickname.

Mascot: A student costumed as a golden eagle is the school mascot.

Northern Arizona

Nickname: Lumberjacks
Mascot: Louie the Lumberjack
Colors: Blue and Gold

Conference: Big Sky
Location: Flagstaff
Year founded: 1899

Nickname: Since athletics began at Northern Arizona University in 1909, teams have been called the Lumberjacks. The name was selected because of the importance of the logging industry to the area. Women teams were referred to as Lumberjills until 1985; then they changed their name to the Lady Jacks.

Mascot: Louis the Lumberjack is the costumed mascot. He has a papier-mâché head with a lumberjack outfit which includes a plaid shirt and blue jeans.

Interesting Facts: Northern Arizona is one of seven colleges and universities that own their own domed stadiums. NAU's Skydome is the largest covered stadium in Arizona, covering 6.2 acres. The roof spans more than 500 feet and rises to 142 feet above the playing surface. Several sports—football, basketball, track and field, and ice hockey—are played in the 15,000-seat arena.

Northern Arizona's biggest football win was the 21-20 victory over West Texas State in 1969. Then an NAIA school, Northern Arizona went to Canyon, Texas, to meet the NCAA Division I Buffaloes, who had several future pro players. NAU was a 38-point underdog, but won, 21-20. NAU had an all-time high 10 players sign professional contracts following that season.

NAU basketball player Wayne See was the first player from Arizona to play in the NBA when he signed with the Iowa Hawks (now the Atlanta Hawks) in 1947.

Peggy Kennedy, a NAU Lady Lumberjack from 1976-79, was the first woman from an Arizona college to play professionally. She joined with the Chicago Hustle and the Milwaukee Does of the Women's Professional League from 1979-81.

Mike Mercer, a Lumberjack in 1960, kicked the first field

goal in Super Bowl history in Super Bowl I as his Kansas City team lost, 35-10, to Green Bay.

The Lumberjacks were the first collegiate team from Arizona to appear in a nationally televised sporting event. The 1958 Lumberjack football team played Northeastern Oklahoma in the Holiday Bowl that year in St. Petersburg, Florida. The game was telecast nationally by CBS.

Northern Colorado

Nickname: Bears
Mascot: Bear
Colors: Blue and Gold
Conference: North Central
Location: Greeley
Year founded: 1890

Nickname: The University of Northern Colorado has been known as the Bears since 1925, when the teachers of Colorado Teacher's College (the school's former name) chose the nickname. The origin of Bears goes back to 1914 when Andrew Thompson, a CTC graduate, donated Totem Teddy, an Alaskan totem pole, to the college. Totem Teddy included a large brown bear on its top—hence the name Bears.

Over the years, several versions of bears were used for athletic logos. In 1980, athletic director Joe Lindahl declared the charging bear UNC's official athletic symbol.

Mascot: A student costumed as a bear performs at sporting events.

Interesting Facts: UNC's highest football season-ending national ranking was in 1969 when its record was 10-0. The team was ranked 3rd in the the final UPI poll and 5th in the AP poll for Division II schools.

Jackson Field has been home to the Bears since 1926. The biggest game at the stadium came in 1934 when quarterback

Roy Hardin led the Bears to a 13-7 win over the Colorado Buffaloes in the final game played between the two teams. The win gave the school its first-ever Rocky Mountain Conference title.

Northern Illinois

Nickname: Huskies
Mascot: Victor E. Huskie
Colors: Cardinal and Black
Conference: Independent
Location: DeKalb
Year founded: 1895

Nickname: Northern Illinois University has been identified with several nicknames during its history. Because the school was known as Northern Illinois State Teachers College in its early history, Profs was used. In the 1920s, Cardinals was popular. In the 1930s, Evansmen was used in recognition of athletic pioneer George G. "Chick" Evans. Northerners and Teachers were other provincial terms used to identify NIU athletic teams.

In 1940, a four-man committee of Evans, Harold Taxman, Walter Lorimer, and Harry Telman—all members of the Varsity Club—was appointed to choose a nickname. After much debate and research, a final decision was made as reported in a story in the January 25, 1940, *Northern Illinois*, the student newspaper and forerunner of the current *Northern Star*:

"Not only does the term have color and meaning, but it is particularly apt as in regard to NI's varsity teams," the article noted. "From now on the word 'Huskies' will be used constantly in this paper and in other papers to indicate our athletic squads."

Mascot: Victor E. Huskie is the costumed mascot.

NIU does not currently have a live husky. In recent seasons, though, a local family brought a husky dog named Tundra for pre-game line-ups and introductions.

Interesting Facts: Quarterback Bob Heimerdinger—known as "Huskie humdinger"—became NIU's first national statistical champion, winning the college football total offense record in both 1950 (1,782 yards) and 1951 (1,775 yards). As a senior, Heimerdinger led the Huskies to a 9-0-0 record as he rallied NIU from a 26-0 halftime deficit to a thrill-packed 27-26 victory at the University of Nebraska-Omaha.

Fullback Mark Kellar won the 1973 NCAA Division I-A rushing championship, beating national runner-up Tony Dorsett by 133 yards.

On September 17, 1988, placekicker John Ivanic booted four field goals—including a 31-yarder with 1:24 left in the game to give Northern Illinois a historic 19-17 triumph over the University of Wisconsin before 46,869 spectators in Madison. The win marked the Huskies' first grid victory against a Big Ten Conference opponent in 14 attempts dating back to 1971.

Northern Iowa

Nickname: Panthers
Mascot: Panther
Colors: Purple and Old Gold
Conference: Missouri Valley; Gateway
Location: Cedar Falls
Year founded: 1876

Nickname: The College Eye, the University of Northern Iowa's school newspaper, held a contest in 1931 to name the school's athletic teams. Burl Berry, a Most Valuable Player for the football team, submitted the winning entry—Purple Panthers. For his winning selection, Berry won a briefcase from a local drug store. Today, Northern Iowa's players are known simply as the

Panthers.

Mascot: A costumed panther entertains at sporting events.

Interesting Facts: The UNI-Dome is home to Northern Iowa's football and basketball games (as well as other sporting events). The Dome is air-supported, meaning that plenty of natural light is available during daylight hours to sizeably reduce utility costs. The roof is made of about 49 tons of woven fiberglass.

Northern Michigan

Nickname: Wildcats
Mascot: Willie the Wildcat
Colors: Old Gold and Olive Green
Conference: Great Lakes
Location: Marquette
Year founded: 1899

Nickname: The origin of the nickname is unknown.

Mascot: Willie the Wildcat is the student mascot dressed in a NMU jersey who performs at sporting events.

Interesting Facts: The only Olympic facility located on a university campus is at Northern Michigan University. On February 9, 1985, the U.S. Olympic Committee established its third Olympic Training Center at the school. On February 19, 1989, the Olympic Training Center was redesignated as the nation's first and only Olympic Education Center (OEC). Northern Michigan houses the nation's only Olympic resident athlete program, where top athletes in several sports can continue their education while training for top national and international competition.

Northern Michigan won the NCAA-Division II football championship in 1975.

The school won the 1991 NCAA-Division I hockey championship.

Northwestern

Nickname: Wildcats
Mascot: Willie the Wildcat
Colors: Purple and White
Conference: Big 10
Location: Evanston, Ill.
Year founded: 1851

Nickname: Wallace Abbey, a Chicago *Tribune* sports writer, was responsible for Northwestern University's nickname. In 1924, after the Northwestern football team performed valiantly in losing efforts to Chicago and Notre Dame on successive weeks, Abbey wrote, "football players had not come down from Evanston: Wildcats would be a name better suited to (Coach) Thistleth's boys..."

Mascot: The athletic department teamed with a commercial advertising firm in 1933 to develop the first caricature of Willie. Fourteen years later a costumed Willie was created when four members of the Alpha Delta Phi fraternity dressed up as Willie for their homecoming float. In 1986, Willie the Wildcat was chosen as one of the country's top mascots in a competition run by the Universal Cheerleaders Association.

Interesting Facts: The Sweet Sioux Tomahawk goes annually to the winner of the Northwestern-Illinois football game. When first instituted, the trophy was actually designed as a wooden Indian; today, it is in the form of a tomahawk. In its first year (1945), the trophy was awarded to Northwestern after a 13-7 victory over Illinois.

Notre Dame

Nickname: Fighting Irish

Mascot: Leprechaun
Colors: Gold and Blue
Conference: Independent
Location: South Bend, Ind.
Year founded: 1842

THE FIGHTING ■ IRISH

Nickname: The origin of Notre Dame's nickname is one of dispute. Several stories exist. One explanation suggests the moniker came about in 1887 during Notre Dame's first season of football. With Notre Dame leading Northwestern, 5-0, at halftime of a game in Evanston, Illinois, the Wildcat fans began to chant, "Kill the Fighting Irish, kill the Fighting Irish," as the second half opened. Another story links the origin of the nickname to halftime of the 1909 Notre Dame-Michigan game. With his team trailing, Notre Dame quarterback John Murphy yelled to his teammates—who happened to have Irish names like Dolan, Kelly, and Duffy—"What's the matter with you guys? You're all Irish and you're not fighting worth a lick." Notre Dame came back to win the game, and the press, after overhearing the remark, reported the game as a victory for the Fighting Irish.

The most generally accepted explanation is that the press coined Fighting Irish because it characterized the players' never-say-die fighting spirit and their Irish qualities of grit, determination, and tenacity.

Mascot: Notre Dame's mascot is a costumed leprechaun. A different student each year is chosen in April during cheerleader tryouts to represent the school. The school logo is the leprechaun, fists raised in a fighting posture.

Interesting Facts: Notre Dame leads the nation with the most national football championships in the AP college football poll. Notre Dame's winning years were 1943, 1946, 1947, 1949, 1966, 1973, 1977, and 1988. Notre Dame also won the national championship in 1923, 1929, and 1930 before the AP polls.

Football Coach Frank Leahy trails only Bear Bryant of Alabama as the coach whose teams have won the most national championships. Leahy coached the four Notre Dame teams of the 1940s.

Notre Dame has had seven Heisman Trophy winners.

The most famous quartet in college football is Notre Dame's "Four Horsemen." The backfield of quarterback Harry Stuhldreher, left halfback Jim Crowley, right halfback Don Miller, and fullback Elmer Layden was immortalized by sportswriter Grantland Rice. After Notre Dame's 13-7 victory over Army on October 18, 1924, Rice penned the most famous passage in the history of sports journalism:

"Outlined against a blue, gray October sky the Four Horsemen rode again.

"In dramatic lore they are known as famine, pestilence, destruction and death. These are only aliases. Their real names are: Stuhldreher, Miller, Crowley and Layden..."

Ohio

Nickname: Bobcats
Mascot: Mr. Bobcat; Bobkitten; Paws
Colors: Kelly Green and White
Conference: Mid-American
Location: Athens
Year founded: 1804

Nickname: For more than 100 years, fans knew Ohio University as the Green and White. On December 7, 1925, however, Bobcats became the official nickname. The bobcat—a sly, scrappy animal—won out over hundreds of names suggested in a contest. Hal H. Rowland, a former student and Athens resident, submitted the name.

Mascot: Mr. Bobcat and Bobkitten are the costumed mascots. Students in Ohio University's Lincoln Hall began the tradition in 1960. The first appearance of Mr. Bobcat ended a 15-game winless streak against Miami University. The feline costume—Bobkitten—originated in the mid-1960s.

Paws, a live bobcat, in recent years replaced another bobcat, Sir Winsalot.

Interesting Facts: Ohio University was Ohio's first university.
Athletic director Harold "Mack" McElhaney originated the

Bobcat Paw. His wife Gloria came up with PAWS (Providing Athletes with Scholarships), which has been in the forefront of Ohio University's athletic donations.

Ohio State

Nickname: Buckeyes
Mascot: Brutus Buckeye
Colors: Scarlet and Grey
Conference: Big 10
Location: Columbus
Year founded: 1870

Nickname: Not only are Ohio State University athletic teams referred to as Buckeyes, but Ohioans in general are labeled Buckeyes. Known as the Buckeye State, Ohio is home to two species of the buckeye tree. Long before it was established as the official tree of Ohio in 1953, General William Henry Harrison made the buckeye famous. During his presidential campaign in 1840, buckeye wood cabins and buckeye walking sticks became emblems of Ohio's first citizen to win the White House.

The most commonly accepted explanation about the origin of the nickname is that it was used to refer to the buckeye tree. However, all accounts generally agree that the name of the buckeye originated from its close resemblance to the eye of the buck deer. One story goes back to 1788.

Colonel Ebenezer Sproat opened the first court in the Northwest Territory. Large and well-proportioned, Colonel Sproat greatly impressed the Indians. In admiration, they named him Hetuch, their name for the eye of the buck deer. The nickname stuck, and Colonel Sproat became familiarly known as Big Buckeye. The name later was passed on to other Ohioans and eventually to the state. The University's athletic board recommended the use of the buckeye emblem in 1950.

The buckeye nut is bitter and, if eaten in quantity, is poisonous to man. According to folklore, the buckeye is a good luck charm and has the ability to cure rheumatism and other ailments.

Mascot: The costumed student mascot is known as Brutus Buckeye. The giant likeness of the buckeye seed first appeared in 1965. The original Brutus costume weighed 85 pounds, but now it only weighs a few pounds.

Interesting Facts: Ohio State's football team won the national championship in 1942, 1954, and 1968.

Recipient of the Heisman Trophy in 1974 and 1975, Archie Griffin is college football's only two-time Heisman winner. Ohio State's other Heisman winners were Les Horvath (1944), Vic Janowicz (1950), and Howard Cassady (1955).

The Woody Hayes Athletic Center is named after the legendary coach who led Ohio State to national championships in 1954 and 1968.

OSU was the national basketball champion in basketball in 1960 with a 25-3 record.

Since 1945, OSU has won 11 national championships in men's swimming and diving.

Oklahoma

Nickname: Sooners
Mascot: None
Colors: Crimson and Cream
Conference: Big Eight
Location: Norman
Year founded: 1890

Nickname: University of Oklahoma teams were called the Rough Riders or Boomers for 10 years before Sooners emerged as a nickname in 1908. That year, the name came from a pep club called The Sooner Rooters.

Historically, a Sooner was a settler who slipped into Oklahoma Territory before the official opening of land rushes, in which thousands of homesteaders entered to stake claims. Oklahoma is known as the Sooner State.

Interesting Facts: The University of Oklahoma won the national football championship in 1950, 1955, 1956, 1974, 1975, and 1985.

The school has had outstanding halfbacks to win awards. Three were Heisman Trophy winners—Billy Vessels in 1952, Steve Owens in 1969, and Billy Sims in 1978.

Rickey Dixon won the Jim Thorpe Award for top defensive back in 1987. Brian Bosworth won the Butkus Award for top linebacker in both 1985 and 1986.

Lee Roy Selmon in 1975 and Tony Casillas in 1985 received the Lombardi Award for top lineman. Jim Weatherall (1951), J.D. Roberts (1953), Lee Roy Selmon (1975), and Greg Roberts (1978) won the Outland Trophy for top interior lineman.

Former coach Barry Switzer had three national champion football teams—1974, 1975, and 1985.

Oklahoma has made 29 football bowl appearances, trailing only Alabama, Southern Cal, Texas, and Tennessee. It has had 11 Orange Bowl wins—more than any other school.

Along with football, its national championships include the College World Series in 1951 (beating Tennessee, 3-2); wrestling seven times—1936, 1951, 1952, 1957, 1960, 1963, and 1974; men's gymnastics in 1977, 1978, and 1991; and golf in 1989.

Oklahoma Baptist

Nickname: Bison
Mascot: Bison
Colors: Green and Gold
Conference: Sooner Athletic
Location: Shawnee
Year founded: 1910

Nickname: Bison is an appropriate nickname for Oklahoma Baptist University. The 125-acre campus, called Bison Hill, is located where bison once roamed.

Mascot: A student dresses as a bison for athletic events.

Interesting Facts: OBU won the NAIA basketball championship in 1966 and the national track and field championship in 1990.

Oklahoma State

Nickname: Cowboys
Mascot: Pistol Pete
Colors: Orange and Black
Conference: Big 8
Location: Stillwater
Year founded: 1890

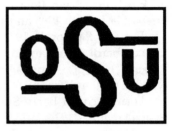

Nickname: In the early years of its history, Oklahoma State University teams were known as the Tigers. Aggies was also a popular name that reflected the fact that the school—then known as Oklahoma A&M—was an agricultural college. The nickname then evolved into Cowboys, an appropriate name for a school in Oklahoma, where cattle is one of the main industries. The Cowboy Hall of Fame is also located in Oklahoma City.

Mascot: Before 1923, the mascot was an orange and black tiger. That year, the student body of Oklahoma A&M, the former name of the University, voted on finding a new mascot more appropriate for the area of the country. At the same time, students were looking for someone to lead the Armistice Day parade in Stillwater. They asked a lawman from the Stillwater area by the name of Francis "Frank" Boardman Eaton. On the day of the parade, he showed up looking like a "crusty old cowboy." Upon seeing Eaton, a hometown legend who went by the nickname Pistol Pete, students obtained his permission to use him as a model for a mascot. A caricature was designed to resemble Pete's craggy face, complete with a prominent nose, mustache, and a huge western hat. A mascot was born, and each year OSU holds a tryout for students wishing to wear the Pistol Pete costume and appear at all major sporting events as well as other special events sponsored by the University.

Interesting Facts: Football player Barry Sanders won the Heisman Trophy in 1988. Sanders broke or tied 34 NCAA records during his career.

A leader in wrestling, Oklahoma State has won 29 national championships. Iowa trails OSU with 12 championships.

OSU won the College World Series in 1959 defeating Arizona, 5-3.

OSU won the national championship in basketball in 1945 and 1946, the first team to win back-to-back titles.

The University has been the NCAA men's champion in golf eight times.

Old Dominion

Nickname: Monarchs
Mascot: Lion
Colors: Slate Blue and Silver
Conference: Colonial Athletic
Location: Norfolk, Va.
Year founded: 1930

Nickname: For years athletic teams of the Norfolk Division of the College of William and Mary (as Old Dominion University was formerly called) were known as the Braves. This was a derivation of the William and Mary nickname of Indians. As Old Dominion achieved its own four-year status and then its independence in 1962, a new name was in order. The name Monarchs was chosen because of the king and queen who ruled England at the time William and Mary College was founded in 1693.

Mascot: The symbol of the school is a royal crown on a lion's head. A student costumed as a lion is an appropriate mascot.

Interesting Facts: Old Dominion won the men's basketball NCAA Division II national championship in 1975. Women's basketball won the NCAA Division I national championship in 1979, 1980, and 1985.

The women's field hockey team won the NCAA-Division I national championship in 1982, 1983, 1984, 1988, 1990, and 1991.

Old Dominion has been a leader in national sailing titles, winning seven from 1982-1990.

Oregon

Nickname: Ducks
Mascot: Duck
Colors: Yellow and Green
Conference: Pacific 10
Location: Eugene
Year founded: 1876

Nickname: University of Oregon athletic teams did not have a nickname until the 1920s when the local media coined the term Webfooters, a take-off on mudders, which indicated the common problem that rain causes on poorly cared turf fields. Although the University objected to the label, Webfooters caught on. An election in 1926 retained the nickname in a slightly altered form—Webfoots. It was still known to be grammatically incorrect—it should be Webfeet—but no one seemed to mind. Because the nickname was continually questioned, a second election in 1932 was held. Webfoots won out again over Pioneers, Yellowjackets, and Spearsmen, a reference to Football Coach "Doc" Spears.

The name Ducks slowly began creeping into the sports headlines. By the 1940s, Ducks was equally referred to as the Webfoots, and by the 1950s had become more popular.

Mascot: An official live mascot, Puddles, accompanied Oregon athletic teams in the late 1940s and lasted well into the 1960s. The duck finally vanished after repeated complaints filed with the Humane Society.

The University of Oregon and Walt Disney have an agreement regarding the Oregon Duck. The Los Angeles studio supplies artwork in the Donald Duck caricature, adapted to the Oregon Duck for use on decals and in non-profit athletic department promotion. It is believed to be the only such agreement between a university and Walt Disney. A costumed Donald is the student mascot.

Interesting Facts: Oregon was the men's national basketball champion in 1939.

Oregon won the men's cross-country national championship in 1971, 1973, 1974, and 1977; the women were cross-country champions in 1983 and 1987.

Oregon won five men's track and field national championships—1962, 1964, 1965, 1970, and 1984. Women's track and field winners were in 1985.

Autzen Stadium, the home of the Ducks, has several outstanding features. There is no track in the stadium, the first row of seats is just 30 feet from the sideline, and the 50-yard line is six feet from ground level. This gradually rises to a height of 12 feet from ground level in the end zone. Thus, every spectator has a good view of the entire field.

Oregon State

Nickname: Beavers
Mascot: Benny Beaver
Colors: Orange and Black
Conference: Pacific 10
Location: Corvallis
Year founded: 1868

Nickname: When Oregon State University was known as Oregon Agricultural College, athletic teams were called Aggies. Orange replaced the drab school colors of sweat shirt gray and tan, and Orangemen became the nickname.

In 1916, when the yearbook *Orange* was renamed *The Beaver*, the name Beavers became associated with athletic teams. L.H. Gregory of the *Oregonian* newspaper also may have popularized the new name. The November 16, 1920, issue of the student newspaper *Barometer* said that "Beaver accepted as the emblem only a a few years ago." Beavers may also have been a popular choice for the school since the official animal of the state of Oregon is the beaver.

Mascot: Benny Beaver was introduced to the student body on September 18, 1952, in an effort to increase school spirit. The costumed student mascot stands six feet tall, wears bright orange knickerbockers, and a black jersey.

Many years before Benny, around 1893, a coyote named Jimmie represented the school. In 1921, there was an attempt to make a live beaver named Bevo into the school mascot, but this gesture met with little success.

Interesting Facts: An early football coach, W.H. "Bill" Hargis, is credited with the first huddle—it was used against the University of Washington in Seattle on November 18, 1918. Hargis also is considered to be the first coach to use the forward pass—it was thrown in the fall of 1918.

Oregon State won the men's cross-country championship in 1961.

Otterbein

Nickname: Cardinals; Otters
Mascot: Cardinal
Colors: Cardinal and Tan
Conference: Ohio Athletic
Location: Westerville, Ohio
Year founded: 1847

Nickname: The origin of Otterbein College's nicknames is unknown. Although athletic teams officially are called the Cardinals, they are sometimes referred to as the Otters, with the latter being a play on the school name.

Mascot: A student costumed as a cardinal is the school's mascot.

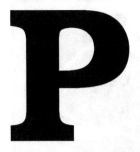

P

Pacific

Nickname: Tigers
Mascot: Tommy Tiger
Colors: Black and Orange
Conference: Big West
Location: Stockton, Calif.
Year founded: 1851

Nickname: Details about the origin of Tigers as a nickname for the University of Pacific teams are unknown. One theory says that the school copied Princeton University's nickname and colors.

Mascot: Tommy Tiger is the costumed student mascot.

Interesting Facts: The women's volleyball team won the national championship in 1985 and 1986.

Penn State

Nickname: Nittany Lions
Mascot: Lion
Colors: Blue and White

Conference:
Independent; Big
Ten
Location:
University Park
Year founded: 1855

Nickname: Penn
State University stu-
dents in 1906 chose
as their nickname the
mountain lion, once said to have roamed the central Pennsylvania mountains. The school is believed to be the first college
to adopt the lion as an athletic symbol. H.D. "Joe" Mason, Class
of 1907, conducted a one-man campaign to choose a mascot after
seeing the Princeton tiger on a baseball game trip to that
campus. A student publication sponsored the campaign.

The lion was designated as a Nittany Lion because Penn State
is located in the Nittany Valley at the foot of Mount Nittany. In
regional folklore, Nittany was a brave Indian princess in whose
honor the Great Spirit caused Mount Nittany to be formed. A
later namesake, daughter of Chief O-Ko-Cho who lived near the
mouth of Penn's Creek, fell in love with a trader named Malachi
Boyer. The tearful maiden and her lost lover became legend, and
her name was given to the mountain and to Penn State's athletic
teams.

Mascot: A student costumed as a lion performs at sporting
events.

Interesting Facts: Penn State's Nittany Lion shrine rests in a
natural setting of trees near Recreation Building on the school's
campus. The shrine was dedicated on October 24, 1942. Animal
sculptor Heinz Warneke and stonecutter Joseph Garatti molded
a 13-ton solid block of Indiana limestone into the lion, a gift of
the Class of 1940.

Penn State, under Joe Paterno, won the national championship in football in 1982 and 1986. The University had an undefeated season in 1968 (11-0), 1969 (11-0), and 1973 (12-0), but
did not win the national title.

John Cappelletti won the Heisman Trophy and the Maxwell Award in 1973. Mike Reid won the Outland Trophy for top interior lineman in 1969. Bruce Clark won the Lombardi Award for top lineman in 1978. Todd Blackledge won the Davey O'Brien Award for top quarterback in 1982.

Penn State has been a leader in men's gymnastics, winning the national title nine times.

Penn State won the men's cross-country title in 1942, 1947, and in 1950.

In 1983, Penn State won the women's fencing national championship. It won the women's lacrosse title in 1987.

Pepperdine

Nickname: Wave
Mascot: Willie the Wave
Colors: Blue, Orange, and White
Conference: West Coast
Location: Malibu, Calif.
Year founded: 1937

Nickname: Waves seems a natural nickname for Pepperdine University, which is located on a bluff cradled by the rugged Santa Monica Mountains and the Pacific Ocean. Malibu Beach, world-famous because of its surf, is within walking distance.

The nickname, though, originated a significant distance from the ocean. In 1937, prospective students of Pepperdine College found the concrete a bit wet, and were eventually treated by the Pepperdine family to a week-long stay at the William Penn Hotel in south-central Los Angeles. Among the tours created by founder George Pepperdine was a visit to the seashore, a sight never seen by most of the enrolled Midwesterners. Captivated by it all, some Tennessee students suggested the name Waves, and the name stuck.

Mascot: Willie the Wave is the costumed mascot.

Interesting Facts: Pepperdine's first president, Batsell Baxter, explained Pepperdine's colors. Blue represents the ocean, and orange, the abundant orange groves in the area.

Pepperdine won the NCAA men's volleyball championship in 1978, 1985, and 1986.

Pittsburgh

Nickname: Panthers
Mascot: Panther
Colors: Blue and Gold
Conference: Big East
Location: Pittsburgh, Pa.
Year founded: 1787

Nickname: Students and alumni leaders adopted Panthers as the nickname of the University of Pittsburgh at a 1909 meeting. According to George M.P. Baird, Class of 1909, who made the suggestion, the nickname was chosen for several reasons. First, the panther was the most formidable creature once indigenous to the Pittsburgh area. Second, it had ancient, heraldic standing as a noble animal. Third, the name provided alliteration. Fourth, the close approximation of its hue would go well with the old gold of the University's colors. Finally, the panther was selected because no other college or university at the time had the animal as a symbol.

Mascot: A student costumed as a brown, furry panther is the mascot.

Interesting Facts: Pittsburgh has had a rich football tradition. Under the legendary Pop Warner, the school won national championships in 1916 and 1918. Coach Jock Sutherland's team won in 1937, and Johnny Majors led his team to a championship in 1976.

Glen "Pop" Warner coached at Pitt from 1915-1923. In his first three years, he went undefeated—8-0 in 1915, 8-0 in 1916, and 9-0 in 1917. Under his command, the Panthers went 59-12-4.

Tony Dorsett, a running back for Pittsburgh from 1973-1976,

is the only four-time All-American in the history of Pitt football. In 1976, he became the only Pitt player ever to win the Heisman Trophy. Dorsett became the first player in NCAA history to reach the 6,000-yard mark. He is also Pitt's all-time leading scorer with 380 points.

Pro coach Mike Ditka was an All-American in 1960 at Pitt. Called "The Hammer," Ditka also played basketball and baseball.

Quarterback Dan Marino, All-American in 1981, became Pitt's all-time leading passer after only three years and finished with with 8,597 yards.

Defensive end Hugh Green was a three-time All-American for Pitt. In 1980 he won the Lombardi Award, the Maxwell Award, and the Walter Camp Award. He is the only defensive player to win the Walter Camp Award since its inception in 1969.

Pittsburgh won the national championship in basketball in 1928 with a 23-2 season. Doc Carlson, who was an All-American end in football for Pop Warner, was the winning coach.

Pittsburg State

Nickname: Gorillas
Mascot: Gus and Gussie Gorilla
Colors: Crimson and Gold
Conference: Mid-America Intercollegiate
Location: Pittsburg, Kan.
Year founded: 1903

Nickname: Pittsburg State University is the only college in the nation with Gorillas as its nickname. The moniker originated in 1920, when a group of young men dissatisfied with the lack of school spirit organized themselves as the Gorillas in order to "accelerate college spirit and enthusiasm until it shall permeate the state." The

Gorillas (a 1920s slang term for roughnecks) sponsored such events as pep rallies, picnics, freshman hazing, special trains to athletic events, and "night-shirt stampedes" through downtown Pittsburg. In 1923, art student Helen Waskey made a drawing of the new mascot. On January 15, 1925, the student body adopted Gorillas as the school nickname. When women athletics began at the school in 1974, teams were called Gussies. On October 31, 1989, the women's teams voted to change their name also to Gorillas.

Mascot: Gus and Gussie are student mascots costumed as gorillas.

Interesting Facts: Pittsburg State won the NCAA Division II national football championship in 1991. Its 23-6 win over Jacksonville State in the championship game completed a 13-1-1 season which gave the Gorillas their third national title. In the six years since 1986, the PSU football team has won more games than any other college football program at any level, posting a 70-6-1 overall record, winning a percentage of .916.

Portland State

Nickname: Vikings
Mascot: Victor Viking
Colors: Green and White
Conference: Western; PAC 10 North
Location: Portland, Ore.
Year founded: 1946

Nickname: When Portland State was known as Vanport College, the student body selected Vikings as the nickname. The name was chosen in 1947 became of Vanport's proximity to the Columbia River and the legend associated with Vikings as fighters and warriors who sailed into battles of conquest. The name also fit alliteratively with Vanport. When the school became Portland State College in 1955, Vikings remained as the moniker.

Mascot: Victor Viking is the costumed student who wears Viking attire, complete with helmet and sword.

Interesting Facts: Since 1984, Portland State has won NCAA Division II volleyball and wrestling championships.

Prairie View A&M

Nickname: Panthers
Mascot: Panther
Colors: Purple and Gold
Conference: Southwestern Athletic
Location: Prairie View, Tex.
Year founded: 1876

Nickname: Prairie View A&M Uni-versity's nickname was for-merly Tigers, but because anoth-er school in the conference had the same nickname, the moniker was changed to Panthers in 1926.

Mascot: A student costumed as a panther is the school's mascot.

Interesting Facts: Prairie View won national championships in football in 1953, 1954, 1958, 1963, and 1964.

The school won the NAIA national basketball championship in 1962.

Prairie View won the NAIA national championship in men's indoor track in 1968 and the men's outdoor championship in 1968 and 1969. The women's track team won the NAIA national championship in 1984, 1987, and 1991. The women's team won the outdoor titles in 1982-1990.

Barbara Jacket, athletic director, was the Women's Olympic Head Track and Field Coach at the 1992 Olympic Games in Barcelona, Spain.

Presbyterian

Nickname: Blue Hose
Mascot: Scotsman
Colors: Garnet and Blue
Conference: South Atlantic
Location: Clinton, S.C.
Year founded: 1880

Nickname: Early Presbyterian University teams were known by the nickname, Blue Stockings, which coach Walter Johnson always said was because his players wore long blue socks similar to stockings. Another explanation is probably more accurate. The phrase "Blue Stocking Presbyterian" goes back to 17th century England, when Puritans wore coarse blue stockings. The Little Parliament of 1653, called together by Oliver Cromwell, was referred to as "that blue-stocking Parliament" because of their plain attire and strict morals. When Puritans arrived in America, the phrase followed them. That nickname was shortened to Blue Hose in 1954.

Mascot: A student dressed in a kilt and other Scottish attire performs at school athletic events.

Interesting Facts: The annual Presbyterian-Newberry football game is known as the Bronze Derby Classic. The winner of the game gains possession of a derby hat, which has been bronzed for preservation.

Princeton

Nickname: Tigers
Mascot: Tiger
Colors: Orange and Black
Conference: Ivy League

Location: Princeton, N.J.
Year founded: 1746

Nickname: The Princeton football team in 1880 adopted an orange-and-black-striped jersey with alternating stripes on both the body and full-length sleeves. About this time, a newspaper account reported that the team was fighting like Tigers.

The Tiger Cheer might also account for the nickname. The cheer, which is still a major yell at Princeton athletic events, dates back to the Civil War. It was reportedly picked up by Princeton students when the New York Seventh Regiment passed through town and gave a version of this cheer in response to the students' applause. The cheer stemmed originally from the British Navy's "three cheers and a tiger" which didn't include shouting "tiger" at the end, but rather concluding the triple round of yells with a tiger-like roar. Somewhere through the years, the cheer was written out in soundless words and the writer, to designate the roar, simply put down "tiger." By the time it reached Princeton, via the Seventh Regiment, it was in form very much like that heard today at Princeton games.

Mascot: A student dressed as a tiger is the costumed mascot.

Interesting Facts: Princeton and Rutgers played in the first-ever intercollegiate football game on November 6, 1869, in New Brunswick. Rutgers won, 6-4, but Princeton gained revenge a few weeks later with an 8-0 win.

Princeton played a major role in the evolution of early football rules. The system of downs and the fixing of players into a line and backfield was started at Princeton.

The school's colors have an interesting history. Orange was chosen because Princeton's original college building, Nassau Hall (built in 1756), was named for William of Orange of the House of Nassau. Black was used because it was the only color ink available when the Class of 1869 wanted their class numerals printed on orange badges to wear for a baseball game with Yale in 1868. Orange and black have been the recognized school colors since Princeton crews wore them at the Saratoga Regatta in 1874.

The second-oldest football stadium in the nation is the

45,725 Palmer Memorial Stadium at Princeton. The stadium opened October 24, 1914, when Princeton defeated Dartmouth, 16-12, before an estimated crowd of 7,000.

Princeton won the national football championship in 1885, 1889, 1893, 1896, 1903, 1906, and 1911. In 1951, Dick Kazmaier won the Heisman Trophy, the only Princeton player to ever have the honor.

Princeton was national champion in basketball in 1925.

Purdue

Nickname: Boilermakers
Mascot: Boilermaker Special
Colors: Old Gold and Black
Conference: Big Ten
Location: West Lafayette, Ind.
Year founded: 1869

Nickname: Boilermakers, the unique Purdue nickname, was among several derisive terms applied to the school by Wabash College supporters following their 18-4 loss to Purdue in 1889. Located just 30 miles from Lafayette and a bitter athletic rival, Wabash College was a liberal arts school whose students were inclined to shun the cultural background of Purdue players who represented a school devoted to the practical arts of engineering and agriculture. Boilermakers struck the fancy of the Purdue players, who were also being called cornfield sailors, black-smiths, pumpkin shuckers, hayseeds, farmers, and rail splitters.

An unsubstantiated story says that in the late 1880s during the football season, Purdue once enrolled eight boilermakers from the shops of the Monon Railroad.

Mascot: The Boilermaker Special claims to be the world's largest mascot. A part of Purdue football since 1940, the 23-foot vehicle is fashioned to look like an old-time locomotive. Built by the

Buick Division of General Motors in 1960, the current 9,000 pound Special is the third model in the series and is powered by a 350 cubic inch, V-8 engine. Capable of highway speeds, the Special finds its way to most of Purdue's Big Ten Games. Special III was presented to the University at halftime of the Purdue-Ohio State game on October 15, 1960. The operation and maintenance of the Boilermaker Special is the responsibility of the Purdue Reamer Club, an independent honorary.

The Boilermaker X-tra Special, the toned-down version of Boilermaker Special, was inaugurated in 1979. The X-tra Special serves to lead the football team on to the stadium field.

Boilermaker Pete, also known as Purdue Pete, is the costumed mascot that is a regular at football, basketball, and volleyball games.

Interesting Facts: Purdue won the national championship in basketball in 1932. Led by coach Piggy Lambert, guard John Wooden was the outstanding player.

The Old Oaken Bucket, a bucket that legend says was used during the Civil War, goes annually to the winner of the Purdue-Indiana football battle. The Cannon is the trophy that goes to the Purdue-Illinois winner.

Quincy

Nickname: Hawks
Mascot: The Hollering Hawk
Colors: Brown and White
Conference: Independent
Location: Quincy, Ill.
Year founded: 1860

Nickname: Sometime before 1956, a contest was held to select a nickname for athletic teams at Quincy College. It is believed that the nickname Hawks was chosen along with the slogan "The Hawks are Flying." This saying referred to a squadron of planes called "The Hawks" that flew over the Quincy area during the 1930s.

Mascot: A student costumed as The Hollering Hawk performs at athletic events.

Interesting Facts: Founded by Franciscan priests, Quincy College is rich in Franciscan tradition and spirit and carries that legacy into its athletic events.

Radford

Nickname: Highlanders
Mascot: Rowdy Red
Colors: Red, Blue, Green, and White
Conference: Big South
Location: Radford, Va.
Year founded: 1910

Nickname: Radford University athletic teams have been called the Highlanders since the 1970s. The nickname reflects the influence of the Scottish immigrants who settled southwestern Virginia over 300 years ago. A Highlander was an inhabitant of the mountainous regions of northern and western Scotland. The people were known for their firm decision-making, resourcefulness, friendship, enthusiasm, and love of country.

Mascot: The Radford mascot at home games, Rowdy Red got his name from one of the school colors and from the Radford Rowdies. This was a group of vocal students who organized themselves into a cheering section at home basketball games in the small Peters Hall gym on campus in the late 1970s. Rowdy made his initial appearance at the Highlanders' first basketball game in the Dedmon Center on December 9, 1981.

Interesting Facts: The school adopted as its colors the red, navy blue, and forest green colors which were woven into the tartan kilt formerly worn by the Highlander band. The Marching Highlander band first wore their Scottish attire in the mid-1950s when Radford was an all-women's college.

Randolph-Macon

Nickname: Yellow Jackets
Mascot: Yellow Jacket
Colors: Lemon Yellow and Black
Conference: Old Dominion Athletic
Location: Ashland, Va.
Year founded: 1830

Nickname: Yellow Jackets was chosen as Randolph-Macon's nickname in 1900. The football team's yellow and black uniforms reminded students of yellow jackets.

*Mascot:*A student dressed in a yellow jacket costume is the mascot.

*Interesting Facts:*The South's oldest small college football rivalry is between Randolph-Macon College and Hampden-Sydney College (Virginia). The two schools first played in 1893 with Randolph-Macon winning, 12-6.

Rice

Nickname: Owls
Mascot: Owl
Colors: Blue and Gray
Conference: Southwest
Location: Houston, Tex.
Year founded: 1912

Nickname: Rice University's nickname originated from the school's heraldic shield. The designer of the crest noted that the arms of several families named Houston and Rice had both chevrons (designs used in coats of arms) and three avian charges. He adapted those for Rice Institute, the former name of Rice University. In the official shield, a double chevron divides the field, and the charges are the Owls of Athena as they appear on an ancient Greek coin.

When athletic activities began at Rice Institute in 1912, teams were named for the bird on the seal. Rice has been historically known as an institution of high academic standards. Like Athena, Greek goddess of wisdom who had the owl for her symbol, Rice also fittingly claims the owl.

Mascot: Rice's Sammy the Owl has an interesting origin. An early symbol of Rice's athletic teams was a large canvas owl. Students from Texas A&M kidnapped the owl in 1917, and Rice students sent a private detective to College Station to find the mascot's location. When the detective sent a cryptic telegram with the message, "Sammy is fairly well and would like to see his parents at eleven o'clock," the Rice Owl had a name.

The canvas owl was safely returned to campus. Other Sammies over the years have included a large fiberglass figure, a student costumed as an owl, and live owls. Presently, Lovett College, named for Rice's first president, supervises the care of three great horned owls.

Interesting Facts: One of the newest traditions at Rice is the Coaches' Table. The original tradition of the table began more than 60 years ago. Rice coaches would take their daily coffee breaks at Ye Olde College Inn, a famous Houston restaurant located across South Main from the old Rice Fieldhouse. The site of the breaks was a table in the restaurant's loft area. Rice coaches and players, as well as visiting coaches such as Bear Bryant, John Heisman, and Darrell Royal, would engrave their names on the table. The tradition continued until Ye Olde College Inn closed in the early 1960s. The table was lost for many years until it was rediscovered in 1990. The original table and a new duplicate, used for current signatures, are both on display in the Owl Club.

Rice's Marching Owl Band, known as MOB, differs from

traditional marching bands. Halftime shows integrate field action and formations with a script to present an entertaining and often thought-provoking experience.

Richmond

Nickname: Spiders
Mascot: Spider
Colors: Red and Blue
Conference: Yankee
Location: Richmond, Va.
Year founded: 1830

Nickname: The University of Richmond is the only school in the nation referred to as Spiders. In 1876, Richmond teams were called Colts. The name remained until the early 1890s when a baseball team comprised of University athletes and city residents used the name Spiders in a summer league. Star pitcher Puss Ellyson's lanky arms and stretching kick confused batters to such an extent that Richmond *Dispatch* reporter Ragland Chesterman aptly used the name Spider in his sports stories.

Mascot: A student dresses in a spider costume.

Interesting Facts: The Spider Athletic Fund accepts donations for several "Web" levels—gold, silver, bronze, blue, red, or white.

Rider

Nickname: Broncs
Mascot: Bronc
Colors: Cranberry and White
Conference: Northeast
Location: Lawrenceville, N.J.

Year founded: 1865

Nickname: In Rider College's early days, athletic teams were appropriately known as the Rough Riders. Legend says, however, that newspaper headline writers couldn't fit the name onto a line and so changed the nickname to Broncs.

Mascot: A costumed bronc (horse) parades the floor at Rider basketball games.

Interesting Facts: Legendary Clair Bee founded the Rider sports program in 1927, serving as the school's first football, basketball, and baseball coach. In later years, he coached the NBA's Baltimore Bullets. He died in 1983.

Jack Madden, holder of scoring and rebounding records at Rider, is still active in sports today as the NBA's senior referee.

The student section at Rider home games is called the Broncs' Zoo.

Robert Morris

Nickname: Colonials
Mascot: Colonial
Colors: Blue and White
Conference: Northeast
Location: Coraopolis, Pa.
Year founded: 1921

Nickname: Robert Morris College chose its nickname to honor its namesake. Robert Morris (1734-1806) was a Pennsylvania signer of the Declaration of Independence who was known for his financial genius. A merchant who served in the Continental Congress, Morris gave of his own fortune to finance the Colonial Patriots' cause. As superintendent of finance from 1781-1784, he guided the organization of a national bank.

Mascot: A student costumed as a colonial patriot is the mascot.

Interesting Facts: Robert Morris was a charter member of the Northeast Conference which was founded in 1981. Started as a basketball-only league, Northeast now sponsors 14 athletic championships.

Rutgers

Nickname: Scarlet Knights
Mascot: Scarlet Knight
Colors: Scarlet
Conference: Big East
Location: New Brunswick, N.J.
Year founded: 1766

Nickname: Prior to 1956, athletic teams at Rutgers University were known as the Chanticleers. Because of the bad connotation associated with a fighting bird, a contest was held to come up with a new name. Scarlet Knights was the winner.

Mascot: During the campus-wide contest to select a new name for Rutgers, English professors required all composition students to write essays about their choice. Sophomore Oscar Karl Huh conceived the idea of the Scarlet Knight. Huh became the first Scarlet Knight mascot riding his steed, Duke, at the Rutgers-Lafayette football game on November 3, 1956.

A student mascot wears a Scarlet Knight costume at athletic events.

Interesting Facts: Rutgers was a pioneer in establishing a college color. The school adopted the color scarlet on May 17, 1869, after the idea had been proposed in the Rutgers *Daily Targum* earlier in the month. Scarlet was the color that was universally designated for the theology degree, not inappropriate since the Dutch Reformed Church established the school.

Rutgers and Princeton played the first-ever intercollegiate football game on November 6, 1869, with Rutgers winning, 6-4.

The men's fencing team were national champions in 1949.

Saint Bonaventure

Nickname: Bonnies;
Brown Indians
Mascot: Indian
Colors: Brown and White
Conference: Atlantic 10
Location: Saint Bonaventure, N.Y.
Year founded: 1856

Nickname: Bonnies is a derivation of Bonaventure. It is the preferred nickname. Brown Indians is the older, more traditional nickname. Its origin stems from the brown robes of the Franciscan friars and the Indian heritage of the surrounding Seneca Nation in Salamanca, New York.

Saint Bonaventure (1221-1274) was an Italian theologian who was one of the leading mystic writers of medieval times. He was canonized in 1482.

Mascot: A student dressed as an Indian symbolizes the school's ties with the Seneca Indians.

Interesting Facts: Saint Bonaventure University won the 1977 NIT Championship in basketball.

All-American Bob Lanier, Class of 1970, was the first player chosen in the 1970 NBA draft (by the Detroit Pistons).

Two baseball players—John J. McGraw, who became one of

baseball's most famous managers with the New York Giants, and Hugh Jennings—graduated from Saint Bonaventure in the late 1800s. Both are enshrined in the National Baseball Hall of Fame in Cooperstown, New York.

St. Cloud State

Nickname: Huskies
Mascot: Husky
Colors: Cardinal Red and Black
Conference: North Central
Location: St. Cloud, Minn.
Year founded: 1869

Nickname: St. Cloud State University's athletic teams have gone by five nicknames in its history. In October 1896, six years after the school played its first football game, a student publication referred to teams as the Normals. The University was then known as St. Cloud Normal School. Renamed St. Cloud Teachers College in 1921, teams went by Teachers for four years. Then in 1925, the nickname was changed to Bear Cats, although no one knows the reason. All athletic teams were called Peds in 1929, originating from pedagogues (teachers). In the 1930s, St. Cloud was known as Flying Clouds. In 1939, the *Talahi* yearbook first referred to teams as Huskies, the name that still identifies them. No one knows exactly who originated Huskies. One source says students voted on the name in a contest. A 1930s football coach and his team as well as a 1930s Letterman's Club also claim credit for the name.

Mascot: A student dressed as a gray husky dog is the school's mascot. Live huskies appeared at homecoming events in the 1960s.

Interesting Facts: The first football game (and also the first athletic contest at the school) was played in October 1890 at the

Central Minnesota Fair. The St. Cloud Normal School team defeated the alumni team, 4-0.

Saint Francis

Nickname: The Red Flash
Mascot: Friar Frankie
Colors: Red and White
Conference: Northeast
Location: Loretto, Pa.
Year founded: 1847

Nickname: Saint Francis College of Pennsylvania has a unique nickname that can be traced to 1927. The school, one of the first Catholic colleges in the East, boasted that year one of the fastest football ground attacks. Because SFC wore predominantly red uniforms, the fans and the *Loretto* (SFC's student newspaper) called the team The Red Flashes. That winter the basketball team earned the same nickname. The Red Flashes evolved into the present form of The Red Flash with sports publicist Simon (Cy) Bender receiving credit for the name. Before athletic teams were known as The Red Flash, they were called Franciscans and Frannies.

A popular unofficial nickname, which is still in use, is Frankies. This name was first used during the 1938-39 basketball season.

Mascot: Friar Frankie is the costumed mascot. Donning a red habit and size 19 sneakers, the mascot was created by Otto Bruno of Creative Critters in Warminster, Pennsylvania, in 1983.

Interesting Facts: The first athletic team at Saint Francis, formed in 1867, was baseball. Football was first played in 1892, and basketball during the 1905-06 season.

St. Joseph's

Nickname: Hawks
Mascot: Hawk
Colors: Crimson and Gray
Conference: Atlantic 10
Location: Philadelphia, Pa.
Year founded: 1851

Nickname: St. Joseph's University traces its nickname back to 1929. The yearbook editor decided that year to sponsor a contest among the student body to choose a school symbol. Nearly 100 names were submitted. Hawks was selected because "it is suggestive of the aerial attack which made our football team famous," according to *The Hawk,* the school newspaper. Ironically, football was discontinued as an intercollegiate sport following the 1939 season.

Mascot: A costumed hawk debuted on January 4, 1956, in the St. Joseph's-LaSalle game. It has become one of the most unique mascots in the country. The student mascot is best known for staying in constant motion by flapping its "wings" from tip-off to final buzzer of every basketball game.

Interesting Facts: St. Joseph's motto is "The Hawk will never die!"

St. Louis

Nickname: Billikens
Mascot: Billiken
Colors: Blue and White
Conference: Midwestern
Location: St. Louis, Mo.

Year founded: 1818

Nickname: The origin of Billikens, one of the most unique of college nicknames, has been well researched over the last 40 years by writer-historian Dorothy Jean Ray.

Ray found that on October 8, 1908, Florence Pretz, a Kansas City, Missouri, art teacher and illustrator, was given a patent for an image that she designed. This "good luck image" was given a name by its distributors—a "billiken." In 1909, the Billiken was manufactured as a bank and statuette and in 1910 as a doll. The Billiken likeness took the shape of basque dolls, clay incense burners, marshmallow candies, metal banks, hatpins, watchfobs, pickle forks, belt buckles, salt and pepper shakers, and glass bottles. The Billiken, like pet rocks and other such fads, was a rage for only about six months. But not at St. Louis University.

Several stories exist as to when the nickname was first used by St. Louis. It is generally conceded that the coach of the SLU football team, John Bender, sometime between 1910 and 1911, at the height of Billikenmania, was associated with the likeness. One story revolves around the owner of a drug store, Billy Gunn. Gunn's obituary reported in 1946, "Gunn gave the Saint Louis University athletic teams their nicknames. Coach Bender walked into Mr. Gunn's drugstore one afternoon and was greeted by the proprietor with: 'Bender, you're a real Billiken!' Billy O'Connor, noted sportswriter, who was there, took up the name for Bender and eventually the university teams became known as the Billikens."

Another story revolves around a football practice that Billy O'Connor and law student Charles Z. McNamara were watching. Coach Bender's broad grin and squinty eyes so impressed O'Connor that he exclaimed: "Why Bender's a regular Billiken!" McNamara later drew a cartoon of Bender in the form of a Billiken and posted it in Gunn's drugstore. Members of the football team soon became known as Bender's Billikens.

Tracking down the origin of the billiken becomes difficult. Tradition says that Billy O'Connor was working for the St. Louis *Post Dispatch* when the name spread. The first mention of Bender's Billikens in the *Post* occurred on October 23, 1911. Billy O'Connor, though, didn't join the *Post* until November 26, 1911.

Mascot: A student costumed as a billiken is the mascot.

Interesting Facts: St. Louis has been a leader in collegiate soccer since winning the national championship in 1959, the first year the contest was held. St. Louis has won nine other soccer championships.

The men's basketball team at St. Louis won the 1948 NIT Championship.

Saint Mary's

GAELS

Nickname: Gaels
Mascot: Gael
Colors: Red and Blue
Conference: West Coast
Location: Moraga, Calif.
Year founded: 1863

Nickname: The football team at Saint Mary's College of California was known as the Saints, and the baseball team was known as the Phoenix until 1926. During that year's successful football season, Saint Mary's defeated archrival California-Berkeley, 26-7, due to a sophomore running back named Boyd "Cowboy" Smith who scored runs of 80 and 55 yards. The day after SMC's win, Pat Frayne, a sports writer for the San Francisco *Call-Bulletin*, applauded Smith's accomplishments and a roster that included many Irish names by writing, "The Lone Horseman and the Galloping Gaels trampled the Golden Bears of California in a flurry of speed and strength." The Lone Horseman designation was soon forgotten, but the Galloping Gaels stuck. Within a year, head coach Ed "Slip" Madigan applied for a copyright, and a new nickname was born.

Frayne chose an appropriate label for the school, because according to the dictionary, Gaels refers to "the Celtic peoples, especially the Irish."

Mascot: A student costumed as a Gael represents the school at sporting events.

Interesting Facts: Coach Madigan led his 1939 team to the Cotton Bowl, defeating Texas Tech, 20-13.

St. Peter's

Nickname: Peacocks
Mascot: Peacock
Colors: Teal Blue and White
Conference: Metro Atlantic
Location: Jersey City, N.J.
Year founded: 1872

Nickname: At its founding, St. Peter's College was an all-male school. With America's entry into World War I, many students and faculty joined the army or worked in defense industries which caused the college to cease day school from 1918 to 1930. In 1930, Father Gannon, dean of St. Peter's, chose the peacock as the school's symbol because in mythology, when the peacock committed itself to the flames of a funeral pyre, it was reborn with colorful beauty. This image was in keeping with the school's aim to become bigger and more attractive than it had been before the war.

Mascot: A student dresses in a cartoon-like peacock costume.

Interesting Facts: St. Peter's is most noted for its successful men's basketball teams, which have scored a series of upsets over better known and bigger foes. The school has experienced eleven 20-win seasons and 12 NIT bids, along with an NCAA Division I Tournament bid in 1990-91.

St. Peter's biggest victory came in the 1968 NIT quarterfinals when the school crushed heavily favored Duke, 100-71.

Sam Houston State

Nickname: Bearkats

Mascot: Sammy/Samantha Bearkat
Colors: Orange and White
Conference: Southland
Location: Huntsville, Tex.
Year founded: 1879

Nickname: Sam Houston State University's athletic teams have been known as the Bearkats since 1923. During that year, the school's name was changed by the Texas state legislature from Sam Houston Normal Institute to Sam Houston State Teachers College. Prior to 1923, sports teams were known as the Normals. Early references to Bearkats spelled the name either Bearcats, Bear Cats, or Bearkats.

A bearcat is a kinkajou, a carnivorous mammal native to South America which is 10 to 12 inches in length with whiskers like a cat that sits up on its hind haunches like a bear. A nocturnal animal, it can be ferocious when provoked. It is doubtful that whoever coined the Bearkat nickname had a kinkajou in mind. The name probably came from a popular local saying of the time, "tough as a Bearkat!"

In the late 1940s, school president Harmon Lowman tried to change the nickname from Bearkats to Ravens after General Sam Houston's Cherokee nickname. When the alumni were polled, Bearkats won out.

Mascot: Sam Houston State had a live kinkajou in 1952, but the animal did not fare well in captivity and was quickly dropped as a mascot. Sammy Bearkat is the costumed student mascot who has appeared at sporting events since 1959. In the mid-1980s, Sammy was joined by Samantha Bearkat.

Interesting Facts: Bowers Stadium may be the nation's finest NCAA I-AA football facility. Dedicated in 1986, it seats 14,000.

Samford

Nickname: Bulldogs
Mascot: Spike

Colors: Blue and Red
Conference: Independent
Location: Birmingham, Ala.
Year founded: 1841

Nickname: The origin of the nick-name is unknown.

Mascot: A costumed bulldog named Spike is the school's mascot.

Interesting Facts: Coach Terry Bowden is the son of Florida State coach Bobby Bowden, who played football and basketball at Samford. The older Bowden also coached football at Samford.

San Diego State

Nickname: Aztecs
Mascot: Monty Montezuma
Colors: Scarlet and Black
Conference: Western Athletic
Location: San Diego, Calif.
Year founded: 1897

Nickname: Little is known about why San Diego State University is known as the Aztecs. The Aztecs were Indians in Central Mexico who ruled a large empire before conquest by the Spaniards in 1521. San Diego State's location in southern California and proximity to Mexico and the Mexican culture may account for the nickname.

Mascot: Monty Montezuma is the student mascot dressed as an Aztec. Montezuma was the best-known Aztec chief who ruled from 1502 to 1520.

Interesting Facts: Todd Santos, who played from 1983-1987, threw for 11,425 yards in his career at San Diego State. No other quarterback in major college football has ever surpassed 11,000 yards in a career.

San Diego State was the NAIA men's basketball champion in 1941.

San Diego State won the men's volleyball championship in 1973.

Forward Milton "Milky" Phelphs led the Aztec basketball squad in scoring from 1939-41. He was the only small-college player named to the Helms All-American squad that year.

San Francisco State

Nickname: Gators
Mascot: Gator
Colors: Purple and Gold
Conference: Northern Calif. Athletic
Location: San Francisco, Calif.
Year founded: 1899

Nickname: San Francisco State University's athletic teams were originally known as the Golden Gaters. The name was dropped to Gaters in the 1960s. In the late 1970s, the name was changed to Gators.

Mascot: Al E. Gator is the school's costumed mascot.

Interesting Facts: San Francisco played unsuccessfully for the Division II football championship in 1960.

San Jose State

Nickname: Spartans
Mascot: None
Colors: Gold, White, and Blue

Conference: Big West
Location: San Jose, Calif.
Year founded: 1857

Nickname: The San Jose State University student body chose Spartans as the nick-name for its athletic teams in 1924. SJSU teams have also been known as the Golden Raiders, a name applied by San Jose *Mercury* sports writer Fred Merrick, who covered campus sports in the late 1930s.

Interesting Facts: Men's cross-country teams were national champions in 1962 and 1963. The women's golf team won the national title in 1987 and 1989. The men's outdoor track and field team was national champions in 1969. In 1948, the men's golf team won the national title.

Seton Hall

Nickname: Pirates
Mascot: Pirate
Colors: Blue and White
Conference: Big East
Location: South Orange, N. J.
Year founded: 1856

Nickname: Seton Hall University's nickname originated with the baseball team. On April 24, 1931, the Newark *Evening News* reported Seton Hall's five-run ninth inning that beat Holy Cross of Worcester, Massachusetts. The story ran, "One of the sportswriters was so excited in the turn of events that he exclaimed with disgust, 'That Seton Hall team is a gang of Pirates.'" The name stuck, and Seton Hall has been the Pirates ever since.

Mascot: A student dressed in a blue pirate uniform is the mascot.

Interesting Facts: Baseball was the first intercollegiate sport at Seton Hall. The first game played was on October 22, 1863, when the Pirates beat Fordham, 20-16. Seton Hall has played in College World Series in 1964, 1971, 1974, and 1975. The baseball program has sent 21 players to the major leagues.

The University has produced two Olympic champions. Andrew Valmon, Class of 1987, won a gold medal as a member of the 4 X 400-meter relay team in the 1988 Olympic Games in Seoul, Korea. Andy Stanfield won the 200 meters in the 1952 games in Helsinki, Finland.

Seton Hall won the NIT Championship in men's basketball in 1953.

The Seton Hall basketball team holds an annual Midnight Madness event called "Hall Hoop Hysteria" each fall. A full house packs Walsh Gym to watch the team go through drills and then compete in an intrasquad scrimmage.

Seton Hall has had two players to be inducted into the Naismith Memorial Basketball Hall of Fame. Bob Davies, a two-time All-American in the 1940s, led the Pirates to a three-year 55-5 record as a member of the vaunted "Wonder Five." Known as the "Harrisburg Houdini," and the "Blonde Bomber," Davies played 10 years in the NBA, all with the Rochester Royals. Credited with inventing the behind-the-back dribble, he became the first pro player to dish off 20 assists in a single game.

Bobby Wanzer, inducted into the Hall of Fame in 1987, was a standout on the 1946-47 squad. He played with the Rochester Royals 10 years and averaged 11.7 points per game. Wanzer was one of the greatest free throw shooters in NBA history.

Shippensburg

Nickname: Red Raiders
Mascot: Red Raider
Colors: Red and Blue
Conference: Pa. State Athletic

Location: Shippensburg, Pa.
Year founded: 1871

Nickname: Red Raiders was chosen for Shippensburg University's nickname because of the Indian heritage that existed in the Cumberland Valley of Pennsylvania.

Mascot: A student dressed in Indian clothes is the school mascot.

Interesting Facts: The only national championship won by Shippensburg was in 1979 when the field hockey team was the Division III winner.

    In 1981, the football team went 12-1. It was the last team to win the Lambert Cup, a trophy representing the best Division I-AA or Division II team in the East. Today, Division II winners receive the Lambert Plaque.

Siena

Nickname: Saints
Mascot: None
Colors: Green and Gold
Conference: Metro Atlantic
Location: Londonville, N.Y.
Year founded: 1937

Nickname: In 1988, Siena College decided to drop its nickname of forty years when it was decided that Indians was offensive to Native Americans. Jim Dalton, faculty member and chair of Siena's minority task force project, stated in referring to the name that "it's oversimplifying Indian culture...the name is culturally demeaning." During the 1988 season, Siena went without a nickname, and sportscasters referred to the school as Siena No-Names. Saints was chosen in 1989 after many suggested monikers—Warriors, Capitals, Green Tide, Eagles, Green, Gold, and Friars—were considered.

Mascot: During the 1988 season, a "temporary" leprechaun mascot cheered fans at sporting events. He had replaced the school's Indian mascot who had danced to drum rhythms for years at athletic games.

Interesting Facts: After dropping the Indian nickname, the Tee Pee Rowdies basketball cheering section simply became known as the Rowdies.

Slippery Rock

Nickname: Rockets
Mascot: Rocky
Colors: Green and White
Conference: Western Division PC
Location: Slippery Rock, Pa.
Year founded: 1889

Nickname: The origin of the official nickname Rockets is unknown. The unofficial nickname Rock was added during the early 1970s. The nickname could have been used for its alliterative value—Slippery Rock Rockets.

Mascot: Rocky is the costumed student mascot.

South Alabama

Nickname: Jaguars
Mascot: Southpaw; Miss Pawla
Colors: Red, Blue, and White
Conference: Sun Belt
Location: Mobile

Year founded: 1963

Nickname: Jaguars was selected by a vote of the student body in the mid-1960s.

Mascot: The costumed mascot, Southpaw, originated 20 to 25 years ago when the school first began competing in intercollegiate athletics. The costumed mascot, Miss Pawla, made her appearance during the 1991-92 basketball season.

South Carolina

Nickname: Fighting Gamecocks
Mascot: Cocky
Colors: Garnet and Black
Conference: Southeastern
Location: Columbia
Year founded: 1831

Nickname: The University of South Carolina is the only major college athletic program that uses the nickname Fighting Gamecocks. At the turn of the century, after struggling for more than a decade under numerous nicknames, the school's football team was first referred to unofficially as Game Cocks. In 1903, *The State,* Columbia's morning newspaper, shortened the name to one word.

Gamecock was an appropriate name since the state of South Carolina has long been connected with the breeding and training of fighting gamecocks. General Thomas Sumter, famed Revolutionary War guerilla fighter, was known as the Fighting Gamecock.

A gamecock is a fighting rooster known for its spirit and courage. A cock fight, which was a popular sport throughout the United States in the 19th century, would last until the death of one of the roosters. Although cock fighting is now outlawed in most states, it is still held surreptitiously in many areas.

Mascot: Dressed in a deep red (garnet) costume, Cocky the Gamecock helps cheer South Carolina teams to victory. A favorite of fans, he has been named one of the most popular mascots in the nation.

Interesting Facts: South Carolina's only Heisman Trophy winner was George Rogers, who won the honor in 1980. First team All-American in 1979 and 1980, Rogers was the NCAA Back of the Year. He was the outstanding offensive player in the Gator Bowl in 1980. Rogers finished his career at South Carolina as the holder of numerous records including a career rushing of 5,204 yards.

Rogers is one of three Gamecocks to have their jersey numbers retired. The other two were Steve Wadiak and Mike Johnson. Wadiak, running back from 1948-51, held the school record for all-time rushing leader for 28 years after his senior season. Center Mike Johnson's number was retired after he died in an automobile accident before his junior year in 1965.

South Carolina played for the College World Series baseball title in 1975, losing to the University of Texas, 5-1.

South Carolina State

Nickname: Bulldogs
Mascot: Bulldog
Colors: Garnet and Blue
Conference: Mid-Eastern Athletic
Location: Orangebur
Year founded: 1896

Nickname: South Carolina State University's faculty and students chose the Bulldog nickname in 1919. It was selected because the bulldog is known equally for its power, tenacity, and equable disposition.

Mascot: Although South Carolina State doesn't have a live mascot now, it had bulldogs named Ess Cee in the past. Also, the school doesn't currently have a costumed mascot; the last one was Reggie the Bulldog.

Interesting Facts: The football team has won the National Black championship twice—in 1976 and 1981.

The school's fiercest rival is with Florida A&M University. In 1966, the Bulldogs ended a 22-year losing streak by defeating the Rattlers, 8-3, on a 96-yard kickoff return for a touchdown.

South Dakota

Nickname: Coyotes
Mascot: Coyote
Colors: Red and White
Conference: North Central
Location: Vermillion
Year founded: 1862

Nickname: Little is known about the origin of the University of South Dakota's nickname. The name is appropriate, however, since the state animal is the coyote.

Mascot: A student dressed in a coyote uniform serves as the mascot.

Interesting Facts: The school won the NCAA Division II men's basketball championship in 1958.

Coyotes is pronounced KI-YOTES, not KI-YOH-TEES.

South Dakota State

Nickname: Jackrabbits
Mascot: Bulldog
Colors: Yellow and Blue

Conference: North Central
Location: Brookings
Year founded: 1881

Nickname: According to South Dakota State University's sports information director, the origin of the nickname Jackrabbits is unknown. Jackrabbits are, however, a common animal in the state. The nickname is often shortened to Jacks when referring to athletic teams.

Mascot: A costumed bulldog named Spike entertains the crowds at athletic events.

Interesting Facts: South Dakota State has won more overall North Central Conference championships than any other member, with at least one championship in every sanctioned sport.

On the national level, the Jackrabbits won the NCAA Division II basketball championship in 1963 and was runnerup in 1985. They have also won national championships in men's and women's cross country.

In an interesting tie-in with the Jackrabbits nickname, former athletic director Reuben Frost was affectionately called Jack. He served as AD from 1947 to 1960 and was internationally known. The home of the Jackrabbits' basketball team is Frost Arena.

South Florida

Nickname: Bulls
Mascot: Rocky the Bull
Colors: Green and Gold
Conference: Metro
Location: Tampa
Year founded: 1956

Nickname: The University of South Florida's student body chose the nickname Golden Brahmans to honor the state's cattle industry. In the mid-1980s, newspapers shortened the name to Bulls for better headline space. The University then officially adopted the nickname Bulls.

Mascot: Rocky the Bull is the costumed student mascot. Rocky was named for the popular character in the *Rocky* movies.

Interesting Facts: South Florida plays its basketball games in the Sun Dome. The facility's unique feature is its air-supported roof which is made of 21 tons of woven Teflon-coated fiberglass.

Southeast Missouri State

Nickname: Indians; Otahkians
Mascot: None
Colors: Red and Black
Conference: Ohio Valley
Location: Cape Girardeau
Year founded: 1893

Nickname: Men's athletic teams at Southeast Missouri State University had long been called the Indians when women's sports were organized in the spring of 1973. Because officials wanted a different nickname for the female squads, a contest was held. Cape Girardeau resident Don Jewell recommended the winning name of Otahkians. The name comes from Princess Otahki, a Cherokee Indian princess who died on the legendary Trail of Tears march from the Allegheny Mountains to Oklahoma during the winter of 1838-39. Hundreds of Cherokees died on the trek, several in the area now called the Trail of Tears State Park near Cape Girardeau. A permanent shrine at the park serves as a memorial to the princess and others who died.

Interesting Facts: The men's basketball team won the NAIA championship in 1943. In 1986, the school played for the NCAA Division II basketball championship game against Sacred Heart

(Conn.), but lost, 93-87.

Southeastern Lousiana

Nickname: Lions
Mascot: Roomie
Colors: Green and Gold
Conference: Trans America Athletic
Location: Hammond
Year founded: 1925

Nickname: A student vote was held in the 1940s to choose Southeastern Louisiana University's nickname. Lions was the winner.

Mascot: A student vote also selected Roomie the Lion as the mascot. Roomie was named after former faculty member Hollis "Roomie" Wilson. A live lion was used at one time. Currently, Roomie is a student costumed as a lion.

Interesting Facts: Southeastern Louisiana's large University Center is home to men's and women's basketball as well as conferences, trade shows, and concerts.

Southern California

Nickname: Trojans
Mascot: Traveler IV; Tommy Trojan
Colors: Cardinal and Gold
Conference: Pacific 10
Location: Los Angeles
Year founded: 1888

Nickname: Prior to 1912, University of Southern California athletic teams were known as the Methodists or Wesleyans. Because school officials weren't pleased with the names, Warren Bovard, director of athletics and son of USC president George Bovard, asked Los Angeles *Times* sports editor Owen Bird to choose an appropriate nickname. Bird recalled later:

"At this time, the athletes and coaches of the university were under terrific handicaps. They were facing teams that were bigger and better-equipped, yet they had splendid fighting spirit. The name 'Trojans' fitted them. I came up with an article prior to a showdown between USC and Stanford in which I called attention to the fighting spirit of USC athletes and named them 'Trojans.' From then on, we used the term 'Trojan' all the time, and it stuck."

Mascot: Traveler, the white horse that appears at all USC home football games with a regal Trojan warrior astride, is the mascot. At football games, whenever USC scores, the band plays "Conquest" and Traveler gallops around the Coliseum track.

Traveler IV is the current mascot. Traveler I, who began the tradition in 1961, was the brother of a famous television horse, Silver, ridden by the Lone Ranger.

Richard Saukko was Traveler's longtime rider who performed at athletic events from 1961-1988.

Tommy Trojan is a statue of a bronzed Trojan warrior that has been a symbol at USC since it was unveiled in 1930.

Interesting Facts: Trojan teams have won more national championships than any other university in the nation.

USC won the national championship in football in 1928, 1931, 1932, 1962, 1967, 1972, 1974, and 1978.

Four Heisman Trophy winners played at USC—Mike Garrett (1965), O.J. Simpson (1968), Charles White (1979), and Marcus Allen (1981). Brad Budde won the Lombardi Award in 1979.

USC won the baseball College World Series in 1948, 1958, 1961, 1963, 1968, 1970-1974, and 1978,

It won the men's national basketball championship in 1940.

USC has also won national titles in men's gymnastics, men's indoor track, men's outdoor track and field, men's swimming and diving, and men's and women's volleyball.

Southern Illinois

Nickname: Salukis
Mascot: Saluki
Colors: Maroon and White
Conference: Missouri Valley
Location: Carbondale
Year founded: 1869

Nickname: Southern Illinois University's athletic teams were known as the Maroons until 1951. The nondescript name had been in use since the first year the school formally sponsored teams in 1913-14. Because they wanted a more imaginative name, the student body overwhelmingly voted in favor of adopting Salukis on March 19, 1951. Salukis beat out Rebels, Knights, Flyers, Marauders, and Maroons.

The unique nickname may never be understood completely, but for native southern Illinoisans who know that the area is frequently referred to as "Egypt," Salukis has a logical connection. Author Baker Bownell in his *The Other Illinois* gives an explanation:

"...Although the legend probably was invented after the fact, it is persistent. There was a drought in the northern counties of Illinois in the early 1800s...the wheat fields dried up, the streams died in their beds. But in southern Illinois rain fell and there were good crops, and from the north came people seeking corn and wheat as to Egypt of old. Thus the name, Egypt."

The "Egypt of old" refers to the biblical story found in Genesis when Jacob during a famine sent his sons to Egypt to get corn. In Egypt at that time, Salukis were accepted as the finest animals a family could possess. Known for their speed and hunting skills, Salukis are the oldest pure-breed dog in the world. Records date them back to 3600 B.C.

Mascot: SIUC has a live Saluki and also a student costumed as a Saluki who performs at sporting events.

Interesting Facts: Gayle Sayers, the former NFL running back, was athletic director at SIUC from 1976 to 1981. He left the school to become a Chicago businessman.

SIUC won the NCAA Division I-AA men's basketball national championship in 1983 defeating Western Carolina, 43-7. SIUC won the NIT Championship in 1967.

The University has won national championships in men's gymnastics four times: 1964, 1966, 1967, and 1972.

Southern Methodist

Nickname: Mustangs
Mascot: Peruna
Colors: Red, Blue, and White
Conference: Southwest
Location: Dallas, Tex.
Year founded: 1914

Nickname: Southern Methodist University students voted on October 25, 1917, to make Mustangs the school nickname. The moniker was a fitting one since mustangs, wild horses, were found in early Texas.

Mascot: A live horse made its first appearance at a SMU game on November 4, 1932. T.E. Jones, the owner of Arlington Downs, donated the four-year-old show horse along with a red blanket. A pep club called the Saddle Burrs, formed shortly after Peruna I came to SMU, took care of the horse and kept the stable site a secret to keep away pranksters. Unfortunately, only two years after coming to the University, Peruna ran out onto Mockingbird Lane and was hit by a car and killed. The horse was buried at Ownby Stadium where a small statue of a mustang marks his grave. Peruna II, as well as all subsequent Perunas, was given to SMU by Cully Culwell, a former SMU student and owner of Culwell & Son men's store near campus.

The name Peruna has an interesting origin. The peppy fight song that inspires Mustang fans at sporting events was established at what probably was SMU's first pep rally. In 1915, when SMU student George Sexton asked Vivian Weeks to play "Comin' Around the Mountain," he substituted the words, "She'll be loaded with Peruna when she comes..." Peruna, in those days, was the name of the most famous elixir in Texas. It had a reputation as a cure-all. Years later the words of the song were changed, but Peruna remained as the name of the mascot.

A student in a mustang costume was added in 1984.

Interesting Facts: SMU won the national championship in football in 1935. The only Southwest Conference team to ever play in the Rose Bowl, SMU lost to Stanford, 7-0, in 1936.

SMU's only Heisman Trophy winner was Doak Walker, who was All-American three times (1947-1949). The Doak Walker Award honors him.

Quarterback Don Meredith, who went on to play for the Dallas Cowboys, still holds the Southwest Conference season completion percentage record of .695 set in 1957 and the SMU career record (minimum of 300 pass attempts) with .610.

SMU football player Eric Dickerson was All-American in 1982.

SMU won the men's indoor track championship in 1983 and the men's outdoor track championship in 1983 and 1986.

Southwest Missouri State

Nickname: Bears
Mascot: Boomer Bear
Colors: Maroon and White
Conference: Gateway Collegiate Athletic
Location: Springfield
Year founded: 1905

Nickname: Very early in Southwest Missouri State University's history, sports writers for the school newspaper gave the athletic teams the nickname Bears. The tradition is that the name was chosen because a bear is on Missouri's state seal and state flag.

Mascot: The costumed student is known as Boomer Bear.

Interesting Facts: SW Missouri State won the NAIA men's basketball championship in 1952 and 1953.

Southwest Texas State

Nickname: Bobcats
Mascot: The Bobcat
Colors: Maroon and Gold
Conference: Southland
Location: San Marcos
Year founded: 1899

Nickname: Bobcats is an appropriate nickname for Southwest Texas State University since the bobcat is an animal native to the Texas Hill Country where the campus is located. Spurgeon Smith, a biology professor, is thought to have first called athletic teams Bobcats in 1919. He noted then that the bobcat is "often aroused to a fighting fury in defense of its home territory."

Mascot: The student mascot dresses as The Bobcat.

Interesting Facts: Southwest Texas State won the Division II national football championship in 1981 and 1982 under Coach Jim Wacker. The school won the NAIA basketball championship in 1960. The golf team won the national championship in 1983, and the tennis team won the title in 1981-82.

Southwestern Louisiana

Nickname: Ragin' Cajuns
Mascot: Bulldog

Colors: Vermilion and White
Conference: Sun Belt
Location: Lafayette
Year founded: 1898

Nickname: The University of Southwestern Louisiana has one of the most unique nicknames in college sports—Ragin' Cajuns. Formerly called the Bulldogs, USL football teams were first called Ragin' Cajuns in 1961, shortly after Russ Faulkinberry was named head football coach. The name originated because more than 90 percent of Faulkinberry's teams were composed of Louisiana high school players, many with French-speaking Arcadian backgrounds. The nickname became popular, and soon all USL athletic teams were called the Ragin' Cajuns.

Mascot: A bulldog became the USL mascot in the late 1980s. Because fans wanted a live mascot and because of varied opinions of what a Ragin' Cajun would look like, a bulldog was selected. It was an appropriate selection because athletic teams went by Bulldogs prior to 1961.

The "Fabulous Cajun Chicken" is not an official mascot but does perform at home athletic events. He is paid by the USL athletic department for his performances.

Interesting Facts: Cajun Field is affectionately called "The Swamp." The largest football crowd—36,133—to watch USL play there was October 6, 1990, when USL played host to Alabama. This record broke the previous mark by almost 6,000 fans.

Before Christian Keener "Red" Cagle went on to West Point All-American fame, he played at USL from 1922-1925. Cagle's career scoring record at USL was not broken until 1989.

The most spectacular building on the USL campus is the Cajundome that serves as home to the Ragin' Cajun basketball team. The $60 million multi-purpose facility is one of the most impressive arenas in the country.

USL's basketball history dates back to 1911. Among its most famous players is Dwight "Bo" Lamar. The three-time All-American became the only player in NCAA history to lead the nation in scoring at the small college level (1,044 points in 1970-

71) and at the university level (1,054 in 1971-72).

Andrew Toney was USL's standout in the 1980s. Toney, who received his degree in three and one-half years, finished his fourth year at USL while attending graduate school. He was a first-round draft choice by the Philadelphia 76ers.

Stanford

Nickname: Cardinal
Mascot: None
Colors: Cardinal
Conference: Pacific 10
Location: Stanford, Calif.
Year founded: 1891

Nickname: Stanford University's student body voted in 1891 to make gold the school's official color. However, another student assembly chose Cardinal as the school color. A few days after the vote, local sportswriters began using Cardinal in their stories. When Stanford defeated Cal on March 19, 1891, the headline ran "Cardinal Triumphs O'er Blue and Gold."

Sometime between 1891 and 1930, Indian began to be used widely by sportswriters. The change may have come about because of the large Indian population of the area. Stanford University officially adopted Indian as the nickname on November 25, 1930. The Indian symbol was dropped in 1972 following meetings between Stanford Native American students and school president Richard Lyman. The 55 students, supported by the other 358 American Indians enrolled in California colleges, felt the mascot was an insult to their culture and heritage. The Stanford Student Senate voted, 18-4, to drop the Indian symbol, and Lyman agreed.

On November 17, 1981, Donald Kennedy, president of Stanford, declared that all teams "will be represented and symbolized exclusively by the color cardinal. Thus, the old designation once again became the nickname.

Mascot: No official Stanford mascot exists. A redwood tree does appear, though, on the school logo. It is representative of El Palo Alto, the Redwood tree which is the logo of the city of Palo Alto. Since Stanford and Palo Alto are almost inextricably intertwined in interests and location, the tree is a natural outgrowth. The tree actually exists—it stands by the railroad bridge beside San Francisquito Creek. This site was where early explorers first camped when settling the area.

Interesting Facts: Stanford's only Heisman Trophy winner was quarterback Jim Plunkett in 1970.

Stanford played in the first Rose Bowl in 1902, losing to Michigan, 49-0.

Stanford won the men's national basketball championship in 1937 and in 1942. In 1991, the University won the NIT championship.

It won the College Baseball World Series in 1987 and 1988.

In 1967 and in 1985-1987, Stanford won the men's swimming and diving championships. The school also won the women's diving championship in 1983 and 1989.

Stanford players were men's outdoor track and field champions in 1925, 1928, and 1934. Also, the school held six water polo championships in the 1970s and 1980s.

Stephen F. Austin

Nickname: Lumberjacks
Mascot: Lumberjack
Colors: Purple and White
Conference: Southland
Location: Nacogdoches, Tex.
Year founded: 1923

Nickname: Stephen F. Austin University athletic teams are called the Lumberjacks because the campus is located in the Piney Woods of East Texas which is home to many lumberjacks.

Mascot: A student dressed as a lumberjack and carrying an ax is the mascot.

Interesting Facts: Bum Phillips, former Houston Oilers and New Orleans Saints coach, is a 1950 graduate of Stephen F. Austin. Mark Moseley, former Washington Redskins kicker, is a 1969 graduate of SFA.

The "wildest" game played at the William R. Johnson Coliseum, home of Lumberjack basketball, was January 10, 1980, at the SFA-Louisiana College game when the contest was stopped with 2:15 remaining after seven technical fouls were called on the Louisiana College bench.

Stetson

Nickname: Hatters
Mascot: Hatter
Colors: Green and White
Conference: Trans America
Location: Deland, Fla.
Year founded: 1883

Nickname: Stetson University, Florida's oldest private university, has an unusual but appropriate nickname. Hatters honors John B. Stetson, the famous maker of the Stetson hat and the namesake of the University. In 1886, three years after Henry Deland founded the school, a disastrous freeze left it in financial trouble. Stetson, a Philadelphia hat maker who had a winter home in Deland, became interested in the school. In 1889, Stetson became chairman of trustees, and the school was renamed in his honor. Hatters soon became the nickname.

Mascot: A student dressed in a huge stetson hat is the popular mascot at sporting events. A picture of a hat is the official school symbol.

Interesting Facts: In 1901, Stetson University was the first school in Florida to field a football team.

Sul Ross State

Nickname: Lobos
Mascot: None
Colors: Scarlet and Grey
Conference: Texas Intercollegiate Athletic
Location: Alpine, Tex.
Year founded: 1917

Nickname: Sul Ross State University's nickname is Lobos, another word for gray wolves. The student body chose Lobos over Rangers for the football team's name in an election on October 11, 1923.

Interesting Facts: Sul Ross is the birthplace of the National Intercollegiate Rodeo Association. Men's and women's rodeo teams have won a number of national titles. The school's annual fall rodeo features top collegiate cowboys and cowgirls in the NIRA's Southwest Region.

Syracuse

Nickname: Orangemen
Mascot: None
Colors: Orange
Conference: Big East
Location: Syracuse, N.Y.
Year founded: 1870

Nickname: The nickname Orangemen reflects Syracuse University's color, which is orange.

Mascot: An Indian was used for many years as a mascot, but because of protests, it was discontinued. The school has no official mascot.

Interesting Facts: Syracuse won the national football championship in 1959 with a 11-0-0 record. The University's only Heisman Trophy winner was halfback Ernie Davis in 1961.

Syracuse's Carrier Dome is the largest arena in Division I college basketball. It seats 32,683.

The school won the men's national basketball championship in 1918 and in 1926.

Syracuse won the men's cross-country championship in 1951.

The school won four men's lacrosse championships—in 1983 and 1988-1990. Rowing championships were won in 1904, 1908, 1913, 1916, and 1920.

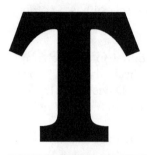

Tarleton State

Nickname: Texans
Mascot: None
Colors: Purple and White
Conference: Independent
Location: Stephenville, Tex.
Year founded: 1899

Nickname: Tarleton State University's athletic teams were once known as the Plowboys. When the school became a senior college in 1961, the student body voted to change to Texans. Women's teams are called TexAnns.

Interesting Facts: While a junior college, the Plowboys won 86 straight basketball games between 1934 and 1937.

Temple

Nickname: Owls
Mascot: Owl
Colors: Cherry and White
Conference: Atlantic 10
Location: Philadelphia, Pa.

Year founded: 1884

Nickname: Temple University was the first school in the nation to adopt the owl as its symbol. A popular story about the nickname's origin is attributed to Temple's founder, Russell Conwell. A Baptist minister, Conwell founded Temple as a night school for ambitious young people of limited means. He encouraged these students with the remark: "The owl of the night makes the eagle of the day."

The owl, a universal symbol for wisdom and knowledge, is an appropriate nickname for athletic teams. Besides being perceptive, resourceful, quick, and courageous, it is a fierce fighter.

Mascot: A student costumed as an owl entertains at sporting events.

Interesting Facts: Temple's colors—cherry and white—are unique as college colors. Only one other school, Rensselaer Polytechnic Institute in Troy, New York, claims cherry and white as its school colors.

One of Temple's traditions is Cherry and White Day when past and present students compete in a series of athletic contests.

Temple's football team played in the first Sugar Bowl in 1935, losing to Tulane, 20-14.

The men's basketball team was NIT Tournament champions in 1938, defeating Colorado, 60-36. The University also won the NIT Tournament in 1969, defeating Boston College, 89-76.

All-American basketball player Bill Mlkvy, known as "The Owl without a vowel," is remembered most for scoring 73 points, including 54 consecutive ones against Wilkes in 1951. The night he scored 43 points during Temple's stunning 70-67 upset of North Carolina was probably his greatest individual effort. Mlkvy led the nation in scoring and rebounding in 1951.

The men's gymnastics team won the national championship in 1949.

The women's lacrosse team was national champion in 1984.

Temple's Center for Sports Medicine was the first such facility to be directly connected with a university. It brings together experts from many health disciplines to help treat and rehabilitate injured athletes.

Tennessee

Nickname: Volunteers or Vols
Mascot: Smokey VII
Colors: Orange and White
Conference: Southeastern
Location: Knoxville
Year founded: 1794

Nickname: The University of Tennessee's nickname is derived from the name most associated with the state. Tennessee acquired its nickname, "The Volunteer State" in the early 1800s when General Andrew Jackson mustered large armies from his home state to fight the Indians and later the British at the Battle of New Orleans. The name became even more significant in the Mexican War when Tennessee governor Aaron V. Brown issued a call for 2800 men to battle Santa Ana; some 30,000 men volunteered, including the famous Davy Crockett. The dragoon uniform worn by Tennessee regulars during the Fight for Texas Independence is still adorning the color guard at UT athletic events.

Mascot: The UT Pep Club held a contest in 1953 to select a mascot. A blue tick coon hound, a native breed of the state, was chosen. Rev. W.C. Brooks of Knoxville provided the school with the first six canine mascots. The current Smokey VII succeeds Smokey VI, who passed away during the 1991 season.

Interesting Facts: Charles Moore, a member of the first football team in 1891, selected the school colors of orange and white. Approved by a school vote, the colors were those of the common American daisy which was native to the area. Tennessee players did not appear in their orange jerseys until the season opening game in 1922. Legend says that the uniforms may have been instrumental in helping the team defeat Emory and Henry by a score of 50-0.

The Tennessee football team won the national championship

in football in 1951 under coach R.R. Neyland.

Tennessee player Steve DeLong won the Outland Trophy for the nation's outstanding interior lineman in 1964.

The men's cross-country team was national champion in 1972. The University won the men's swimming and diving championship in 1974 and 1991.

The Beer Barrel is the annual trophy given to the winner of the Tennessee-Kentucky football game. Although the series between the two schools started in 1893, the trophy was not conceived until 1925 by a Wildcat booster group. Painted with the words "Ice Water" to satisfy the local temperance union, the Wildcats retained the keg with a 23-20 win.

Tennessee-Martin

Nickname: Pacers
Mascot: Pacer Pete; Pacer Polly
Colors: Royal Blue, Orange, and White
Conference: Ohio Valley
Location: Martin
Year founded: 1900

Nickname: University of Tennessee-Martin athletic teams were known as Volunteers until 1971. That year Pacers was selected as the official school nickname because it symbolized UT-Martin as a pacesetter university. The symbol of the pacer horse, a proud and spirited breed, represents the strength and pride associated with the school.

Mascot: The school has two costumed student mascots. Pacer Pete, representing men's athletics, and Pacer Polly, representing women's sports, are modeled after the San Diego Chicken.

Interesting Facts: UT-Martin added royal blue as one of its colors in 1970. Previously, orange and white had represented the school—the same colors used by the Knoxville campus.

Tennessee Tech

Nickname: Golden Eagles
Mascot: Golden Eagle
Colors: Purple and Gold
Conference: Ohio Valley
Location: Cookeville
Year founded: 1915

Nickname: In the early part of this century, Tennessee Polytechnic Institute was a tiny school located in the rugged, mountainous Upper Cumberland region. Golden Eagles were plentiful. It's easy to understand how the early students and faculty could narrow their choices for a school nickname to Golden Eagles or Mountaineers.

On February 14, 1925, Golden Eagles was officially adopted. The school newspaper, *The Oracle,* printed a story which outlined the efforts of a committee to suggest several possible nicknames to Athletic Association members for their consideration. The two most popular names were Golden Eagles and Mountaineers. The Association, by a vote of 139-18, proudly declared its preference.

Mascot: A student costumed as a golden eagle is chosen during cheerleading tryouts each year to represent the school as its mascot.

In 1952, several Tech students braved a night rainstorm to steal a huge block-tin eagle statue from the charred ruins of a resort hotel in Monteagle. They painted the eagle—which had a wingspan of over six feet—a glistening gold and suspended it from the rafter for public inspection at the following day's basketball game in Memorial Gym. Governor Frank G. Clement, a life-long friend of the hotel owner, was in Cookeville to speak. He worked out an agreement between his friend and the students who wanted to retain the eagle for their mascot.

Interesting Facts: Tennessee Tech's three most famous football players had their jerseys retired and are in the Tech Hall of Fame. All-American Larry Schreiber, 1969 stand-out, had three 1,000-yard seasons. Jim Youngblood, two-time All-American, holds the record for Tech tackles. Elois Grooms was an All-American in 1974.

Tech was the men and women's national rifle champions three times (1980-1982).

The Robert Hill Johnson Award has been given each year since 1951 to the football player who, according to team members, makes the largest contribution to the squad. The award is named after Robert Hill Johnson, a native of Sparta, Tennessee, who was a student and assistant football coach when he was killed in an auto accident on January 14, 1952.

Texas

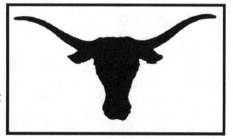

Nickname: Longhorns
Mascot: Bevo
Colors: Burnt Orange and White
Conference: Southwest
Location: Austin
Year founded: 1883

Nickname: In 1943, D.A. Frank explained in a letter to "The Firing Line" column in *The Daily Texan,* the school newspaper, the origin of the University of Texas' nickname. One day in 1903, Alex Weisburg, who was editor-in-chief of *The Texan,* told Frank, "D.A., hereafter, in every sports article, call the team 'The Longhorns,' and we'll soon have it named." According to Frank, the name became official around 1906 or 1907.

Longhorns was a fitting choice for a nickname because Longhorn cattle roamed the Texas plains in the 1800s. Longhorns were big-boned, rangy animals with horns that often measured five to eight feet from tip to tip. Because the bulls were so tough and courageous that they seldom hesitated to battle wolf packs or even grizzly bears, the name Longhorns seems appropriate for competitive athletic teams.

Mascot: The University's present mascot is a steer named Bevo XIII. UT's first Bevo was brought to campus by Steve Pinckney, who served as a football manager in 1911. Engaged in fighting Mexican rustlers along the Rio Grande after graduation, Pinckney found an orange-and-white colored steer, which was paid for by ex-students' subscriptions. Bevo I made his debut in 1916 during the school's 21-7 victory over A&M in Austin. Bevo I had a short career, for some Aggies branded him with "13-0," signifying the score of the previous year's upset win. Bevo I made his next public appearance in the form of steak at a UT-A&M dinner to honor the Horns' 1920 team, which had upset A&M, 7-3, to win the SWC title. The Aggies got the portion that bore the shameful brand, and Texas retained the other half. Legend says that "BEVO" derived from that 13-0 Aggie branding. The story says that Texas fans turned the 13 into a "B," made the hyphen an "E," inserted the "V," and the "O" was already there.

A student costumed as a longhorn serves as a mascot at basketball games only.

Interesting Facts: Former football coach Darrell Royal led the Longhorns to national championships in 1963, 1969, and 1970. Royal won national Coach of the Year honors in 1963 and 1970.

Running back Earl Campbell won the 1977 Heisman Trophy.

The world's biggest bass drum, Big Bertha, is a feature attraction when the Longhorn Band performs at football games. Big Bertha is eight feet in diameter, 54 inches in width, and weighs 500 pounds. Four bandsmen called Drum Wranglers look after it.

The roar of Smokey the Cannon is heard when the cannon fires two blank 10-gauge shotgun shells after each Texas football score.

The Longhorn baseball program won the College World Series in 1949, 1950, 1975, and 1983.

Texas won the women's national indoor track title in 1988 and 1990.

The women's swimming and diving team has claimed seven national titles since 1984; the men's team has won five titles since 1981.

Texas-Arlington

Nickname: Mavericks
Mascot: Sam Maverick
Colors: Royal Blue ad White
Conference: Southland
Location: Arlington
Year founded: 1895

Nickname: Mavericks is the University of Texas-Arlington's fifth nickname. Hornets (1921-1923), Junior Aggies (1923-1949), Blue Riders (1949-1951), and Rebels (1951-1971) were previous monikers.

Mavericks became the official UTA mascot in 1971. The name comes from one of the largest landholders in Texas in the 1800s, Samuel Augustus Maverick. Mayor of San Antonio in 1839 and signer of the Texas Declaration of Independence, Maverick owned 340,000 acres of land which he purchased at five cents an acre. The Washington *Daily Globe* in 1854 called Maverick "the largest landholder in the world and by far the wealthiest citizen in Texas."

Mascot: Sam Maverick, the student mascot who is costumed as a cowboy, is a popular fixture at UTA athletic events.

Interesting Facts: Willie Brand became the all-time leading basketball scorer at UTA in his junior year. He finished his career with 1,907 points, and his jersey #22 was retired at his final game in 1991.

Texas at El Paso

Nickname: Miners
Mascot: Paydirt Pete

Colors: Orange, White, and Blue
Conference: Western Athletic
Location: El Paso
Year founded: 1914

Nickname: The University of Texas at El Paso, better known as UTEP, took its nickname from the original name of the school, the Texas School of Mines.

Mascot: The mascot is Paydirt Pete, a student costumed as a rugged looking miner, complete with a pick ax.

Before the current mascot, a Walt Disney-type character served as mascot, but fans soon decided that they needed a more macho-looking representative for a school known as Miners.

Interesting Facts: UTEP won the men's cross-country national championship in 1969, 1975, 1976, and 1978-1981.

UTEP won the men's indoor track championships in 1974-1976, 1978, and 1980-1982. The University claimed the men's outdoor track and field titles in 1975 and 1978-1982.

Texas-Pan American

Nickname: Broncs
Mascot: Bucky the Bronc
Colors: Green, White, and Orange
Conference: Sun Belt
Location: Edinburg
Year founded: 1927

Nickname: A coach in the 1920s who came from Southern

Methodist was responsible for the nickname at the University of Texas-Pan American. The coach, who liked SMU's nickname—Mustangs—chose Broncs for Pan American.

Mascot: A student dresses as Bucky the Bronc.

Interesting Facts: Texas-Pan American has an old tradition that when other teams misname them—call them Broncos instead of Broncs—they win. At least, it worked for the Bronc basketball players in December 1981. They upset the Indiana Hoosiers, 66-60. It was a sweet victory because the Hoosiers, led by Isiah Thomas, went on to the win the NCAA basketball championship that season.

Texas-San Antonio

Nickname: Roadrunners
Mascot: Rowdy
Colors: Orange, Navy, Blue, and White
Conference: Southland
Location: San Antonio
Year founded: 1969

Nickname: A student election in 1977 chose Roadrunners as the nickname of the University of Texas-San Antonio. Roadrunners, birds representative of the Texas Hill Country and the Southwest, defeated Armadillos, another animal native to Texas. Roadrunners was officially adopted in 1978.

Mascot: Rowdy the Roadrunner is the costumed student.

Texas A&I

Nickname: Javelinas

Mascot: Porky
Colors: Blue and Gold
Conference: Lone Star
Location: Kingsville
Year founded: 1925

Nickname: Since its doors were opened for classes in 1925, Texas A&I University has been known as the Javelinas. According to an article in an early edition of the *South Texan*, the campus newspaper, students voted to accept the javelina "after hearing some almost unbelievable but highly interesting tales of the fighting spirit of the javelina." The article went on to describe the javelina:

"Wherever the javelina is known, his reputation as an intrepid and relentless fighter also is known. The word javelina (pronounced hah-vay-lee-nah, with the accent on the third syllable) is the Spanish name for the peccary, a species of wild hog indigenous of the New World and ranging from Texas to Pantagonia.

"They are small animals, seldom attaining 40 inches in length and more than 20 inches in height. Biologically, they are related to swine, though their teeth are different and their stomachs are in some respects characteristic of a ruminant. They also vary from swine in that the young are born in pairs. They usually range in pairs, although it is not uncommon to find them in blocks of eight to ten.

"When attacked, they boldly face their enemy and begin crowding in on him with a short, driving rush and with their jaws snapping with the suddenness of steel traps, and the animal is a sorrowful plight that fails to keep his carcass out of range of their knife-like teeth."

Flocks of the javelinas are frequently found near the school, and the animals still venture on campus. They can be easily driven into nearby fields.

Mascot: Live javelina mascots are a tradition at the University. The present javelina is Porky. At one time, the mascots were allowed to run loose on campus; today the animals are caged. In 1929, Dr. R.B. Cousins, the first president of the school, was attacked by one of the two mascots kept on campus. It was found to be rabid, and Cousins underwent the Pasteur treatment for rabies.

The University also has a student costumed as a javelina.

Interesting Facts: Texas A&I claims seven NAIA Division I championships in football.

Texas A&I holds the record for the small college with the longest victory streak—42 games without a defeat from 1973 to 1977. The only other team in history that has ever won more in a row is the University of Oklahoma with 47 straight victories from 1953 to 1957.

Texas A&M

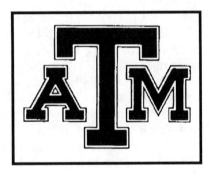

Nickname: Aggies
Mascot: Reveille
Colors: Maroon and White
Conference: Southwest
Location: College Station
Year founded: 1876

Nickname: Aggies is the name used to refer to students and former students, as well as Texas A&M University's athletic teams. Aggies is an appropriate nickname because A&M is short for Agricultural and Mechanical.

Mascot: The official mascot of Texas A&M University is Reveille V, a full-bred collie. The mascot's origin goes back to 1931. Some cadets accidentally ran over a black and white dog in their Model T on the way back to campus. They took the injured dog back to their dormitory. The next morning when the bugler sounded reveille, the dog started barking and promptly received her name. Reveille was soon adopted by the Corps and the band. She followed them to all formations and led them when they marched. At the first football game, she marched to the field with the band. Reveille died in 1944 and is buried at the north entrance of Kyle Field along with three subsequent mascots.

Interesting Facts: Traditions abound at Texas A&M. One of the most popular traditions occurs after the Aggie football team scores a field goal or touchdown. The Aggie gets to kiss his/her date. An old saying goes: "When the Aggies score on the field, the Aggies score in the stands too." One Aggie legend says that during the team's lean years, Aggies got to kiss their dates after every first down.

To a newcomer to Aggie football games, one tradition soon becomes apparent: Aggies stand for the entire game. This practice is linked to "The Twelfth Man." In January, 1922, the SWC champion Aggies played in the Dixie Classic against Centre College in Dallas. Gill, a student on the basketball team, was asked by Coach Bible to suit up just in case he was needed to replace injured players. Gill stood ready to play but was not needed. In the same way, Aggie students stand during games to remember the spirit and loyalty of the Twelfth Man.

The school doesn't have cheerleaders, nor are there any cheers: yell leaders yell. All yells at football games are done from a "humping it" position (bending over with hands placed just above the knees, properly aligning the back, mouth, and throat for maximum volume). During games, the yell leaders use hand signals to indicate what yell will occur next. They tell the "Twelfth Man" what yell is coming up, and students on the bottom row pick up the signal and repeat it, passing it upward until the entire student body knows what is coming up.

Texas A&M won the national football championship in 1939.

The school won two women's softball titles—in 1983 and 1987.

Texas Christian

Nickname: Horned Frogs
Mascot: Super Frog
Colors: Purple and White

Conference: Southwest
Location: Fort Worth
Year founded: 1873

Nickname: A committee from two student literary societies at AddRan College in Waco chose Horned Frog for their school annual. The plural Horned Frogs then became the nickname for AddRan's athletic teams. The moniker remained after the college moved to Fort Worth and became Texas Christian University.

The 1897 committee considered horned frogs and cactus to be the two most typically Texas subjects. The committee chose Horned Frog after the University of Texas had already chosen Cactus as the name for its yearbook.

W.O. Stephens, an AddRan faculty member, is also reported to have suggested the horned frog for the school annual's name.

A horned frog is a lizard-like creature with hornlike spikes that resides in the southwestern United States and is on the endangered species list.

TCU is the only college or university in the nation that has the distinctive nickname. In 1980, the moniker was selected as the #1 sports nickname in the nation by ESPN Cable Systems.

Mascot: Since keeping a live horned frog, which grows to be about six inches long, on the sidelines at athletic events hardly strikes fear in the hearts of opposing players, students at TCU have come up over the years with various costumed characters as mascots. In 1979, Super Frog originated. The brainchild of John Grace, TCU's athletic promotions director at the time, the super-animated costumed mascot performs at football and basketball games. According to Grace, Super Frog was created "to provide TCU with a mascot which people could laugh with, instead of laughing at."

Interesting Facts: A student committee chose the school colors of purple and white in 1896. Purple was selected because it stood for royalty and white because it symbolized a "clean game."

TCU won the national football championship in 1938 with a

11-0-0 season.

Quarterback Davey O'Brien won the 1938 Heisman Trophy Award and the Maxwell Award. The first Davey O'Brien Award, named after the TCU player, was given in 1981 to Jim McMahon of Brigham Young. The Award is given annually by the Educational and Charitable Trust of Fort Worth.

Texas Lutheran

Nickname: Bulldogs
Mascot: Bulldog
Colors: Black and Gold
Conference: Heart of Texas
Location: Seguin
Year founded: 1891

Nickname: The men's athletic teams at Texas Lutheran College were called Bulldogs for the first time in 1926 by first-year coach John M. "Jack" Doerfler. He stated that he wanted his boys to be "strong and tenacious" like bulldogs. Prior to that time, the men's teams had no nickname. In those early years, the women's teams played under a number of names including Amazons, Robins, Bullets, and Bullettes. Today all teams are called Bulldogs.

Mascot: Although no live bulldog is currently the mascot, Texas Lutheran has had several since the first bulldog, Lucky, came in 1938. Garfield Kiel, a TLC student, brought the bulldog who was a fixture on campus well into the 1950s. He was a very friendly dog who attended morning chapel services with students on a regular basis and was cared for by various students and faculty. In 1975, J.C. Boone, a TLC alumnus, presented his bulldog, Golden Hope, to the school. He and the mascot faithfully attended almost every game. When Hope died, Boone was given another bulldog by students who named him Telsey after the initials of the college—T.L.C. Currently, a student costumed as a bulldog serves as mascot.

Interesting Facts: Texas Lutheran's football team won the NAIA Division II national championship in 1974 and 1975.

The women's volleyball teams were the AIAW national champions in 1975 and 1976.

In 1967, John Bohmann was the NAIA men's individual golf champion, and in 1991, Cameron Beckman won the same title.

Three TLC students were selected as members of U.S. Olympic teams—Patricia Dowdell in volleyball (1980), Laurie Flachmeier in volleyball (1980 and 1984), and Tim Funk in team handball (1984).

Texas Lutheran athletics had meager beginnings. Well into the 1920s, the athletic budget was $50 per year or less, and the participants had to furnish their own shoes and other equipment. Nevertheless, those early teams won many victories with the most stellar performances occurring during the 1921-22 academic year when the men's football, basketball, and baseball teams all went undefeated.

Verne Lundquist, Class of 1963, went on to a career at CBS. Lisa Burkhardt, Class of 1979, is now sports anchor for the Madison Square Garden Cable Network in New York and does specials for HBO and ESPN.

Texas Tech

Nickname: Red Raiders
Mascot: Raider Red; Midnight Raider
Colors: Scarlet and Black
Conference: Southwest
Location: Lubbock
Year founded: 1923

Nickname: The Fort Worth *Star Telegram* in 1925 suggested that Doggies would be a good nickname for Texas Tech University. Mrs. E.Y. Freeland, the head coach's wife, though, had other ideas. Influenced by the Spanish architecture at Tech, she suggested that the football team be called Matadors. School colors of scarlet and black were chosen because they represented a full matador's colors of red cape and black costume.

During the 1930s, Collier Parrish, then the sports editor of the Lubbock *Morning Avalanche Journal*, began to call the team the Red Raiders because of Tech's coast-to-coast schedule and all red uniforms. Coach Pete Cawthon and the team liked the nickname, and it has been Tech's name ever since.

Mascot: Texas Tech has a live mascot and a costumed one. Midnight Raider is the black horse ridden by the Masked Rider who is dressed in a scarlet and black cape, a black hat, and a black mask. The horse and rider, originating in 1936, circle the football field in celebration of Tech touchdowns. The twosome also represent the school at many other functions.

Raider Red is the costumed mascot who first made his appearance in 1978 because of the need for a mascot that could attend all athletic events. In 1977, the Southwest Conference passed a rule that prohibited live mascots, such as the masked rider, from the playing field. Therefore, Tech came up with an additional mascot that was the brainchild of a local cartoonist Dirk West and Saddle Tramp (see below) Jim Gasperd.

Interesting Facts: The hand sign of Texas Tech is the "guns up" sign. It is made by extending the index finger outward while extending the thumb upward to form a gun.

The Saddle Tramps is a male spirit organization. The group forms a big circle on the field before each football game, rings cowbells, and chants "go-fight-win." After each Tech football score, the Tramps ring Bangin' Bertha, a large bell that is located in the south end zone of the field. After each Tech win, they ring the victory bells located in the administration building for 30 minutes. A Saddle Tramp serves as Raider Red.

The Red Raider Club is the fund-raising branch for Tech athletics. Started in 1929, it has 50 chapters throughout the state.

Toledo

Nickname: Rockets

Mascot: Rocky the Rocket
Colors: Blue and Gold
Conference: Mid-American
Location: Toledo, Ohio
Year founded: 1872

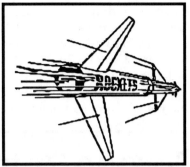

Nickname: Before 1923, The University of Toledo had no nickname. The nameless football team was referred to in sports stories as the Blue and Gold, Munies (for municipal), and Dwyer's Boys (after head coach James Dwyer). Many suggestions for a nickname were considered and rejected, including Toreadors or Bulls (referring to Toledo's sister relationship with its namesake in Spain), Commodores, Turtles, Bancroft Highwaymen, and Jeeps.

When the University of Toledo football team played once-powerful Carnegie Tech in 1923, local Pittsburgh sportswriters were surprised to learn that UT didn't have a nickname. As the underdog, Toledo fought hard against Carnegie Tech by recovering a series of embarrassing fumbles. Sportswriters pressed James Neal, a student working in the press box, to come up with a nickname for his team. Despite UT's 32-12 loss, Neal labeled the team Skyrockets, obviously impressed by his alma mater's flashy performance against a superior team. The name was shortened to Rockets and has been used ever since.

Mascot: Rocky the Rocket is the costumed mascot who performs at athletic events.

Another symbol stands in front of the school's stadium. In 1961, the University of Toledo acquired a rocket from the U.S. Army missile program for Glass Bowl Stadium. The one-ton rocket, carrying two sets of fins and a propellant booster capable of guiding the missile to supersonic velocity, was donated because of the University's affiliation with the Ordnance Corps of the U.S. Department of Army in training officers for the command management system.

Interesting Facts: The first game played at basketball arena Savage Hall in 1976 is probably the most memorable. Toledo snapped Indiana's 33-game winning streak by defeating the Hoosiers, the defending NCAA champion, 59-57.

Toledo's basketball program has resulted in three legendary players. Chuck Chuckovits played in 1937 and 1938 and achieved All-American status twice. Bob Gerber (1941-42), also two-time All-American, led the nation in scoring with 532 points. All-American Steve Mix led UT to a 23-2 record in 1966.

Towson State

Nickname: Tigers
Mascot: Tiger
Colors: Black, Gold, and White
Conference: Independent
Location: Towson, Md.
Year founded: 1866

Nickname: When Towson State University was a two-year normal school, the Baltimore media referred to its athletic teams as the Teachers. As the school grew to a four-year program, the Baltimore papers began calling the teams Professors, a nickname which was shor-tened to Profs. Later, Schoolmasters was used as a nickname.

Towson was also called Indians and Golden Knights. It took a soccer game to designate a permanent nickname.

One autumn afternoon a local sportswriter was covering the Towson State soccer team in an uphill struggle. The next day the reporter wrote that while the team had lost the game "they played like tigers." The soccer team liked the nickname and adopted it. Soon other varsity teams followed suit, and it became the official nickname.

Mascot: A student costumed as a tiger serves as the mascot.

Troy State

Nickname: Trojans
Mascot: Trojan
Colors: Black and Silver
Conference: Gulf South
Location: Troy, Ala.
Year founded: 1887

Nickname: Sportswriters referred to Troy State as the Teachers or Bulldogs in the 1920s. Late in the decade, Trojans became a popular moniker. In 1932, when former Alabama football star Albert Elmore became coach, the name was changed to Red Wave.

When the 1973 football team left for Monroe, Louisiana, to play its season opener against Northeast Louisiana University, the squad didn't have a nickname. On the Troy campus that Saturday, students were voting on choosing one. The two names on the ballot were Red Wave and Trojans; by a 2-1 margin, Trojans won. By kickoff time in Monroe, the football team had a name once again.

Mascot: A student dresses in a Trojan costume.

Interesting Facts: Troy State University has won three national football championships. The 1984 and 1987 teams were the NCAA Division II winners, and in 1968, the school won the NAIA Division I championship.

TSU baseball teams were NCAA Division II national champs in 1986 and 1987.

The men's golf teams won national titles in 1976, 1977, and 1984. Women's golf teams claimed titles in 1984, 1986, and 1989.

Tufts

Nickname: Jumbos

Mascot: Elephant
Colors: Brown and Blue
Conference: New England Small College
Location: Medford, Mass.
Year founded: 1854

Nickname: Tufts University owes its nickname to a train collision. P.T. Barnum's famed elephant, Jumbo, who was the largest captured African elephant at the time, was killed by a train in 1885. The circus owner donated his elephant—which he had stuffed—to the University. Jumbo stood in Barnum Hall until the building was destroyed by fire in 1975. The athletic department's administrative secretary at the time, Phyllis Byrne, rushed up to the ruined building after the fire and scooped up Jumbo's ashes in a peanut butter jar. The jar is now prominently displayed in the athletic director's office. Over the years, football players have rubbed the jar for good luck. Before the fire, students put pennies and other items in the elephant's trunk for good luck during exams.

Mascot: A student costumed as an elephant is the mascot. At homecoming games, Tufts has a live elephant.

Interesting Facts: Tufts University was the only eastern college to have a nickname listed in "The Top 25 College Nicknames" in the 15th edition of *The National Directory of College Athletics.* The school's nickname ranked #18.

Tulane

Nickname: Green Wave
Mascot: Green Wave
Colors: Olive Green and Sky Blue
Conference: Independent
Location: New Orleans, La.

Year founded: 1834

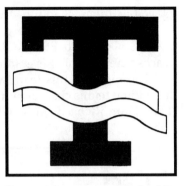

Nickname: Athletic teams at Tulane University were known as the Olive and Blue from 1893 to 1919. In 1919, the college newspaper, *Hullabaloo*, began calling the football team the Greenbacks. On October 20, 1920, Earl Sparling, a Tulane student from Oklahoma City who was editor of the student newspaper, wrote a football song that was published in the paper. The song was entitled "The Rolling Green Wave." The name, although not immediately adopted, began to receive acceptance, and on November 19, 1920, Green Wave was used in a report of the Tulane-Mississippi A&M game in the student newspaper. By the end of the 1920-1921 season, the name seemed to have been accepted by the *Hullabaloo* and most of the daily newspapers. As late as 1923, though, the name Greenbacks was still being alternately used with Green Wave.

Mascot: Rix Yard became Tulane's athletic director in 1963. He and others felt Tulane needed a more virile symbol for its teams. (Since 1955, the school's symbol had been Greenie, a pelican riding a surf board.) Working through Elton Endacott, the manager of the Tulane Bookstore, Art Evans, art director for the Angelus-Pacific Company in Fullerton, California, submitted several sketches. (Evans created mascots for many of the nation's colleges including the Purdue Boilermaker and the Southern Cal Trojan.) Evans' angry-looking Green Wave came into being in 1964, and it has been the symbol of Tulane's athletic teams ever since.

Interesting Facts: Tulane played in the first Sugar Bowl in 1935. Coach Ted Cox's SEC Co-Champions defeated Pop Warner's Temple team, 20-14.

Tulane's Green Wave plays home football games in the huge Louisiana Superdome in downtown New Orleans. When the Superdome was completed in August, 1975, it became the largest enclosed stadium in the world. The dome roof reaches as high as a 27-story building. Before the 1975 season, Tulane played in Tulane Stadium. The facility, before being demolished in 1980, was the world's largest steel stadium. It was located on the site of the Old Etienne de Bore plantation, one of the first places where sugar was granulated in the nation.

The men's tennis team was the 1959 national champions. Individual tennis champions from Tulane include Jack Tuerno in 1949, Ham Richardson in 1953 and 1954, and Jose Aguero in 1955.

Tulsa

Nickname: Golden Hurricane
Mascot: None
Colors: Old Gold, Royal Blue, and Crimson
Conference: Independent
Location: Tulsa, Okla.
Year founded: 1894

Nickname: University of Tulsa athletic teams have been known by several nicknames through the years. Teams were called Kendallites (after the former name of the University of Tulsa—Henry Kendall College), Tigers, Orange and Black, and the Presbyterians (after the founder, a Presbyterian minister). During the 1922 football season, the head coach remarked that his team had roared through their opponents "like tornadoes." This prompted a change to the nickname Golden Tornado. When it was discovered that Georgia Tech already was known by that nickname, there was a change to the next closest choice, the Golden Hurricane. The school's logo consists of hurricane warning flags.

Interesting Facts: Tulsa won the NIT Championship in 1981 defeating Syracuse, 86-84.

Utah

Nickname: Utes
Mascot: Indian Rider
Colors: Crimson and White
Conference: Western Athletic
Location: Salt Lake City
Year founded: 1850

Nickname: The University of Utah's athletic teams are known as the Utes. The nickname and the state of Utah were named for the Ute Indians. The Utes were a tribe of Great Basin Indians who spoke a Shoshonean language. They once occupied western Colorado and adjacent territory in Utah and New Mexico. Originally, they lived in domed grass houses. Their scanty clothing was generally made of sagebrush, though they sometimes wore deerskins. After getting horses from the Spanish, many soon adopted customs of the Plains Indians and lived in tipis, dressed in skins, and hunted buffalo. They now live in Utah, Colorado, and Arizona.

Mascot: An Indian rides a horse at football games.

Interesting Facts: The women's gymnastics teams have dominated the sport over the last decade. They won six national championships from 1982 to 1986 and again in 1990. Utah's skiing teams also were national champions six times in the 1980s.

Valparaiso

Nickname: Crusaders
Mascot: Chuckie
Colors: Brown and Gold
Conference: Mid-Continent
Location: Valparaiso, Ind.
Year founded: 1859

Nickname: The plumed knight, with his fists raised, evolved from the original Valparaiso University symbol of the uhlan. An uhlan is a medieval German cavalryman who is armed with a lance. This symbol represented VU's role as a German Lutheran school. However, VU replaced the uhlan with the Crusaders during World War II when anti-Nazi sentiment discouraged any association with Germany.

Mascot: A student costumed as Chuckie the Crusader performs at sporting events.

Interesting Facts: On December 17, 1988, Valparaiso beat the then #19 Notre Dame Fighting Irish, 71-68, in overtime. This was only the second time in VU's 73-year history that it had beaten the Fighting Irish.

Vanderbilt

Nickname: Commodores
Mascot: Fightin' Commodore
Colors: Black and Gold
Conference: Southeastern
Location: Nashville, Tenn.
Year founded: 1873

Nickname: Commodores was first applied to Vanderbilt University athletic teams in 1897 by William E. Beard, a member of the editorial staff of the Nashville *Banner.* Beard was a quarterback on the 1892 Vanderbilt team. Commodore Cornelius Vanderbilt (1794-1877) was an American steamship and railroad magnate who was popularly known as Commodore. He gave a million dollars to found Vanderbilt University in 1873.

Mascot: The costumed mascot is called Fightin' Commodore or Mr. Commodore.

Interesting Facts: Vanderbilt's football history goes back over a hundred years. In November 1890, Peabody Normal College challenged Vanderbilt to a football game on Thanksgiving Day. Dr. William L. Dudley, president of the Vanderbilt Athletic Association and chemistry professor, called a mass meeting of students to the gymnasium. A motion was made and passed unanimously that Elliott Jones, a student from Kansas City who had seen some Harvard football games, organize a team and serve as its captain and coach. Jones rounded up 13 players—11 starters and two subs. Vanderbilt players wore padded breeches, long stockings, tightly-laced sleeved canvas jackets, and hockey caps. The game was played at Sulphur Dell, the city's professional baseball field; Vanderbilt won, 40-0. Vanderbilt players soon became campus heroes. Elliott Jones agreed to remain captain and coach, and by September 1891, four games had been scheduled with Sewanee and Washington University. The only loss of the 1891 season was to Washington University, 24-6.

Dr. William Dudley, dean of the School of Medicine, organized the Southern Intercollegiate Athletic Association in 1893 and served as president until his death in 1914. Vanderbilt's Dudley Field is named in his honor.

Dan McGugin became Vanderbilt coach in 1904; he would coach at the University for 30 years. His first team scored a total of 196 points in its first three games, shutting out Mississippi A&M, Georgetown, and Ole Miss. For the entire 1904 season, 452 points were scored against eight opponents' four points!

McGugin's 1910 Commodores played Yale to a 0-0 tie, the first time in history that Yale, who dominated early football, had been held scoreless on its home field.

Villanova

Nickname: Wildcats
Mascot: Wildcat
Colors: Blue and White
Conference: Big East; Yankee
Location: Villanova, Pa.
Year founded: 1842

Nickname: The Villanova University student body chose Wildcats as its nickname in 1926 after a contest was conducted by that year's senior class. The name was suggested by Edward Hunsinger, an assistant football coach at the school. Prior to that time, Villanova's teams were called the Blue and White or the Main Liners.

Mascot: The identity of the costumed mascot changes from game to game since the cheerleaders take turns being the Wildcat.

Interesting Facts: Villanova won the men's national basketball championship in 1985.

The women's cross-country team won the national championship in 1989, 1990, and 1991. The men's cross-country team was winners in 1966, 1967, 1968, and 1970.

The men's indoor track team won national titles in 1968, 1971, and 1979. The men's outdoor track and field team was winners in 1957.

Virginia

Nickname: Cavaliers; Wahoos
Mascot: Cavalier
Colors: Orange and Blue
Conference: Atlantic Coast
Location: Charlottesville
Year founded: 1819

Nickname: The University of Virginia has been known by several nicknames. The most widely accepted monikers have been Cavaliers and Wahoos. V-men, Virginians, and Old Dominion also have been associated with athletic teams.

In 1923, the college newspaper, *College Topics*, held an alma mater contest. It failed to produce an alma mater, but the winning entry, "The Cavalier Song," written by Lawrence Lee, Jr., with original music by Fulton Lewis, Jr., Class of 1924, did inspire the creation of one of the current names for University athletes, the Cavaliers. It is an appropriate nickname since many descendants of Cavaliers, partisans of Charles I of England, settled in Virginia.

The term Wahoos came to be associated with Virginia athletes as a result of a cheer, "Wah-hoo-wah," which made its debut in the early 1890s. Legend has it that Washington and Lee baseball fans stuck the tag Wahoos on Virginia players during the fiercely contested baseball rivalry between the two schools, which are located 70 miles apart. The cheer, "Wah-hoo-wah," later became a part of the "The Good Old Song," written in 1893. The song has served as an unofficial alma mater since that time.

After World War II, the term Wahoo was used to refer to any University student. Although the terms Cavaliers and Wahoos are used interchangeably to refer to University teams and players, Cavaliers is more often used by the media, and Wahoos is often a favorite term of Virginia students and fans.

Mascot: A student costumed as a Cavalier cheers teams on at athletic contests.

Interesting Facts: The 1989 Cavalier football team won more games than any other Virginia football team (10-3) and captured a share of a first-ever conference championship. On January 1, 1991, Virginia met Tennessee in the Sugar Bowl. For 59 minutes and 29 seconds of the game,Virginia was ahead of Tennessee. With 31 seconds left, Tennessee edged Virginia with a touchdown and won, 23-22.

Women's cross-country teams won national championships in 1981 and 1982. The men's lacrosse team won the national championship in 1972, and the women's lacrosse team won in 1991.

Virginia Commonwealth

Nickname: Rams
Mascot: Rodney Ram;
Rhonda Ram
Colors: Black and Gold
Conference: Metro
Location: Richmond
Year founded: 1838

Nickname: The student body of Virginia Common- wealth University selected Rams as a nickname when Richmond Professional Institute and the Medical College of Virginia merged.

Mascot: The school has two student mascots, one male and one female—Rodney Ram and Rhonda Ram.

Virginia Military Institute

Nickname: Keydets
Mascot: Kangaroo
Colors: Red, White, and Yellow
Conference: Southern
Location: Richmond
Year founded: 1839

Nickname: Virginia Military Institute has been identified with several nicknames throughout the years. In 1917, at a football game between VMI and North Carolina, Flying Squadron was first used. The name stuck, and it became more popular during the 1920 football season. It wasn't until the late 1940s and early 1950s that Keydet came into use. The source and meaning of the nickname Keydet is speculative. There is no definite meaning that has been found for the word. Several explanations have been offered, but none have been convincingly substantiated. The United States Military Academy claims that it was a word used to denote the gray of the standard uniform of a cadet. One less factual explanation is, that due to the Southern drawl of some of the VMI Corps members, the common term cadet was transformed into Keydet.

Mascot: A student dressed in a kangaroo costume represents VMI at home and road games.

In 1947, two VMI cheerleaders saw a picture of a kangaroo on the front of a magazine and realized how uncommon the animal was as a mascot. After a kangaroo was finally obtained, a contest was held to give him an appropriate name. The prize-winning name was T.D. Bound. Later the kangaroo's name was changed to Moe in order that he might be associated with all sports at VMI and not only football. There have been four real Moes, the last of which was actually a wallaby (a smaller relative of the kangaroo). VMI currently has no live mascot.

Interesting Facts: The VMI Regimental Band, organized into its own company within the Corps, was formed in 1947. In addition to providing music for athletic events, the band has been involved in parades and festivals across the country and in special events such as the 1989 celebration of the bicentennial of the French Revolution in Paris, France. The band performed at Mardi Gras in New Orleans in 1990 and 1991, winning the Harry Mendelson Award for the best band participating in the Endymion Parade. The band also performs at Inaugural parades in Washington and Richmond.

Virginia State

Nickname: Trojans
Mascot: None
Colors: Orange and Blue
Conference: Central Intercollegiate Athl. Assoc.
Location: Petersburg
Year founded: 1882

Nickname: In 1932, Virginia State University student Lawrence Johnson wrote an article in the school newspaper stating, "The team played like Trojans!" Johnson's remark attracted attention, and the nickname became popular. It soon became the official nickname of athletic teams.

Virginia Tech

Nickname: Hokies; Gobblers
Mascot: Fighting Gobbler
Colors: Maroon and Orange
Conference: Big East; Metro
Location: Blacksburg
Year founded: 1872

Nickname: Virginia Tech's unique nickname Hokies can be

traced back to the last century. Virginia Agricultural and Mechanical College changed its name to Virginia Polytechnic Institute in 1896. With the name change came the necessity for writing a new cheer. A student body contest was held. Senior O.M. Stull won first prize for his Hokie yell, which is still heard today. When asked if Hokie had any special meaning, Stull said that the word was solely a product of his imagination. Hokies soon became a nickname for all the school's athletic teams. In 1912, the Gobbler was officially introduced as a mascot for the football team. As the mascot gained in popularity, Gobblers came to be known as one of the names for all Tech athletic teams.

Mascot: Fighting Gobbler is the mascot, a costumed student dressed as a Hokie bird.

Interesting Facts: Virginia Tech's football teams went to three bowl games in the 1980s. The school scored one of its most thrilling victories over North Carolina State, 25-24, on Chris Kinzer's field goal as time expired in the 1986 Peach Bowl.

Virginia Tech has two bands. The Marching Virginians, 340 members strong, is known as "The Spirit of Tech." Its regimental band members, "The Highty-Tighties," whose heritage can be traced all the way back to 1883, are a company of the Tech Corps of Cadets and are called "The Tradition of Tech."

The *Hokie Huddler,* the newspaper that reports solely on Tech athletics, is in its eighth year of operation. It is published 33 times a year.

Kylene Barker, a cheerleader for the Hokies during the 1977 football season, was crowned Miss America the next year.

Two Tech football players are in the National Football Foundation Hall of Fame. They are Hunter Carpenter, a Hokie back who played at the turn of the century, and Carroll Dale, an All-American in 1959.

Tech's Bruce Smith, "The Sack Man," won the Outland Trophy in 1984. Smith had 46 quarterback sacks at Tech and had a career total of 71 tackles behind the line of scrimmage. Smith went on to be the NFL Defensive Player of the Year in 1987.

Virginia Union

Nickname: Panthers
Mascot: Panther
Colors: Maroon and Steel Gray
Conference: Central Intercollegiate Athl. Assoc.
Location: Richmond
Year founded: 1865

Nickname: No explanation exists as to the origin of the nickname Panthers.

Mascot: A student dressed in a panther costume performs at sporting events.

Interesting Facts: Virginia Union won the national title in NCAA Division II men's basketball in 1980 and 1992. The women's basketball team won the 1983 national championship.

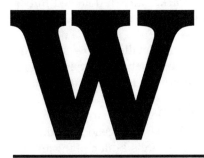

Wabash

Nickname: Little Giants
Mascot: Wally
Colors: Scarlet
Conference: Indiana Collegiate
Location: Crawfordsville, Ind.
Year founded: 1832

Nickname: Coach Francis Cayou, an American Indian and fierce competitor, named his 1904 football team the Little Giants because of its ferocious effort against overwhelming odds. Cayou said, "We're not very big, but we play like Little Giants." Then a school of only 300 students, Wabash College managed a 4-4 record in 1904 against much-favored teams such as Illinois, Notre Dame, Purdue, and Indiana.

Mascot: Wally is the costumed mascot that has a papier mâché head which is approximately three feet high. The mascot began appearing with Wabash cheerleaders in the 1970s. Since Wabash is an all-male school, cheerleaders are also all men from a service fraternity called the Sphinx Club.

The origin of Wally is not known. Wally is the name that Crawfordsville locals pin on out-of-town Wabash students.

Interesting Facts: Wabash has a rich tradition in football. The college played its first football game on Saturday, October 25,

1884, at the Indianapolis Baseball Park. Wabash defeated Butler that day, 4-0. Then in 1886, Wabash was Indiana's first state football champions.

The first football game in Crawfordsville is now a famous one, for it was at that game in 1889 that Wabash gave Purdue its nickname Boilermakers. Wabash used the term in a derogatory fashion when it lost a lopsided game by an 18-4 score. After their defeat, Wabash men chased the Purdue team back to the train station shouting Boilermakers. They accused Purdue of "enlisting" non-students from the school's boiler plant just to win the game. Thus, a heated rivalry began that lasted until 1928.

Wabash and Notre Dame met 11 times from the late 1800s to 1924 with Notre Dame winning 10 of 11 games. Wabash's 5-0 win on October 21, 1905, in South Bend was the last time the Irish were beaten at home until 1928.

The oldest rivalry west of the Alleghenies is between Wabash College and DePauw University (Greencastle, Indiana). They first played in 1890 and have met 98 times.

Wabash won the 1982 NCAA Division III national basketball championship.

Wabash played its first intercollegiate baseball game in 1866.

Wagner

Nickname: Seahawks
Mascot: Seahawk
Colors: Green and White
Conference: Northeast
Location: Staten Island, N.Y.
Year founded: 1883

Nickname: The origin of Wagner College's nickname Seahawks is unknown.

Mascot: The school has a student costumed as a seahawk as its mascot.

Interesting Facts: Wagner won the NCAA Division III football title in 1987.

The women's basketball team won the Northeast Conference Tournament in 1989.

Wake Forest

Nickname: Demon Deacons
Mascot: Deacon
Colors: Old Gold and Black
Conference: Atlantic Coast
Location: Winston-Salem, N.C.
Year founded: 1834

Nickname: As early as 1895, Wake Forest College used its colors, Old Gold and Black, in athletic competition. The college badge was a button designed by John Heck and contained a tiger's head over the letters WFC. Most Wake Forest historians believe that the college's adoption of the colors of Old Gold and Black resulted from the tiger logo. The tiger designation remained until the 1920s, and nicknames up until that time were simply the Baptists (Wake Forest is a Baptist-affiliated university) and the Old Gold & Black.

Beginning in 1923, new head coach Hank Garrity led the football team, which had never had a winning record in the 1900s, to three straight winning seasons. According to many people, including school newspaper editor Mayon Parker, Class of 1924, the current nicknames did not seem descriptive enough of the newfound athletic spirit. After Wake Forest defeated rival Trinity (now Duke) in Garrity's first football season, Parker first referred to the players as Demon Deacons, because of what Garrity termed their "devilish" play and fighting spirit. Wake Forest's news director Henry Belk and Garrity liked the title and began using it. The name stuck.

Mascot: A student dressed as a deacon is the popular mascot at Wake Forest University who over the decades has inspired athletic crowds with his cheering and antics.

Jack Baldwin, Class of 1943, was the original Deacon. The idea for the mascot originated when Baldwin and some of his fraternity brothers were sitting around talking about the need for a Wake Forest mascot. The group decided that someone dressed like a Baptist deacon with a top hat, tails, and a black umbrella, would be appropriate. Baldwin was chosen to don such an outfit, and he agreed to do so at the Wake Forest-North Carolina football game. The "stunt" by the fraternity brothers now is the tradition.

Interesting Facts: The men's golf team won three national championships (1974, 1975, and 1986).

The baseball team won the College World Series in 1955 under Coach Taylor Sanford.

Arnold Palmer was inducted into the Wake Forest Hall of Fame in 1971.

The late Brian Piccolo is probably Wake Forest's most famous athlete. Piccolo, whose battle against cancer was told in the movie, *Brian's Song*, established nine new school records in the 1964 season. *Brian's Song* is shown annually on campus as part of a fund drive to raise money for the Brian Piccolo Cancer Fund Drive.

Washburn

Nickname: Ichabods
Mascot: None
Colors: Yale Blue and White
Conference: Mid-America Intercoll. Ath. Association
Location: Topeka, Kan.
Year founded: 1865

Nickname: Washburn University athletic teams are called Ichabods in honor of the early school benefactor, Ichabod Washburn. There was not a graphic representation associated with Mr. Ichabod until 1938. The editors of the *KAW*, the university yearbook, decided that year to accept suggestions for a design. Bradbury Thompson, Class of 1934, drew the adopted design. The following explanatory material accompanied Ichabod's first representation in the Washburn *KAW*:

"He has courage and enthusiasm as shown by his brisk walk. He is democratic and courteous, for he tips his hat as he passes. Sincere in his search for truth and knowledge, he studiously carries a book under his arm. His friendly smile makes you like him. He is neatly dressed and he fits well into his generation...but adapts himself with equal ease to any change of any age."

Interesting Facts: Washburn's men's basketball team was the 1986-87 NAIA champions.

Washburn lays claim to throwing the first forward pass in football.

Washington

Nickname: Huskies
Mascot: Sundodger; Redoubt
Colors: Purple and Gold
Conference: Pacific 10
Location: Seattle
Year founded: 1861

Nickname: University of Washington athletic teams were known as the Sundodgers until 1921. The nickname originated when a college magazine called *Sundodgers* was banned from campus and, in protest, students adopted the name for their teams. The moniker never was very popular, and many people thought it didn't do much for the Northwest's image of a place where it seemed to rain most of the time.

A committee was formed in 1921 to select a new nickname. After many possible names were submitted, the decision came down to Malamutes and Huskies. These two names were considered appropriate because of Seattle's nearness to the Alaskan frontier. The committee members chose Huskies.

Mascot: Eight Alaskan Malamutes have served as the Husky mascot. They include Frosty I, Wasky, Ski, Denali, King Chinook, Regents Denali, and the current mascots, Sundodger and Redoubt.

Interesting Facts: Washington won the national football championship in 1991 (USA Today/CNN poll).

The school has won the men's Varsity Eights (Intercollegiate Rowing national championship) eleven times; the women's Varsity Eights were winners seven times in the 1980s.

The last Husky football team to go through an entire season with an unblemished record was the 1915 team with a 7-0 season. Coach Gilmour Dobie also led Washington to undefeated seasons in 1909, 1910, 1911, 1912, and 1913.

An interesting story surrounds the choice of purple and gold as the school's colors. The colors were adopted in 1892 by a vote of a student assembly on the original downtown Seattle campus. One patriotic group favored red, white, and blue, reasoning that "since the school was named after the father of our country, our national colors should be the school's colors." The opposing and winning faction argued that national colors should not be degraded for such everyday use. The debate was ended when a young English instructor, Miss Frazier, stood and read from English writer Lord Byron's "Destruction of Senacherib":

The Assyrian came down like the wolf on the fold,
And his cohorts were gleaming in purple and gold;
And the sheen of their spears was like stars on the sea,
And the blue wave rolls nightly on deep Galilee.

Washington & Lee

Nickname: Generals
Mascot: None
Year founded: 1749
Conference: Old Dominion Athletic
Location: Lexington, Va.
Colors: Royal Blue and White

Nickname: Washington & Lee University's nickname pays homage to two great generals—Revolutionary War general George Washington and Civil War general Robert E. Lee. The nickname originated in the 1910s. Prior to that time, athletic teams were known as the White and Blue.

Washington State

Nickname: Cougars
Mascot: Butch the Cougar
Colors: Crimson and Gray
Conference: Pacific 10
Location: Pullman
Year founded: 1890

Nickname: On October 25, 1919, the Washington State College football team played the heavily favored and unbeaten California Bears at Berkeley. Washington State won the game, 14-0. After the contest, a Bay Area sportswriter said the Pacific Northwest team "played like cougars." Back home, the WSC student body promptly took the name Cougars, and on October 28, 1919, officially adopted it as the school's nickname.

Mascot: A student dressed as Butch the Cougar is Washington State University's mascot. Butch attends all football and basketball events as well as community functions.

Interesting Facts: The men's basketball team won the 1917 national championship with a 25-1 record under coach Doc Bohler.
State won the men's indoor track championship in 1977.

Wesleyan

Nickname: Cardinals
Mascot: Cardinal

Colors: Cardinal and Black
Conference: Little Three;
NESCAC
Location: Middletown, Conn.
Year founded: 1831

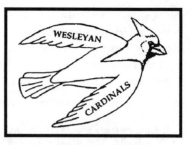

Nickname: The establishment of Cardinals as the nickname for Wesleyan University came about over several years. First, in 1925, the Alumni Council reestablished cardinal red as the school color because the color had gradually shaded off into a crimson or maroon over the years. Second, there were students from other denominations than those of the Methodist Episcopal Church; therefore, the nickname Methodists did not seem appropriate. Third, in 1925, the college literary magazine was named *The Wesleyan Cardinal* with a cardinal bird on the cover. Finally, a group of the 1932 football team never forgot that the newspapers of Rochester, New York, in reporting the game that year with the University of Rochester, had called them "the mysterious ministers from Middletown." Half the team resented the slogan and resolved that something must be done to remedy the situation. The following spring one of the football players, Walter W. Fricke, Class of 1933, who was also the baseball captain, purchased a baseball jacket with a cardinal bird depicted on the breast pocket. Cardinals then became Wesleyan's accepted nickname.

Mascot: A student occasionally dresses in a cardinal costume and goes to football, basketball, and hockey games. The student mascot does not perform on a regular basis, though.

Interesting Facts: Wesleyan's school colors of cardinal and black were adopted in 1884. An editorial in the *Wesleyan Argus* for October 10, 1884, explained the change from the previous color: "Lavender is not a striking color. Waving as a pennant or smoothed into a bow, it has not the brilliant tint which is desirable in a college color. In a uniform it is too neutral....Cardinal and Black make a combination that is rich and striking."

Wesleyan likes to boast about its winning football record (1-0) against the University of Michigan. The school beat Michigan,

14-6, in 1883.

The Little Three Conference (Wesleyan, Amherst, and Williams) gets a lot of attention. Formalized around 1910, it is one of the oldest small college rivalries in the country.

West Chester

Nickname: Golden Rams
Mascot: Rammy
Colors: Purple and Gold
Conference: Pa. State Athletic
Location: West Chester, Pa.
Year founded: 1871

Nickname: West Chester University has had three nicknames.

In the 1925-26 season, West Chester wore new gold jerseys for a mid-season contest at Shippensburg. In the October 28, 1925, edition of the school paper, it was reported that the players "look like huge yellow jackets." Thus, the nickname Yellow Jackets was born.

The second nickname was coined before a championship game with Slippery Rock during the 1929-30 season. Presumably because of their uniforms, West Chester players were called the Golden Avalanches.

In the 1934-35 season, a goat named Elmer was purchased at a local farm for a match between West Chester and La Salle. The team's name became the Golden Rams.

Mascot: Rammy is the student mascot who is dressed in a Golden Ram outfit.

Interesting Facts: West Chester was the NCAA Division I soccer champion in 1961.

During women's basketball coach Carol Eckman's tenure (1967-1972), her teams compiled an astonishing 62-4 record. In 1969, Eckman organized the first National Invitational Women's Basketball Tournament at West Chester, a prelude to the championships that are played today. The Dial Classic/Carol

Eckman Memorial, sponsored by Dial Soap Company, is an annual women's basketball tournament played at West Chester each year. The University is the only Division II site to host a Dial Classic each year.

West Georgia

Nickname: Braves
Mascot: Indian Brave
Colors: Red and Blue
Conference: Gulf South
Location: Carrolton
Year founded: 1933

Nickname: Many people mistakenly believe that West Georgia College's nickname was patterned after the Atlanta Braves baseball team. The college, though, chose its moniker decades before the Milwaukee Braves moved to Atlanta.

Shortly after the Fourth District A&M School became West Georgia Junior College in 1933, Braves was chosen as the nickname. The student body voted for the name in honor of the area's Creek Indian heritage. Although there was a brief movement to change the nickname when West Georgia became a senior college in 1957, the overwhelming sentiment of keeping Braves prevailed.

Mascot: A student dresses in an Indian costume for football games.

Interesting Facts: Football, established in 1946, was discontinued in 1956. It began again in 1980, and in 1982, West Georgia won the Division III national championship.

The school won the men's NAIA basketball championship in 1974, defeating Alcorn State, 97-79.

West Texas State

Nickname: Buffaloes
Mascot: Lady IV; Bucky
Colors: Maroon and White
Conference: Independent
Location: Canyon
Year founded: 1910

Nickname: Because West Texas State University is located on the high plains in buffalo territory, it chose Buffaloes as its nickname. A supporter of the school also donated a buffalo to be used as a mascot.

Mascot: West Texas State has a live buffalo, Lady IV, and a costumed buffalo, Bucky, that serve as mascots.

Interesting Facts: The school has won two national NCAA Division II titles in women's volleyball.

West Virginia

Nickname: Mountaineers
Mascot: Mountaineer
Colors: Old Gold and Blue
Conference: Big East
Location: Morgantown
Year founded: 1891

Nickname: West Virginia University's athletic teams have for years been known as the Mountaineers. The name reflects the rugged individual spirit of the state which is known as the

Mountain State. The state motto is "Mountaineers Are Always Free."

Mascot: The Mountaineer mascot has been around since 1936 when Boyd "Slim" Arnold was chosen as the first student to represent the school at athletic events.

Interesting Facts: In 1921, West Virginia was a participant in the first college football game broadcast on radio. The site was Forest Field in Pittsburgh, and the game was transmitted over KDKA, the nation's first radio station, which made its official debut in November 1920 with the Harding-Cox presidential election returns.

West Virginia won the 1942 men's NIT basketball championship.

The school has been the dominant figure in the men and women's rifle championships since 1983, winning seven times.

Probably the greatest football player to play at West Virginia was Ira Errett Rodgers. He accounted for more touchdowns, 66, with his runs and passes than any other player in the school's history. He ran for 42 scores and passed for 24 in a four-year career that culminated in 1919. He was a consensus selection as fullback and captain of the All-America team that year. Rodgers was also an outstanding shortstop and hitter on the baseball teams and excelled on the basketball team. He holds the distinction as being the only West Virginia player to be named captain in three sports.

Known as the "Fab Five From '55," the top five seniors on West Virginia's 1955 football team were as distinguished a group as the University ever had. Tackles Bruce Bosley and Sam Huff, quarterback Freddy Wyant, and halfbacks Bob Moss and Joe Marconi are legendary names. They led the Mountaineers to 7-2, 8-2, 8-1, and 8-2 seasons. They were responsible for an unprecedented three consecutive victories over Penn State and two conquests of Pitt. A 26-6 upset of nationally ranked South Carolina in the 1954 opener is among WVU's all-time greatest wins. Ironically, the "Fab Five" enjoyed their biggest thrill as sophomores when WVU was invited to play in the 1954 Sugar Bowl on New Year's Day.

Western Carolina

Nickname: Catamounts
Mascot: Catamount
Colors: Purple and Gold
Conference: Southern
Location: Cullowhee, N.C.
Year founded: 1889

Nickname: Western Carolina University held a contest in 1933 to select a new nickname. At that time, the school was called Western Carolina Teachers College, and its teams were known as the Teachers. Everyone on campus was invited to suggest names. The usual names were nominated—Bears, Indians, and Panthers. However, the college wanted an unusual name, a name of an animal that everyone wouldn't copy. The contest came down to two names—Mountain Boomers, a small ground squirrel that scampers in the woods and is difficult to catch, and Catamounts. The latter was the favorite of C.C. Poindexter, the head football coach. Because Poindexter wanted his players to be Catamounts with "fierce spirit, savage attacks, and lightning quick moves," the nickname was chosen.

The dictionary meaning of a catamount is "any of various wild cats such as a cougar or lynx." The name was appropriate for Western Carolina because cats of the catamount variety, including the bobcat, roamed the southern Appalachian Mountains where the University is located.

Western Carolina is the only football-playing school in the nation that uses the nickname Catamounts. The University of Vermont is the only other school playing under that nickname.

Mascot: A student costumed as a catamount entertains spectators at athletic events.

Interesting Facts: Western Carolina played for the NCAA Division 1-AA football championship in 1983, but was defeated, 43-7, by Southern Illinois. Even with the championship defeat, the 1983 season epitomized a Cinderella season. Coach Bob Waters' team got off to an unimpressive start with back-to-back losses at Clemson and Wake Forest. However, a string of 12 straight games without a defeat followed before the streak was snapped by Southern Illinois.

The largest crowd to see the Catamounts play was in 1983 when 13,924 watched the football team battle Appalachian State. The largest crowd at a road game was in 1987 when 72,000 fans attended the Western Carolina-Clemson game.

The largest and most versatile facility of its kind in Western North Carolina is the Liston B. Ramsey Regional Activity Center. Completed in 1986 at a cost of $16 million, the facility not only hosts basketball games but rodeos and cultural events.

Western Illinois

Nickname: Leathernecks
Mascot: Bulldog
Colors: Purple and Gold
Conference: Gateway; Mid-Continent
Location: Macomb
Year founded: 1899

Nickname: Western Illinois University is the only non-military institution in the nation to have as its nickname the Fighting Leathernecks. Longtime coach and athletic director Ray "Rock" Hanson received permission from the U.S. Navy Department in 1927 to use the Marine's official seal, mascot (Bulldog), and nickname. Hanson was formerly in the Marine Corps.

Mascot: Western Illinois has both a live bulldog mascot and a student mascot costumed as a bulldog.

Interesting Facts: Ray "Rock" Hanson was Western Illinois University's athletic director as well as baseball, basketball, and football coach from 1926 to 1964. During his tenure, Western won 29 different league championships. The Western Illinois football stadium bears his name. Inducted into six Halls of Fame, Hanson's contributions extend well beyond the Western Illinois campus. Not only did he write numerous articles on the rules and ethics of competition, but he proposed the 10-second rule in basketball which was adopted by the National Basketball Coaches Association in 1937.

Western Kentucky

Nickname: Hilltoppers
Mascot: Big Red
Colors: Red and White
Conference: Sunbelt
Location: Bowling Green
Year founded: 1906

Nickname: Hilltoppers is an appropriate nickname for Western Kentucky University. On February 4, 1911, Western Kentucky State Normal School moved from the site of its forerunner, Southern Normal School, to a commanding hill in the southwestern part of Bowling Green. During the move, the entire student body marched to the new site, carrying various articles of school equipment. The new school site on "the Hill" was 232 feet above nearby Barren River and the surrounding level plain. It was only natural that athletic teams should come to be known as Hilltoppers. The name, though, did not come into use until the 1925-26 school year. Prior to that, Western Kentucky's teams were referred to Pedagogues or Teachers.

Mascot: Big Red, Western's athletic mascot, began his tenure at the school in the fall of 1979. The huge, furry, lovable creature was originally designed and built by WKU student Ralph Carey, Class of 1980, of Cincinnati, and made its debut during the 1979-80 basketball season.

Big Red won the "Key to Spirit" award, the highest honor presented to team mascots at the time, at the Universal Cheerleading Association competition in 1980, 1981, and 1983.

Interesting Facts: Fans at Hilltopper sporting events wave red towels as they cheer for their team. Western's unique Red Towel originated with the late E.A. Diddle, one of the most successful coaches in history and a member of the Naismith and Helms Athletic Foundation Halls of Fame. Through 1,062 Hilltopper basketball games, Diddle clutched a red towel. He chewed on it, threw it, cried on it, waved it at fans, and used it to signal his players.

Western Kentucky and Murray State have an annual gridiron trophy exchange called the Red Belt. It originated in 1978 when Hilltopper athletic trainer Bill Edwards attended a district trainers' meeting with Murray State trainer Tom Simmons. When Simmons forgot to bring a belt along, he borrowed a red one from Edwards. When Edwards asked about his belt after the meeting, Simmons responded that Western would have to beat Murray State in football to get the belt back. Simmons had the belt mounted on a large plaque, complete with brass plates, to keep Western-Murray scores etched in history.

Western Michigan

Nickname: Broncos
Mascot: Bronco
Colors: Brown and Gold
Conference: Mid-American
Location: Kalamazoo
Year founded: 1903

Nickname: Broncos became the official nickname of the Western Michigan University athletic teams in 1939 after the school dropped its former name, Hilltoppers. John Gill, then WMU assistant football coach, suggested the name. Gill later served as Western's head gridiron coach and then associate athletic director.

Mascot: A student dressed as a bronco cheers on crowds at athletic events.

Interesting Facts: Western Michigan won the men's cross-country national championships in 1964 and 1965.

Whittier

Nickname: Poets
Mascot: Friday the Squirrel
Colors: Purple and Gold
Conference: Southern Calif.
Location: Whittier, Calif.
Year founded: 1887

Nickname: Whittier College was named for the American poet, Quaker scholar, and abolitionist John Greenleaf Whittier. Thus, the nickname Poets was a suitable selection for Whittier's athletic teams.

Mascot: Friday the Squirrel is the costumed mascot of the school. John Greenleaf Whittier had a pet squirrel named Friday that inspired him in his writings.

Interesting Facts: Whittier College, alma mater of President Richard M. Nixon (Class of 1934), has won more SCIAC championships than any other school.

Wichita State

Nickname: Shockers
Mascot: WuShock
Colors: Yellow and Black
Conference: Missouri Valley
Location: Wichita, Kans.
Year founded: 1895

Nickname: Wichita State University acquired the nickname Shockers when the school was known as Fairmount College. Football manager R.J. Kirk, Class of 1907, made posters in 1904 to advertise a game with the Chilocco Indians. Since Kirk had paired Indians with Chilocco, a press agent for the Wichita Fall Festival who was helping publicize the contest demanded that Kirk produce a nickname for Fairmount. Kirk then invented the name Wheatshockers to go with Fairmount's name. Kirk chose a nickname appropriate to the state since Kansas is the #1 wheat-producing state in the nation. When wheat was shocked or headed, the majority of the Fairmount football players earned money for college expenses by working all summer in the harvest. Although it was never officially adopted, the nickname caught on and later was shortened to Shockers.

Mascot: WuShock is the costumed student mascot.

Interesting Facts: Wichita State won the 1989 College Baseball World Series defeating the University of Texas, 5-3.

Widener

Nickname: Pioneers
Mascot: None
Colors: Widener Blue and Gold
Conference: Middle Atlantic
Location: Chester, Pa.
Year founded: 1821

Nickname: A student vote in 1971 selected Pioneers as the school nickname. The moniker had been the Cadets since the 1860s. At that time, the school was known as PMC Colleges (Pennsylvania Military College and Penn Morton College combined). The school's name changed to Widener University in 1972.

Interesting Facts: Widener won the NCAA Division III football championship in 1977 and 1981 under head coach Bill Manlove.

The National Football League's all-time leading punt returner, Billy "White Shoes" Johnson played football at Widener from 1971 to 1973.

William & Mary

Nickname: Tribe; Indians
Mascot: Indian
Colors: Green, Gold, and Silver
Conference: Independent
Location: Williamsburg, Va.
Year founded: 1693

Nickname: The College of William & Mary took Indians as its nickname because of the school's association with Indians early in its history. In the early 1700s, the college established an Indian School in the Brafferton, one of the campus buildings. While it has used Indians as a symbol for many years, the school currently prefers to emphasize the word Tribe, which now appears on all athletic uniforms, including the football helmet.

There was discussion at the school in 1989 to changing the nickname because the moniker might be insensitive and demeaning to Native Americans. After chiefs of the nine Indian tribes in Virginia came out strongly in favor of maintaining the nickname, the controversy waned.

Mascot: An Indian princess serves as the school's mascot.

Interesting Facts: William & Mary won the men's NCAA Division I tennis championship in 1947 and 1948.

Williams

Nickname: Ephmen; Purple Cows
Mascot: None

Colors: Purple
Conference: Little Three
Location: Williamstown, Mass.
Year founded: 1793

Nickname: Williams College is known by two unusual nicknames—Ephmen and Purple Cows.

Williams was founded with funds bequeathed by Colonel Ephraim Williams, commander of a detachment of the Massachusetts militia, who was killed in 1755 during the French and Indian Wars. Thus, the nickname Ephmen honors Williams.

The other designation used for Williams' athletic teams, Purple Cows, was first used after a student humor magazine called *The Purple Cow* made its debut in 1907.

Williams adopted purple as the team's color in 1860 when Jennie Jerome couldn't tell the difference between Williams and Amherst in a baseball game. Because there were no uniforms, Jerome purchased purple ribbons and gave them to the Williams players to wear. Jerome is also noteworthy because she was the mother of Winston Churchill.

Mascot: Williams has no mascot. The Purple Cow logo, though, does symbolize the school.

Interesting Facts: The longest Division III football rivalry in the nation is between Williams College and Amherst College. The series started in 1884. Williams/Amherst is the fourth longest rivalry in NCAA football behind Lehigh/Lafayette, Yale/Princeton, and Yale/Harvard.

Williams won the NCAA Division III women's swimming titles in 1981 and 1982.

Well-known alumni include former New York Yankees' owner George Steinbrenner, Class of 1952, and baseball commissioner Fay Vincent, Class of 1960.

Wisconsin

WISCONSIN T.M.

Nickname: Badgers
Mascot: Bucky
Colors: Cardinal Red and White
Conference: Big 10
Location: Madison
Year founded: 1849

Nickname: The state of Wisconsin has long been known as the Badger State. In keeping with the state nickname, the University of Wisconsin adopted Badgers as its moniker. Contrary to what many people believe, the nickname did not come about as a result of badgers found within the state. The name originated in the 1820s during a lead-mining rush in the southwestern part of the state. Hundreds of miners from Missouri, Tennessee, Kentucky, and Illinois made their way to Wisconsin to prospect the mines that the Indians had already discovered. When cold weather came, the miners, who had been living in tents and who were too busy to build houses, moved like badgers into holes tunneled in the hillsides and into abandoned mine shafts.

Badgers are burrowing animals in the same family as weasels, skunks, and wolverines. They have broad, flat bodies, small heads, short tails, and short legs. About two and one-half feet long, they are gray to reddish in color. Their heads are distinctively marked with white stripes extending from their nose tips to their shoulders and with black patches on their faces and cheeks.

Mascot: Buckingham V. Badger (commonly known as Bucky) is the school's costumed mascot. The student mascot first appeared at the Wisconsin-Iowa game in 1949. Six students now take turns wearing the Badger costume.

The University once had live badgers. They were brought to football games in cages or on chains. Like any normal badger, they were feisty and belligerent, and especially so when held captive. Their scrappy performance symbolized the threat of the fighting Badgers. It also resulted in their not being kept long. The last time an animal served as team mascot was in 1947. The badger didn't endear himself to the cheering squad—he had the worrisome habit of fighting and biting the cheerleaders.

In 1948 the caricature Bucky attained official recognition when it was placed on the cover of the centennial-year football facts book.

Interesting Facts: Wisconsin won the men's national basketball championship in 1912, 1914, 1916, and 1941.

The school was men's cross-country champions in 1982, 1985, and 1988; women's teams won in 1984 and 1985.

Wisconsin won the Intercollegiate Rowing Varsity Eights in 1951, 1959, 1966, 1973, 1974, 1975, and 1990.

The University has been national champions in hockey five times.

Wisconsin-Green Bay

Nickname: Phoenix
Mascot: Phoenix
Colors: Green, Phoenix Red, and White
Conference: North Star
Location: Green Bay, Wis.
Year founded: 1966

Nickname: The University of Wisconsin-Green Bay athletic teams were first known as the Bay Badgers, a tie-in with the school's parent campus at Madison. However, UW-Green Bay students and administrators wanted a separate identity. A campus-wide vote in 1970 chose Phoenix over several other contenders.

The phoenix has its origins in Egyptian, Greek, and Roman mythologies. The phoenix is said to be a large and magnificent bird, similar to an eagle, with red and gold plumage. According to ancient myths, only one phoenix lives at one time in 500-year cycles. When the time of its death approaches, the bird builds a next of branches and incense. The sun then ignites the nest, and the flames engulf the bird. Out of the ashes of the old bird, a young renewed phoenix arises.

Mascot: A student costumed as a phoenix is the mascot.

Interesting Facts: The first women's basketball team in 1973, comprised of 14 women, had only four players who had played high school basketball. The program blossomed under the guidance of coach Carol Hammerle, to win the North Star Conference regular season championship in 1990-91.

Wofford

Nickname: Terriers
Mascot: Terrier
Colors: Old Gold and Black
Conference: Independent
Location: Spartanburg, S.C.
Year founded: 1854

Nickname: The origin of Wofford College's nickname goes back to the early 1900s. A picture of the 1909 Wofford baseball team shows a terrier named Jack in the center of the front row. Wofford professor E.H. Shuler recalled seeing a terrier at baseball games in the early 1910s. About the same time, a cartoon drawing of a terrier doing gymnastics appeared in the Wofford *Journal*, the college literary magazine. By 1914, when football resumed after an 11-year absence, the nickname Terriers was firmly established.

To Wofford fans, the terrier is an appropriate name for athletic teams. A small, wiry dog noted for its courage and eagerness, the terrier is willing to take on and wear down bigger and stronger opponents no matter what the odds.

Mascot: A live terrier served as the school's mascot for many years. Spike, a bull terrier in the 1950s, was once photographed peering through a telescope at his Russian cousin, the Laika, orbiting in Sputnik II. In the early 1960s, Jocko, a registered Kerry Blue terrier, hated crowds, noise, and football. He had to be carried into the stadium in a tranquilized condition. Stymie was a popular mascot during the 1972-73 season.

A student mascot costumed as a terrier now has taken the place of a live one.

Interesting Facts: Wofford played for the NAIA Division I football national championship in 1970, but lost to Texas A&I.

Wyoming

Nickname: Cowboys
Mascot: Cowboy Joe
Colors: Brown and Yellow
Conference: Western Athletic
Location: Laramie
Year founded: 1886

Nickname: The nickname Cowboys identified University of Wyoming athletic teams as early as 1891. According to the March 4, 1964, issue of the *Branding Iron*, the student newspaper, the nickname originated two years before the first official football game.

The Wyoming pick-up football team appealed to a 220-pound ex-Harvard cowpuncher, Fred Bush, for help in a game against the Cheyenne Soldiers. Bush signed up for a course or two and came out for the team. When Bush came on the field decked out in a checkered shirt and Stetson hat, someone yelled, "Hey, look at the cowboy!" Since many of the members of the team also were ex-cowboys, the name stuck.

Mascot: The first Cowboy Joe was given to the University by the Merrill Farthing family and the Cheyenne Quarterback Club in 1950. Joe II officially took over on Homecoming 1965 when the original mascot was retired to the University Farm. Cowboy Joe III is the present mascot. A brown and white pinto Shetland pony, Joe III began his career in 1981.

Interesting Facts: The University of Wyoming, the only university in the state of Wyoming, is nationally recognized for its ski program. The school won the men and women's skiing championships in 1968 and 1985.

Wyoming's football teams have been to five major bowls and won six Western Athletic Conference crowns. Wyoming's football game with Northern Colorado on November 5, 1949, is a memorable one. In that game, the Cowboys set an NCAA record for the most points scored—103. The record 15 touchdowns are the most scored by rushing and passing in a game and the most touchdowns scored in a game. The 13 extra points made by kicking is also a record.

One of Wyoming's most visible graduates is nationally recognized sportscaster Curt Gowdy, who was a track, baseball, and basketball letterman.

The Wyoming campus, located at 7200 feet, is the highest Division I university in the country. Wyoming's altitude is an obvious training advantage for the cross country team. One of the most noted runners to come out of the Cowboy program is world class marathoner Joe Nzau who represented Kenya in the marathon event in the 1984 Olympics. Nzau resides in Laramie and occasionally helps in the training of Cowboy athletes.

Xavier

Nickname: Musketeers
Mascot: Musketeer
Colors: Blue and White
Conference: Midwestern
Collegiate
Location: Cincinnati, Ohio
Year founded: 1831

Nickname: Francis J. Finn, S.J., then a member of the Xavier University Board of Trustees, proposed the nickname Musketeers in 1925. Father Finn, an assistant pastor at the downtown Cincinnati Church of St. Francis Xavier and director of the St. Xavier Parochial School, wrote 21 books for boys. In choosing Musketeers, Father Finn provided permanent recognition to Xavier's strong ties with French culture. The patron of the University, St. Francis Xavier, a native of Spain, received his education at the College of St. Barbe and at the University of Paris. He also helped found the Jesuit Order in Paris in 1540. Also, the first students at Xavier in the 1830s were French-speaking young men from Louisiana.

Mascot: There was no representation of the Musketeer on the campus for decades after Father Finn named the athletic teams. Then, a committee at Xavier learned about a bronze statue of the most famous of all the Musketeers—D'Artagnan. The statue had been erected at his birthplace in Auch in Southern France. (Many people did not realize that D'Artagnan had been a real swordsman who died in battle in 1673 and not just a figment of Alexandre Dumas' imagination when he wrote *The Three Musketeers*.) The committee wrote to the townspeople at Auch, and the Auch Municipal Council offered to send a statue of the famous D'Artagnan to Xavier. The statue stands in the center of the University Mall.

A costumed Musketeer entertains crowds at sporting events.

Interesting Facts: Xavier won the NIT championship in 1958, defeating Dayton, 78-74.

The men's basketball teams, under coach Pete Gillen, in six years have won four Midwestern Collegiate Conference championships, five MCC tournament titles, and six straight NCAA tournament berths. Gillen is the all-time winningest coach in MCC tournament history.

Byron Larkin, 1988 Second Team All-American, is the only Xavier player ever to lead the team in scoring four straight seasons. His 2,696 career points put him first on the XU all-time list and in the Top 20 on the Division I all-time list.

The Musketeer basketball team has played in the Cincinnati Gardens since 1983. Opened in 1949, the Gardens is also home to the Cincinnati Cyclones, a minor league hockey franchise.

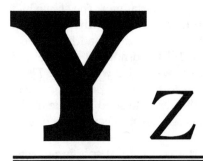

Youngstown State

Nickname: Penguins
Mascot: Pete and Penny Penguin
Colors: Scarlet and White
Conference: Independent
Location: Youngstown, Ohio
Year founded: 1908

Nickname: Youngstown State University is the only school on the college level that has the nickname Penguins.

Although no one has been able to substantiate how the nickname got started, there is a consensus about the origin. On a cold, freezing night in February 1933, the Youngstown basketball team played at West Liberty (West Virginia) State. The spectacle of the players stomping about the floor, swinging their arms, caused someone to remark, "They look like a bunch of penguins."

A member of the 1933 basketball team, Bennett Kunicki, later recorded his memories of that same night. He said that the basketball players had been considering a new name prior to the West Liberty game. The players and other athletic supporters did not like their nickname YoCo (the acronym for Youngstown College). Detractors of the team often jeered Youngstown by slurring Yoco to sound like yokel or loco. Kunicki said Penguins was mentioned by players going to the West Liberty game because they found themselves on roads hit by snowfalls of between one and two feet deep.

The nickname was formally introduced to students in the *Jumbar*, the school newspaper, after the Slippery Rock game on December 15, 1933. It soon became popular with the two local newspapers.

Mascot: Pete and Penny are the two costumed student mascots.

Interesting Facts: Youngstown State won the Division I-AA football championship in 1991, beating Marshall, 25-17.

Dike Beede, the first football coach at Youngstown State, is credited with initiating the usage of the penalty flag on October 16, 1941. The late Beede detailed the facts behind his innovation to the media. "I had this idea for some time," he said. "I came home from practice one day and asked my wife to do a little sewing." His wife, who later earned the title, "The Betsy Ross of Football," bought some red cloth, and sewing it with some white cloth from a bedsheet, made four 16-inch squares. Beede convinced referee Jack McPhee to use the flags in the 1941 game against Oklahoma City. (Before the flags, officials used horns whenever rules were violated.) McPhee started a tradition which in time became a national practice.

Other Colleges and Nicknames

Abilene Christian Wildcats
Adams State College Indians
Adrian College Bulldogs
Alabama A&M University
Bulldogs
Alabama Christian College
Eagles
Alabama State University
Hornets
Alabama-Huntsville Chargers
Alaska-Fairbanks Nanooks
Albany College of Pharmacy
Panthers
Albany State College Golden
Rams
Albion College Britons
Albright College Lions
Alderson-Broaddus College
Battlers
Alice Lloyd College Eagles
Allen University Yellow Jackets
Allentown College Centaurs
Alliance College Eagles
Alma College Scots
American International College
Yellow Jackets
American University Eagles
Anderson College Ravens
Angelo State University Rams
Aquinas College Saints
Arkansas Baptist College
Buffaloes
Arkansas College Scots
Arkansas Tech University
Wonder Boys
Arkansas-Pine Bluff Golden
Lions
Armstrong State College Pirates
Asbury College Eagles
Ashland College Eagles
Assumption College
Greyhounds

Athens State College Bears
Atlanta Christian College
Chargers
Atlantic Christian College
Bulldogs
Auburn-Montgomery Senators
Augsburg College Auggies
Augusta College Jaguars
Aurora College Spartans
Averette College Cougars
Azusa Pacific College
Babson College Beavers
Baker University Wildcats
Baltimore, U. of, Super Bees
Baptist Bible College Patriots
(Mo.)
Baptist Bible College Defenders
(Pa.)
Baptist College Buccaneers
Baptist Christian College
Warriors
Baptist Univ. of America Eagles
Barat College Barat-cudas
Barber-Scotia College Sabers
Bard College Bardians
Barnard College Bears
Barrington College Warriors
Bartlesville Wesleyan College
Eagles
Baruch College Statesmen
Bates College Bobcats
Belhaven College Clansmen
Bellarmine College Knights
Bellevue College Bruins
Belmont Abbey College
Crusaders
Belmont College Rebels
Beloit College Buccaneers
Benedict College Tigers
Benedictine College Ravens
Bentley College Falcons
Berea College Mountaineers

Berkshire Christian College Knights
Berry College Vikings
Bethany Bible College Bruins
Bethany College Bisons (W.V.)
Bethany College Swedes (Kan.)
Bethany Nazarene College Redskins
Bethel College Wildcats (Tenn.)
Bethel College Pilots (Ind.)
Bethel College Threshers (Kan.)
Bethel College Royals (Minn.)
Bethune-Cookman College Wildcats
Biola University Eagles
Birmingham-Southern Panthers
Biscayne College Bobcats
Bishop College Fighting Tigers
Black Hills Yellow Jackets
Blackburn College Beavers
Bloomfield College Deacons
Blue Mountain College Toppers
Bluefield College Ramblin' Rams
Bluefield State College Big Blues
Bluffton College Beavers
Boise State University Broncos
Boston State College Warriors
Boston University Terriers
Bowdoin College Polar Bears
Bowie State College Bulldogs
Bradley University Braves
Brescia College Bearcats
Briar Cliff College Chargers
Bridgeport, U. of, Purple Knights
Bridgewater College Eagles
Bridgewater State College Bears
Brigham Young U.-Hawaii Seasiders
Bristol College Monarchs
Bryan College Lions
Bryant College Indians
Buena Vista College Beavers
Buffalo State College Bengals

Buffalo, State U. of New York Bulls
Caldwell College Cougars
California Baptist College Lancers
California Inst. of Technology Beavers
California Lutheran College Kingsmen
California Maritime Academy Keelhaulers
California State Poly Univ. Boncos
California State College Vulcans (Pa.)
California State College (Bakersfield) Roadrunners
California State College (Stanislaus) Warriors
California State University (Chico) Wildcats
California State University (Dominguez Hills) Toros
California State University (Hayward) Pioneers
California State University (Los Angeles) Diablos
California State University (Sacramento) Hornets
California, U. of, (Davis) Mustangs
California, U. of, (Riverside) Highlanders
California, U. of, (San Diego) Tritons
Calvary Bible College Warriors
Calvin College Knights
Cameron University Aggies
Campbell University Camels
Campbellsville College Tigers
Capital University Crusaders
Cardinal Stritch College
Carleton College Knights
Carroll College Fighting Saints (Mont.)

Carroll College Pioneers (Wis.)
Carthage College Redmen
Castleton State College Spartans
Cathedral College Cougars
Cedarville College Yellow
Jackets
Centenary College Gentlemen
Central Methodist College
Eagles
Central State University
Bronchos (Okla.)
Central State University
Marauders (Ohio)
Central Washington University
Wildcats
Central Wesleyan College
Warriors
Centre College Colonels
Chadron State College Eagles
Chapman College Panthers
Charleston, U. of, Golden Eagles
Chatham College Seals
Cheyney State College Wolves
Chicago, U. of, Maroons
Christian Brothers College
Christopher Newport College
Captains
Cincinnati Bible College Golden
Eagles
The Citadel Bulldogs
City College of New York
Beavers
Claflin College Panthers
Claremont Men's-Harvey Mudd
College Stags
Clarion State College Golden
Eagles
Clark College Panthers
Clark University Cougars
Clarke College Crusaders
Clarkson College Golden
Knights
Clinch Valley College Cavaliers
Coe College Kohawks
Coker College Cobras

Colby College White Mules
Colby-Sawyer College Cougars
Colorado College Tigers
Colorado School of Mines
Orediggers
Columbia College Centaurs
Columbia Chrsitian College
Clippermen
Columbus College Cougars
Concord College Mountain
Lions
Concordia College Cardinals
(Mich.)
Concordia College Stags (Tex.)
Concordia College Clippers
(N.Y.)
Concordia College Falcons
(Wis.)
Concordia College Cobbers
(Minn.)
Concordia College Cougars (Ill.)
Concordia College Comets
(Minn.)
Concordia College Bulldogs
(Neb.)
Concordia Seminary Preachers
(Mo.)
Converse College All-Stars
Cornell College Rams
Covenant College Scots
Creighton University Bluejays
Culver-Stockton College
Wildcats
Cumberland College Indians
Curry College Colonels
Daemen College Demons
Dakota State College Trojans
Dakota Wesleyan University
Tigers
Dallas Baptist College Indians
Dallas Bible College Eagles
Dallas Christian College
Crusaders
Dallas, U. of, Crusaders
Dana College Vikings

Daniel Webster Eagles
David Lipscomb College
Davis & Elkins College Senators
Defiance College Yellow Jackets
Denison University Big Red
Denver, U. of, Pioneers
Detroit Bible College Lancers
Detroit College Falcons
Dickinson State College Blue
  Hawks
Dickinson College Red Devils
Dillard University Blue Devils
Columbia, U. of, Firebirds
Doane College Tigers
Dominican College Chargers
Dominican College Penguins
Dorot College Defenders
Dowling College Golden Lions
Dr. Martin Luther College
  Lancers
Drew University Rangers
Drexel University Dragons
Drury College Panthers
Dubuque, U. of, Spartans
Dyke College Demons
D'Youville College Spartans
Earlham College Hustlin'
  Quakers
East Central University Tigers
East Texas Baptist Tigers
Eastern College Golden Eagles
Eastern Connecticut State
  Warriors
Eastern Mennonite College
  Royals
Eastern Michigan University
  Hurons
Eastern Montana College
  Yellowjackets
Eastern Nazarene College
  Crusaders
Eastern Oregon State Mounties
Eastern Washington University
  Eagles
Eckerd College Tritons

Edward Waters College Tigers
Eisenhower College Generals
Elizabeth City State University
  Vikings
Elizabethtown College Blue Jays
Elmherst College Bluejays
Elmira College Soaring Eagles
Embry Riddle Aeronautical
  University Eagles
Emerson College Lions
Emerson University Eagles
Emory and Henry College
  Wasps
Emporia State University
  Hornets
Erskine College Flying Feet
Eugene Bible College Deacons
Eureka College Red Devils
Evangel College Crusaders
Fairmont State College Falcons
Fayetteville State University
  Broncos
Findlay College Oilers
Fisk University Bulldogs
Fitchburg State College Falcons
Flagler College Saints
Florida Institute of Technology
  Engineers
Florida Institute of Technology
  Spurs
Florida International University
  Sunblazers
Florida Memorial College Lions
Fontbone College Griffins
Fort Lauderdale College
  Seagulls
Fort Lewis College Raiders
Fort Valley State College
  Wildcats
Fort Wayne Bible College
  Falcons
Framingham State College
  Rams
Franklin College Grizzlies
Franklin and Marshall College

Diplomats
Franklin Pierce College Ravens
Freed-Hardemen College Lions
Fresno Pacific College Vikings
Friends University Falcons
Frostburg State College Bobcats
Furman University Paladins
Gallaudet College Bisons
Gannon University Golden
Knights
Geneva College Golden
Tornadoes
George Fox College Bruins
George Williams College
Indians
Georgetown College Tigers
Georgia College Colonials
Georgia Southwestern
Hurricanes
Georgian Court Lions
Gettysburg College Bullets
Glassboro State College Profs
Glenville State College Pioneers
Gordon College Fighting Scots
Goshen College Maple Leaves
Grace Bible College Tigers
Grace College Lancers
Graceland College Yellowjackets
Grand Rapids Baptist Comets
Grand Rapids School of Bible
and Music Victors
Grand View College Vikings
Great Falls College Argonauts
Great Lakes Bible College
Crusaders
Greensboro College Hornets
Greensville College Panthers
Grinnell College Pioneers
Grove City College Wolverines
Gustavus Adolphus College
Gusties
Hamilton College Continentals
Hamline University Pipers
Hanover College Panthers
Hardin-Simmons University

Cowboys
Harding University Bisons
Harris-Stowe College Hornets
Hartford, U. of, Hawks
Hartwick College Warriors
Hastings College Broncos
Haverford College Fords
Hawaii Pacific College Sea
Warriors
Hawaii, U. of, Vulcans
Hawthorne College Highlanders
Heidelburg College Student
Princes
Hellenic College Owls
Hendrix College Warriors
Heritage College Minutemen
High Point Panthers
Hillsdale Freewill Baptist Saints
Hiram College Terriers
Hobart College Statesmen
Holy Family Tigers
Hood College Blazers
Hope College Flying Dutchmen
Houghton College Highlanders
Houston Baptist University
Huskies
Howard University Bison
Humboldt State University
Lumberjacks
Hunter College Hawks
Huntingdon College Hawks
(Ala.)
Huntington College Foresters
(Ind.)
Huron College Tribe
Husson College Braves
Huston-Tillotson College Rams
Idaho, College of, Coyotes
Illinois Benedictine College
Eagles
Illinois College Blueboys
Illinois Institute of Technology
Scarlet Hawks
Illinois Wesleyan University
Titans

Immaculata College Mighty
Macs
Immanuel Lutheran College
Knights
Incarnate Word College
Crusaders
Indiana Central University
Greyhounds
Indiana Institute of Technology
Indiana University Grenadiers
Indiana University-Purdue
University Metros
Indiana University-Purdue
University Tuskers
Indiana University of Pa. Big
Indians
Iowa Wesleyan College Tigers
Jamestown College Jimmies
Jarvis Christian College Bulldogs
Jersey City State Gothics
John Brown University Golden
Eagles
John Carroll University Blue
Streaks
John Jay College of Criminal
Justice Bloodhounds
John Wesley College Lancers
Johns Hopkins University Blue
Jays
Jordon College Suns
Judson Baptist College
Crusaders
Judson College Eagles
Juniata College Indians
Kalamazoo College Hornets
Kansas Newman College Jets
Kansas Wesleyan College
Coyotes
Kean College Squires
Kearney State College
Antelopes
Keene State College Owls
Kenyon College Lords
Keuka College Lakesiders
King College Tornadoes

King's College, The, Knights
King's College Monarchs
Knox College Siwash
Knoxville College Bulldogs
Kutztown State College Golden
Bears
La Grande College Panthers
Lake Forest College Foresters
Lake Superior State College Soo
Lakers
Lakeland College Muskies
Lamar University Cardinals
Lambuth College Eagles
Lancaster Bible College
Chargers
Lander College Senators
Langston University Lions
La Roche College Red Devils
La Salle College Explorers
La Verne College Leopards
Lawrence Institute Of
Technology Blue Devils
Lawrence University Vikings
Lebanon Valley College Flying
Dutchmen
Lee College Vikings
Lehman, Herbert College
Lancers
Le Moyne College Dolphins
Le Moyne-Owen College
Magicians
Le Tourneau College
Yellowjackets
Lewis University Flyers
Lewis and Clarke College
Pioneers
Lewis-Clarke State College
Warriors
Life Bible College Vikings
Limestone College Saints
Lincoln Christian College
Preachers
Lincoln Memorial University
Railsplitters
Lincoln University Blue Tigers

(Mo.)
Lincoln University Lions (Pa.)
Lindenwood College Lions
Livingston University Tigers
Livingstone College Fighting
Bears
Lock Haven State College Bald
Eagles
Longwood College Lancers
Los Angeles Baptist College
Mustangs
Louisiana College Wildcats
Lowell, U. of, Chiefs
Lubbock Christian College
Chaparrals
Luther College Norsemen
Lycoming College Warriors
Lynchburg College Hornets
Lyndon State College Hornets
Macalester College Scots
Mac Murray College
Highlanders
Maine Maritime Academy
Mariners
Maine, U. of, (Farmington)
Beavers
Maine, U. of, (Kent) Bengals
Maine, U. of, (Machias) Clippers
Maine, U. of, (Presque Isle) Owls
Malone College Pioneers
Manchester College Spartans
Manhattanville College Valiants
Maranatha Baptist Bible
Crusaders
Marian College Knights (Ind.)
Marian College Sabres (Wis.)
Marietta College Pioneers
Marion College Titans
Marquette University Warriors
Mary College Marauders
Mary Baldwin College Squirrels
Mary-Hardin Baylor College
Crusaders
Mary Washington College Blue
Tide

Marycrest College Eagles
Maryland, U. of, (Eastern Shore)
Hawks
Marymount College of Kansas
Spartans
Maryville College Fighting Scots
(Tenn.)
Maryville College Saints (Mo.)
Marywood College Pacers
Mass. Institute of Technology
(MIT) Engineers
Mass. Maritime Academy
Buccaneers
Mayville State College Comets
McKendree College Bearcats
McNeese State University
Cowboys
McPherson College Bulldogs
Medgar Evers College Gators
Medialle College Marauders
Mercer University Golden
Hawks
Mercy College Flyers
Mesa College Mavericks
Messiah College Falcons
Methodist College Monarchs
Metropolitan State College
Roadrunners
Miami University Redskins
Michigan Tech University
Huskies
Mid-America Nazarene
Pioneers
Middlebury College Panthers
Midland Lutheran College
Warriors
Midwest Christian College
Conquerors
Midwestern State University
Indians
Miles College Golden Bears
Milligan College Buffaloes
Millikin University Big Blue
Millsaps College Majors
Milwaukee School of

Engineering Pats
Milton College Wildcats
Minnesota, U. of, (Duluth)
 Bulldogs
Minnesota, U. of, (Morris)
 Cougars
Minot State College Beavers
Misericordia, College,
 Highlanders
Mississippi Industrial College
 Tigers
Missouri Baptist College
 Spartans
Missouri Southern State Lions
Missouri, U. of, (Rolla) Miners
Missouri, U. of, (St. Louis)
 Rivermen
Missouri Valley College Vikings
Missouri Western State Griffons
Mobile College Rams
Molloy College Lions
Monmouth College (Ill.)
 Fighting Scots
Montana State University
 Bobcats
Montana Tech Orediggers
Montclair State College Indians
Moody Bible Institute Archers
Moravian College Greyhounds
Morehead State University
 Eagles
Morehouse College Maroon
 Tigers
Morgan State University Bears
Morningside College
 Maroonchiefs
Morris Brown College
 Wolverines
Morris College Hornets
Mount Holyoke College Lyons
Mount Marty College Lancers
Mount Mercy College Mustangs
Mount St. Joseph, College of,
 Mounties
Mount St. Mary College Blue

Knights
Mount St. Mary's College
 Mountaineers
Mount Union College Purple
 Raiders
Mt. Vernon Bible College
 Swordsmen
Mt. Vernon Nazarene College
 Cougars
Muhlenberg College Mules
Multnomah School of Bible
 Ambassadors
Muskingum College Fighting
 Muskies
Nasson College lions
National College Mavericks
Nazareth College Moles (Mich.)
Nazareth College Golden Flyers
 (N.Y.)
Nebraska Wesleyan University
 Plainsmen
Neuman Nikes
New England College Pilgrims
New England, U. of, Red Knights
New Haven, U. of, Chargers
New Jersey Institute of
 Technology Highlanders
New Mexico Highlands
 University Cowboys
New York Institute of
 Technology Bears
New York State U. of Maritime
 College Privateers
New York, State U. of (Albany)
 Great Danes
New York, State U. of
 (Binghamton) Colonials
New York, State U. of (Stony
 Brook) Patriots
New York, State U. College of
 (Fredonia) Blue Devils
New York, State U. College of
 (Brockport) Golden Eagles
New York, State U. College of
 (New Paltz) Hawks

New York, State U. College of (Geneseo) Knights
New York, State U. College of (Purchase) Panthers
New York, State U. College of Red Dragons (Cortland)
New York, State U. College of Red Dragons (Oneonta)
New York, State U. College of Technology Wildcats
Newcomb College Green Wave
Nichols College Bisons
Norfolk State University Spartans
North Adams State College Mohawks
North Carolina A&T State University Aggies
North Carolina Central University Eagles
North Carolina, U. of, (Ashville) Bulldogs
North Carolina Wesleyan Battling Bishops
North Central College Cardinals
North Central Bible College Chiefs
North Dakota, U. of, Fighting Sioux
North Florida, U. of, Ospreys
North Georgia College Saints
North Park College Vikings
North Texas State University Mean Greens
Northeast Missouri State University Bulldogs
Northeastern Bible College Lancers
Northeastern Illinois University Golden Eagles
Northeastern Oklahoma State University Redmen
Northern Kentucky University Norsemen
Northern Montana College Lights
Northern State College Wolves
Northland College Lumberjacks
Northland Baptist College Pioneers
Northrop University Knights
Northwest Christian College Crusaders
Northwest Missouri State University Bearcats
Northwest Nazarene College Crusaders
Northwestern College Red Raiders
Northwestern College Eagles
Northwestern College Trojans
Northwestern Oklahoma State University Rangers
Northwestern State University Demons
Northwood Institute Northmen
Norwich University Cadets
Notre Dame, College of, Road Runners (Md.)
Notre Dame, College of Argonauts (Calif.)
Nyack College Fighting Parsons
Oakland City College Mighty Oaks
Oakland University Pioneers
Oberlin University Yeomen
Occidental College Tigers
Oglethorpe University Stormy Petrels
Ohio Dominican College Panthers
Ohio Northern University Polar Bears
Ohio Wesleyan University Battling Bishops
Oklahoma Christian College Eagles
Oklahoma City University Chiefs
Oklahoma University of Science and Arts Drovers

Olivet College Comets
Olivet Nazarene College Tigers
Oral Roberts University Titans
Oregon College of Education
Wolves
Oregon Tech Owls
Ottawa University Braves
Ouachita Baptist University
Tigers
Our Lady of the Lake University
Armadillos
Ozark Bible College
Ambassadors
Ozarks, College of the,
Mountaineers
Ozarks, School of the, Bobcats
Pace University Settlers
Pacific Lutheran University
Lutes
Pacific University Boxers
Paine College Lions
Palm Beach Atlantic Sailfish
Panhandle State University
Aggies
Park College Pirates
Parks College of St. Louis
University Falcons
Paul Quinn College Tigers
Pembroke State University
Braves
Penn State University-Behrend
Cubs
Penn State University-Capitol
Lions
Pennsylvania, U. of, Quakers
Pfeiffer College Falcons
Philadelphia College of
Pharmacy and Science Blue
Devils
Philadelphia College of Textiles
and Science Rams
Philander Smith College
Panthers
Phillips University Haymakers
Piedmont Bible College

Preachers
Pikeville College Bears
Pillsbury Baptist Bible College
Comets
Pittsburgh Mountain Cats
Plymouth State College Panthers
Point Loma College Crusaders
Point Park College Pioneers
Poly Institute of New York Blue
Jays
Pomona-Pitzer College Sage
Hens
Portland, U. of, Pirates
Post Center Pioneers
Pratt Institute Cannoneers
Principia College Indians
Providence College Friars
Puget Sound, U. of, Loggers
Purdue University (Hammond)
Lakers
Purdue University (North
Central) Centaurs
Queens College Knights
Quinnipiac College Braves
Ramapo College of New Jersey
Roadrunners
Redlands, U. of, Bulldogs
Regis College Rangers
Rensselaer Polytechnic Institute
Engineers
Rhode Island College
Anchormen
Rhode Island, U. of, Rams
Rio Grande College Redmen
Ripon College Redmen
Rivier College Raiders
Roanoke College Maroons
Roberts Wesleyan College
Raiders
Rochester Inst. of Technology
Tigers
Rochester, U. of, Yellowjackets
Rockhurst College Hawks
Rockmont College Rockets
Rocky Mountain College Bears

Roger Williams College Hawks
Rollins College Tars
Roosevelt University Lakers
Rosary College Rebels
Rose Hulman Institute of
Technology Fightin' Engineers
Rust College Bearcats
Rutgers University (Camden)
Pioneers
Rutgers University (New
Brunswick) Scarlet Raiders
Sacred Heart University
Pioneers
Saginaw Valley State Cardinals
St. Ambrose College Fighting
Bees
St. Andrews Presbyterian
Knights
St. Anselm College Hawks
St. Augustine's College Mighty
Falcons
St. Catherine, College of, Katies
St. Edward's University
Hilltoppers
St. Francis College Cougars
(Ind.)
St. Francis College Terriers
(N.Y.)
St. John Fisher College Cardinals
St. John's College Eagles
St. John's University Johnnies
(Minn.)
St. John's University Redmen
(N.Y.)
St. Joseph's College Monks
(Maine)
St. Joseph's College Pumas (Ind.)
St. Joseph the Provinder, College
of Saints
St. Lawrence University Saints
St. Leo College Monarchs
St. Louis Christian College
Soldiers
St. Louis Colege of Pharmacy
St. Martin's College Saints

St. Mary of the Plains Cavaliers
St. Mary's College Redmen
(Minn.)
St. Mary's College Belles (Ind.)
St. Mary's College Eagles (Mich.)
St. Mary's University Rattlers
St. Mary's College of MD Saints
St. Mary's, College of, Flames
St. Meinrad College Ravens
St. Michael's College Purple
Knights
St. Norbert College Knights
St. Olaf College Lions
St. Paul's College Lions
St. Rose, College of, Golden
Knights
St. Scholistica, College of Saints
St. Teresa, College of Olympians
St. Thomas Aquinas Spartans
St. Thomas, College of, Tommies
St. Thomas, U. of, Saints
St. Vincent College Bearcats
St. Xavier College Cougars
Salem College Tigers
Salem State College Vikings
Salisbury State College Sea Gulls
San Diego, U. of, Toreros
San Francisco, U. of, Dons
Sangamon State University
Prairie Dogs
Santa Clara, U. of, Broncos
Santa Fe, College of, Knights
Savannah State College Tigers
Schreiner College Mountaineers
Scranton, U. of, Royals
Scripps College Athenas
Seattle Pacific University
Falcons
Seattle University Chieftans
Shaw College Saints
Shaw University Bears
Shenandoah College Hornets
Shepherd College Rams
Shorter College Hawks
Siena College Indians

Simpson College Knights
Simpson College Redmen
Sioux Falls College Cougars
Skidmore College Wombats
Sonoma State University
  Cossacks
South, U. of, Tigers
South Carolina, U. of, (Aiken)
  Pacers
South Carolina, U. of,
  (Spartanburg) Rifles
South Dakota Tech Hardrockers
South Dakota, U. of, Pointers
Southampton College Colonials
Southeastern Baptist College
  Trojans
Southeastern College Crusaders
Southeastern Mass. University
  Corsairs
Southeastern Oklahoma State
  University Savages
Southeastern University Hawks
Southern Arkansas University
  Muleriders
Southern Bible College Lions
Southern California College
  Vanguards
Southern Colorado, U. of,
  Indians
Southern Connecticut State Owls
SIU-Edwardsville Cougars
Southern Maine, U. of, Huskies
Southern Mississippi, U. of,
  Golden Eagles
Southern Oregon State Raiders
Southern Tech Institute Hornets
Southern University & A&M
  Jaguars
Southern University Black
  Knights
Southern Utah State
  Thunderbirds
Southwest Baptist College
  Bearcats
Southwest State University

Golden Mustangs
Southwestern Assemblies of God
  College Lions
Southwestern Baptist Bible
  Eagles
Southwestern College
  Moundbuilders
Southwestern at Memphis
  Lynxcats
Southwestern Oklahoma State
  University Bulldogs
Southwestern University Pirates
Spalding College Pelicans
Spring Arbor College Cougars
Spring Garden College Bobcats
Spring Hill College Badgers
Springfield College Chiefs
Staten Island, College of,
  Dolphins
Stephens College Stars
Sterling College Warriors
Steubenville, U. of, Saints
Stevens Institution of
  Technology Ducks
Stockton State College Ospreys
Stonehill College Chieftans
Strayer College Tigers
Suffolk University Rams
Susquehanna University
  Crusaders
Swarthmore College Little
  Quakers
Sweet Briar College Vixens
Tabor College Bluejays
Talledega College Tornadoes
Tampa, U. of, Spartans
Tarkio College Owls
Taylor University Trojans
Tennessee State University
  Tigers
Tennessee Temple University
  Crusaders
Tennessee, U. of,-Chattanooga
  Moccasins
Tennessee Wesleyan College

Bulldogs
Texas College Steers
Texas Southern University
  Tigers
Texas, U. of,-Dallas Comets
Texas, U. of,-Permian Basin
  Chargers
Texas Wesleyan College Rams
Texas Woman's University
  Pioneers
Thiel College Tomcats
Thomas College Terriers
Thomas More College Rebels
Tiffin University Dragons
Tougaloo College Bulldogs
Transylvania University Pioneers
Trenton State College Lions
Trevecca Nazarene College
  Trojans
Trinity Bible Institute Crusaders
Trinity Christian College Trolls
Trinity College Trojanas (Ill.)
Trinity College Bantams (Conn.)
Trinity University Tigers
Tri-State University Trojans
Tusculum College Pioneers
Tuskekee Institute Golden
  Tigers
Union College Bulldogs (Ky.)
Union College Dutchmen (N.Y.)
Union University Bulldogs
U.S. Coast Guard Academy
  Bears
U.S. International University
  Soaring Gulls
U.S. Marine Corps Academy
  Marines
U.S. Merchant Marine Academy
  Mariners
United Wesleyan College
  Warriors
Unity College Rams
Upper Iowa University Peacocks
Upsala College Vikings
Urbana College Blue Knights

Ursinus College Bears
Utah State University Aggies
Utica College of Syracuse
  University Pioneers
Valdosta State College Blazers
Valley City State College Vikings
Vassar College Brewers
Vermont Catamounts
Villa Maria College Crusaders
Virginia Intermont College
  Cobras
Virginia Wesleyan College
  Marlins
Viterbo College 76ers
Voorhees College Tigers
Walsh College Cavaliers
Warner Pacific College Knights
Warren Wilson College Owls
Wartburg College Knights
Washington College Shoremen
Washington and Jefferson
  College Presidents
Washington University Bears
Wayland Baptist University
  Pioneers
Wayne State College Wildcats
Wayne State University Tartars
Waynesburg College
  Yellowjackets
Webber College Warriors
Weber State College Wildcats
West Coast Christian College
  Knights
West Liberty State College
  Hilltoppers
West Virginia Institute of
  Technology Golden Bears
West Virginia State College
  Yellow Jackets
West Virginia Wesleyan
  College Bobcats
Western Baptist College
  Warriors
Western Connecticut State
  Colonials

Western Maryland College
Terrors
Western Montana College
Bulldogs
Western New England College
Golden Bears
Western New Mexico University
Mustangs
Western Oregon State College
Wolves
Western State College
Mountainers
Western Washington University
Vikings
Westfield State College Owls
Westmar College Eagles
Westminster College Blue Jays
Westminster College Titans
Westmont College Warriors
Wheeling College Cardinals
Wheaton College Crusaders
Whitman College Missionaries
Whitworth College Pirates
Wilberforce University Bulldogs
Wiley College Wildcats
Wilkes College Colonels
Willamette University Bearcats
William Carey College
Crusaders
William Jewell College
Cardinals
William Paterson College
Pioneers
William Penn College
Statesmen
William Smith College Smithies
William Woods College Owls
Wilmington College Wildcats
(Del.)
Wilmington College Quakers
(Ohio)
Wilson College Phoenix
Winona State University
Warriors
Winston-Salem State University

Rams
Winthrop College Eagles
Wisconsin, U. of,-Eau Claire
Blugolds
Wisconsin, U. of,-Lacrosse
Indians
Wisconsin, U. of,-Stout Blue
Devils
Wisconsin, U. of,-Milwaukee
Panthers
Wisconsin, U. of,-Oshkosh
Titans
Wisconsin, U. of,-Parkside
Rangers
Wisconsin, U. of,-Platteville
Pioneers
Wisconsin, U. of,-River Falls
Falcons
Wisconsin, U. of,-Stevens Point
Pointers
Wisconsin, U. of,-Superior
Yellowjackets
Wisconsin, U. of,-Whitewater
Warhawks
Wittenberg University Tigers
Wooster, the College of,
Fighting Scots
Worcester Polytechnic Institute
Engineers
Worcester State College
Lancers
Wright State University Raiders
Xavier University of Louisiana
Gold Rush
Yale University Bulldogs
Yankton College Greyhounds
Yeshiva University Maccabbees
York College Nomads
York College of Pennsylvania
Spartans

11/8/02 WK.